# Busy Ant Maths

# Stretch and Challenge 6

A problem-solving, cross-curricular
programme for children working
above end-of-year expectations

Peter Clarke

Published by Collins

An imprint of HarperCollinsPublishers
The News Building
1 London Bridge Street
London SE1 9GF

Browse the complete Collins catalogue at
**www.collins.co.uk**

10 9 8 7 6 5 4 3 2 1

ISBN 978-0-00-816735-6

British Library Cataloguing in Publication Data
A Catalogue record for this publication is available from the British Library.

Commissioned by Fiona McGlade
Cover and series design by Kneath Associates
Template creation by Ken Vail Graphic Design
Illustrations by Mark Walker, Steve Evans, Gwyneth Williamson and QBS Learning
Typesetting by QBS Learning
Editing and proofreading by Alissa McWhinnie

Printed and bound by CPI Group (UK) Ltd, Croydon, CR0 4YY

**Acknowledgements**
Peter Clarke wishes to thank Brian Molyneaux for his valuable contribution to this publication.

# Contents

| Domain(s) | Topic | Issue number | Teacher's notes page number |
|---|---|---|---|
| Number:<br>– Number and place value | Number | 1 | 100 |
| | Negative numbers | 2 | 103 |
| Number:<br>– Addition, subtraction, multiplication and division | Addition | 3 | 106 |
| | Subtraction | 4 | 110 |
| | Multiplication | 5 | 113 |
| | Division | 6 | 117 |
| | Mixed operations | 7 | 120 |
| | Mixed operations and algebra | 8 | 123 |
| Number:<br>– Fractions (including decimals and percentages) | Fractions | 9 | 126 |
| | Fractions | 10 | 130 |
| | Decimals | 11 | 134 |
| | Percentages | 12 | 137 |
| | Percentages | 13 | 140 |
| Ratio and proportion | Ratio and proportion | 14 | 143 |
| | Ratio and proportion | 15 | 146 |
| | Ratio and proportion | 16 | 149 |
| Algebra | Algebra | 17 | 152 |
| | Algebra – The Financial Issue | 18 | 155 |
| Measurement | Length | 19 | 158 |
| | Mass | 20 | 161 |
| | Volume and capacity | 21 | 164 |
| | Time | 22 | 167 |
| | Area | 23 | 171 |
| | Perimeter | 24 | 174 |
| | Measurement | 25 | 178 |
| Geometry:<br>– Properties of shapes | 2-D shapes | 26 | 181 |
| | 3-D shapes | 27 | 185 |
| | Movement and angle | 28 | 188 |
| Geometry:<br>– Position and direction | Reflections | 29 | 191 |
| | Translations | 30 | 194 |
| Geometry:<br>– Properties of shapes<br>– Position and direction | Geometry | 31 | 197 |
| | Geometry | 32 | 200 |
| | Geometry | 33 | 203 |
| Statistics | Statistics | 34 | 206 |
| | Statistics | 35 | 209 |
| | Statistics | 36 | 212 |

# Introduction

The National Curriculum emphasises the importance of all children mastering the programme of study taught each year and discourages the acceleration of children into content from subsequent years.

The National Curriculum states: *'The expectation is that the majority of pupils will move through the programmes of study at broadly the same pace. However, decisions about when to progress should always be based on the security of pupils' understanding and their readiness to progress to the next stage. Pupils who grasp concepts rapidly should be challenged through being offered rich and sophisticated problems before any acceleration through new content. Those who are not sufficiently fluent with earlier material should consolidate their understanding, including through additional practice, before moving on.'* [1]

However, the National Curriculum also goes on to say that: *'Within each key stage, schools [therefore] have the flexibility to introduce content earlier or later than set out in the programme of study. In addition, schools can introduce key stage content during an earlier key stage, if appropriate.'* [2]

*Stretch and Challenge* aims to provide support in meeting the needs of those children who are exceeding age-related expectations by providing a range of problem-solving and cross-curricular activities designed to enrich and deepen children's mathematical knowledge, skills and understanding.

The series provides opportunities for children to reason mathematically and to solve increasingly complex problems, doing so with fluency, as described in the aims of the National Curriculum:

*'The National Curriculum for mathematics aims to ensure that all pupils:*

- *become **fluent** in the fundamentals of mathematics, including through varied and frequent practice with increasingly complex problems over time, so that pupils develop conceptual understanding and the ability to recall and apply knowledge rapidly and accurately*

- ***reason mathematically** by following a line of enquiry, conjecturing relationships and generalisations, and developing an argument, justification or proof using mathematical language*

- *can **solve problems** by applying their mathematics to a variety of routine and non-routine problems with increasing sophistication, including breaking down problems into a series of simpler steps and persevering in seeking solutions.'* [3]

*Stretch and Challenge* has been designed to provide:

- a flexible 'dip-in' resource that can easily be adapted to meet the needs of individual children, and different classroom and school organisational arrangements

- enrichment activities that require children to use and apply their mathematical knowledge, skills and understanding to reason mathematically and to solve increasingly complex problems

- mathematical activities linked to the entire primary curriculum, thereby ensuring a range of cross-curricular contexts

- an easy-to-use bank of activities to save teachers time in thinking up new enrichment activities

- an interesting, unique and consistent approach to presenting enrichment activities to children.

The *Stretch and Challenge* series consists of six packs, also available digitally on Collins Connect, one for each year group from Year 1 to Year 6.

---

**1** Mathematics programmes of study: key stages 1 and 2 National Curriculum in England, September 2013, page 3

**2** Mathematics programmes of study: key stages 1 and 2 National Curriculum in England, September 2013, page 4

**3** Mathematics programmes of study: key stages 1 and 2 National Curriculum in England, September 2013, page 3

### Printed resources

Containing:

- Pupil activity booklets (Issues)
- Teacher's notes
- Resource sheets

### Online resources at connect.collins.co.uk

Containing printable:

- Pupil activity booklets (Issues)
- Teacher's notes
- Resource sheets

It is envisaged that the activities in *Stretch and Challenge* will be used by either individuals or pairs of children. However, given the flexible nature of the resource, if appropriate, children can work in groups. The activities are intended to be used:

- as additional work to be done once children have finished other set work
- by those children who grasp concepts rapidly and need to be challenged through rich and sophisticated problems
- as in-depth work that is to be undertaken over a prolonged period of time, such as during the course of several lessons, a week or a particular unit of work
- as a resource for promoting mathematical reasoning and problem solving and developing independent thinking and learning
- as a springboard for further investigations into mathematics based on the children's suggestions.

## The features of *Stretch and Challenge*

### Pupil activity booklets (Issues)

- Each of the 36 Issues in *Stretch and Challenge 6* consists of a four-page A5 pupil activity booklet (to be printed double sided onto one sheet of A4 paper).

- The 36 Issues cover the different domains and attainment targets of the Mathematics National Curriculum Programme of Study (see pages 11–20).

- The Issues have been designed to resemble a newspaper, with each of the Issues consisting of between five and eight different activities, all related to the same mathematical topic.

- It is important to note that children are not expected to complete all the activities in an Issue nor work their way through an Issue from beginning to end. For many children not all of the activities offered in an Issue will be appropriate. When choosing which activities a child is to complete, teachers should ensure that the activities do not accelerate the child into mathematical content they may not be familiar with, or are unable to reason more deeply in order to develop a conceptual understanding. Rather, activities should be chosen on the basis that they engage the child in reasoning and the development of mathematical thinking, as well as enriching and deepening the child's mathematical knowledge, skills and understanding.

- The terms 'Issue' and 'Volume' have been used rather than 'Unit' and 'Year group' because they are in keeping with the newspaper theme.

### Types of activities

- Each of the 36 Issues in *Stretch and Challenge 6* are designed to deepen children's mathematical knowledge, skills and understandings, and enhance their use and application of mathematics. There are four different types of 'using and applying' activities in the series:

 What's the Problem?     The Puzzler

 Looking for Patterns     Let's Investigate

- Alongside developing children's problem-solving skills, the series also provides activities with cross-curricular links to other subjects in the primary curriculum. The following shows the *Stretch and Challenge* features and its corresponding primary curriculum subject.

| Curriculum subject | | *Stretch and Challenge* feature |
|---|---|---|
| English | | The Language of Maths |
| Science | | Focus on Science |
| Computing | | Technology Today |
| Geography | | Around the World |
| History | | In the Past |
| | | Famous Mathematicians |
| Art and design / Music | | The Arts Roundup |
| Design and Technology | | Construct |
| Physical Education | | Sports Update |

- As well as the features mentioned above, other regular features in *Stretch and Challenge* include:

 Money Matters     At Home (home–school link activities).

- A chart showing the link between the Issues, the *Stretch and Challenge* features and cross-curricular links can be found on pages 22 and 23.

- Inquisitive ant is a recurring feature of the series. In each Issue there is an ant holding a mathematical word or symbol. Children locate the ant and write about the meaning of the word or symbol.

## Teacher's notes

Each of the 36 Issues includes a set of teacher's notes, including answers.

**Issue number**

**Prerequisites for learning**

Lists the prerequisites for learning that children need to have acquired prior to this Issue.

Lists the associated knowledge and skills that contribute to understanding the Issue topic.

**Simplifications**

Where appropriate, offers suggestions for supporting children who may be experiencing difficulties understanding the main mathematical ideas.

**Extensions**

Where appropriate, offers suggestions for extending children's understanding if you feel they are developing a good understanding of the main mathematical ideas.

**Assessment for Learning**

Each Issue includes a list of questions specifically designed to assist in assessing pupils' understanding of the Issue topic.

**Answers**

These are provided where appropriate.

**Mathematics topic**

**Resources**

To aid preparation, the resources needed for the Issue are listed.

**Teaching support**

Provides teaching points for each of the activities in the Issue. These may be helpful when introducing the Issue to the children, or when children experience difficulty whilst working on a particular activity.

Almost all of the activities in *Stretch and Challenge* can be undertaken either individually or in pairs (or sometimes in small groups).

Where an activity is particularly suitable for pairs to work on, this is denoted by 👤👤.

When children are likely to need access to a computer, this is denoted by 💻.

When children are likely to need access to a computer with Internet access, this is denoted by (www).

**Record of completion**

To assist in keeping a record of which Issues children have completed.

Once a child has completed an Issue you could either put a tick or write the date in the corresponding box.

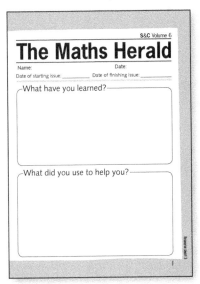

**Pupil self assessment booklet**

Each Resource Pack in the *Stretch and Challenge* series includes an age-appropriate pupil self assessment A5 booklet (to be printed double sided onto one sheet of A4 paper).

This booklet is a generic sheet that can be used for any, or all, of the 36 Issues in the Resource Pack.

The booklet is designed to provide children with an opportunity to undertake some form of self assessment once they have completed the Issue.

After the children have completed the booklet, discuss with them what they have written.

This can then be kept, together with the child's copy of the Issue and their working out and answers, including, if appropriate, 'My notes'.

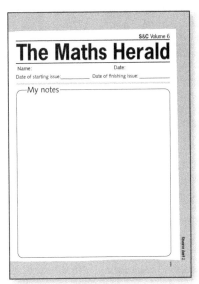

**My notes**

The pupil activity booklets have been designed to resemble a newspaper. This means that quite often there is insufficient space in the booklets for children to show their working and answers.

You may decide to simply provide children with pencil and paper to record their work or an exercise book that they use as their '*Stretch and Challenge* Journal'. Alternatively, you could provide them with a copy of the A5 booklet: 'My notes' (to be printed double sided onto one sheet of A4 paper). This can then be kept, together with the child's copy of the Issue and, if appropriate, their 'Pupil self assessment booklet.'

Whichever method you choose for the children to record their working and answers, i.e. on sheets of paper, using a 'My notes' booklet, in an exercise book, or any other method, children need to be clear and systematic in their recording.

**Other Resource sheets**

For some of the activities, children are required to use a specific Resource sheet.

These are included both in the back of this Resource Pack and the online resources.

# A possible *Stretch and Challenge* teaching and learning sequence

As the diagram on the right illustrates, the process of learning about mathematics can be thought of as the interrelationship between knowledge, understanding and application.

A suggested teaching sequence for working with children based on this model and using the activities in *Stretch and Challenge* is given below.

A complete sequence may occur during a particular lesson if the activity given is designed to be completed during the course of the lesson. Alternatively, the teaching and learning sequence may extend for a longer period of time if the activities are to be completed over the course of several lessons, a week or during a particular unit of work.

Constructing meaning

Transferring knowledge

Using & applying

Understanding

## Briefing

The teacher:

- introduces the topic

- checks prerequisites for learning

- introduces the activity including, where appropriate, reading through the activity with the children

- checks for understanding

- clarifies any misconceptions

- ensures there is easy access to any necessary resources.

## Working

- Children work individually, in pairs, or if appropriate, in groups.

- Teacher acts only as a 'guide-on-the-side'.

## De-briefing

The child / children:

- reports back to others

- reflects on their learning

- identifies the 'next step'.

The teacher evaluates learning.

# Links to the Year 6 Mathematics National Curriculum Programme of Study and Attainment Targets

*Stretch and Challenge Issue*

| | 1 | 2 | 3 | 4 | 5 | 6 | 7 | 8 | 9 | 10 | 11 | 12 | 13 | 14 | 15 | 16 | 17 | 18 | 19 | 20 | 21 | 22 | 23 | 24 | 25 | 26 | 27 | 28 | 29 | 30 | 31 | 32 | 33 | 34 | 35 | 36 |
|---|---|---|---|---|---|---|---|---|---|---|---|---|---|---|---|---|---|---|---|---|---|---|---|---|---|---|---|---|---|---|---|---|---|---|---|---|
| **Number – Number and place value** | | | | | | | | | | | | | | | | | | | | | | | | | | | | | | | | | | | | |
| read, write, order and compare numbers up to 10 000 000 and determine the value of each digit | • | | | | | | | | | | | | | | | | | | | | | | | | | | | | | | | | | | | |
| round any whole number to a required degree of accuracy | | | | | | • | | | | | | | | | | | | | | • | | | | | | | | | | | | | | | | |
| use negative numbers in context, and calculate intervals across zero | | | • | | | | | | | | | | | | | | | | | | | | | | | | | | | | | • | | | | |
| solve number and practical problems that involve all of the above | • | | • | | | | | | | | | | | | | | | | | | | | | | | | | | | | | • | | | | |
| **Notes and guidance (non-statutory)** | | | | | | | | | | | | | | | | | | | | | | | | | | | | | | | | | | | | |
| Pupils use the whole number system, including saying, reading and writing numbers accurately. | • | | • | | | | | | | | | | | | | | | | | | | | | | | | | | | | | | | | | |

*Stretch and Challenge Issue*

## Number – Addition, subtraction, multiplication and division

| | 1 | 2 | 3 | 4 | 5 | 6 | 7 | 8 | 9 | 10 | 11 | 12 | 13 | 14 | 15 | 16 | 17 | 18 | 19 | 20 | 21 | 22 | 23 | 24 | 25 | 26 | 27 | 28 | 29 | 30 | 31 | 32 | 33 | 34 | 35 | 36 |
|---|---|---|---|---|---|---|---|---|---|---|---|---|---|---|---|---|---|---|---|---|---|---|---|---|---|---|---|---|---|---|---|---|---|---|---|---|
| multiply multi-digit numbers up to 4 digits by a two-digit whole number using the formal written method of long multiplication | | | | | • | | | | | | | | | | | | | | | | | | | | | | | | | | | | | | | |
| divide numbers up to 4 digits by a two-digit whole number using the formal written method of long division, and interpret remainders as whole number remainders, fractions, or by rounding, as appropriate for the context | | | | | | • | | | | | | | | | | | | | | | | | | | | | | | | | | | | | | |
| divide numbers up to 4 digits by a two-digit number using the formal written method of short division where appropriate, interpreting remainders according to the context | | | | | | • | | | | | | | | | | | | | | | | | | | | | | | | | | | | | | |
| perform mental calculations, including with mixed operations and large numbers | | | | • | • | • | • | • | | | | | | | | | | | | | | | | | | | | | | | | | | | | |
| identify common factors, common multiples and prime numbers | | | | • | • | • | • | | | | | | | | | | | | | | | | | | | | | | | | | | | | | |
| use their knowledge of the order of operations to carry out calculations involving the four operations | | | | | | • | • | • | | | | | | | | | | | | | | | | | | | | | | | | | | | | |
| solve addition and subtraction multi-step problems in contexts, deciding which operations and methods to use and why | | | | • | • | • | • | • | | | | | | | | | | | | | | | | | | | | | | | | | | | | |
| solve problems involving addition, subtraction, multiplication and division | | | | • | • | • | • | • | | | | | | | | | | | | | | | | | | | | | | | | | | | | |
| use estimation to check answers to calculations and determine, in the context of a problem, an appropriate degree of accuracy | | | | • | • | • | • | • | | | | | | | | | | | | | | | | | | | | | | | | | | | | |

*Stretch and Challenge Issue*

| Notes and guidance (non-statutory) | 1 | 2 | 3 | 4 | 5 | 6 | 7 | 8 | 9 | 10 | 11 | 12 | 13 | 14 | 15 | 16 | 17 | 18 | 19 | 20 | 21 | 22 | 23 | 24 | 25 | 26 | 27 | 28 | 29 | 30 | 31 | 32 | 33 | 34 | 35 | 36 |
|---|---|---|---|---|---|---|---|---|---|---|---|---|---|---|---|---|---|---|---|---|---|---|---|---|---|---|---|---|---|---|---|---|---|---|---|---|
| Pupils practise addition, subtraction, multiplication and division for larger numbers, using the formal written methods of columnar addition and subtraction, short and long multiplication, and short and long division. | | | • | • | • | • | • | • | | | | | | | | | | | | | | | | | | | | | | | | | | | | |
| They undertake mental calculations with increasingly large numbers and more complex calculations. | | | • | • | • | • | • | • | | | | | | | | | | | | | | | | | | | | | | | | | | | | |
| Pupils continue to use all the multiplication tables to calculate mathematical statements in order to maintain their fluency. | | | | • | • | • | • | • | | | | | | | | | | | | | | | | | | | | | | | | | | | | |
| Pupils round answers to a specified degree of accuracy, for example, to the nearest 10, 20, 50 etc., but not to a specified number of significant figures. | | | | | • | • | • | • | | | | | | | | | | | | | | | | | | | | | | | | | | | | |
| Pupils explore the order of operations using brackets; for example, $2 + 1 \times 3 = 5$ and $(2 + 1) \times 3 = 9$. | | | | | | • | • | • | | | | | | | | | | | | | | | | | | | | | | | | | | | | |
| Common factors can be related to finding equivalent fractions. | | | | | | | | | | | | | | | | | | | | | | | | | | | | | | | | | | | | |

*Stretch and Challenge Issue*

## Number – Fractions (including decimals and percentages)

| | 1 | 2 | 3 | 4 | 5 | 6 | 7 | 8 | 9 | 10 | 11 | 12 | 13 | 14 | 15 | 16 | 17 | 18 | 19 | 20 | 21 | 22 | 23 | 24 | 25 | 26 | 27 | 28 | 29 | 30 | 31 | 32 | 33 | 34 | 35 | 36 |
|---|---|---|---|---|---|---|---|---|---|---|---|---|---|---|---|---|---|---|---|---|---|---|---|---|---|---|---|---|---|---|---|---|---|---|---|---|
| • use common factors to simplify fractions; use common multiples to express fractions in the same denomination | | | | | | | | | • | • | | | | | | | | | | | | | | | | | | | | | | | | | | |
| • compare and order fractions, including fractions > 1 | | | | | | | | | • | • | | | | | | | | | | | | | | | | | | | | | | | | | | |
| • add and subtract fractions with different denominators and mixed numbers, using the concept of equivalent fractions | | | | | | | | | | • | | | | | | | | | | | | | | | | | | | | | | | | | | |
| • multiply simple pairs of proper fractions, writing the answer in its simplest form [for example, $\frac{1}{4} \times \frac{1}{2} = \frac{1}{8}$] | | | | | | | | | | • | | | | | | | | | | | | | | | | | | | | | | | | | | |
| • divide proper fractions by whole numbers [for example, $\frac{1}{3} \div 2 = \frac{1}{6}$] | | | | | | | | | • | | | | | | | | | | | | | | | | | | | | | | | | | | | |
| • associate a fraction with division and calculate decimal fraction equivalents [for example, 0·375] for a simple fraction [for example, $\frac{3}{8}$] | | | | | | | | | | | • | | | | | | | | | | | | | | | | | | | | | | | | | |
| • identify the value of each digit in numbers given to three decimal places and multiply and divide numbers by 10, 100 and 1000 giving the answers up to three decimal places | | | | | | | | | | | • | | | | | | | | | | | | | | | | | | | | | | | | | |
| • multiply one-digit numbers with up to two decimal places by whole numbers | | | | | | | | | | | • | | | | | | | | | | | | | | | | | | | | | | | | | |
| • use written division methods in cases where the answer has up to two decimal places | | | | | | | | | | | | | • | | | | | | | | | | | | | | | | | | | | | | | |
| • solve problems which require answers to be rounded to specified degrees of accuracy | | | | | | | | | | | | • | • | | | | | | | | | | | | | | | | | | | | | | | |
| • recall and use equivalences between simple fractions, decimals and percentages, including in different contexts | • | | | | | | | | | | | | | | | | | | | | | | | | | | | | | | | | | | | |

*Stretch and Challenge Issue*

| Notes and guidance (non-statutory) | 1 | 2 | 3 | 4 | 5 | 6 | 7 | 8 | 9 | 10 | 11 | 12 | 13 | 14 | 15 | 16 | 17 | 18 | 19 | 20 | 21 | 22 | 23 | 24 | 25 | 26 | 27 | 28 | 29 | 30 | 31 | 32 | 33 | 34 | 35 | 36 |
|---|---|---|---|---|---|---|---|---|---|---|---|---|---|---|---|---|---|---|---|---|---|---|---|---|---|---|---|---|---|---|---|---|---|---|---|---|
| Pupils should practise, use and understand the addition and subtraction of fractions with different denominators by identifying equivalent fractions with the same denominator. They should start with fractions where the denominator of one fraction is a multiple of the other (for example, $\frac{1}{2} + \frac{1}{8} = \frac{5}{8}$) and progress to varied and increasingly complex problems. | | | | | | | | | | • | | | | | | | | | | | | | | | | | | | | | | | | | | |
| Pupils should use a variety of images to support their understanding of multiplication with fractions. This follows earlier work about fractions as operators (fractions of), as numbers, and as equal parts of objects, for example as parts of a rectangle. | | | | | | | | | • | • | | | | | | | | | | | | | | | | | | | | | | | | | | |
| Pupils use their understanding of the relationship between unit fractions and division to work backwards by multiplying a quantity that represents a unit fraction to find the whole quantity (for example, if $\frac{1}{4}$ of a length is 36 cm, then the whole length is $36 \times 4 = 144$ cm). | | | | | | | | | • | | | | | | | | | | | | | | | | | | | | | | | | | | | |
| They practise calculations with simple fractions and decimal fraction equivalents to aid fluency, including listing equivalent fractions to identify fractions with common denominators. | | | | | | | | | • | | | | | | | | | | | | | | | | | | | | | | | | | | | |
| Pupils can explore and make conjectures about converting a simple fraction to a decimal fraction (for example, $3 \div 8 = 0.375$). For simple fractions with recurring decimal equivalents, pupils learn about rounding the decimal to three decimal places, or other appropriate approximations depending on the context. Pupils multiply and divide numbers with up to two decimal places by one-digit and two-digit whole numbers. Pupils multiply decimals by whole numbers, starting with the simplest cases, such as $0.4 \times 2 = 0.8$, and in practical contexts, such as measures and money. | | | | | | | | | | | • | | | | | | | | | | | | | | | | | | | | | | | | | |

Stretch and Challenge Issue

| Notes and guidance (non-statutory) Continued | 1 | 2 | 3 | 4 | 5 | 6 | 7 | 8 | 9 | 10 | 11 | 12 | 13 | 14 | 15 | 16 | 17 | 18 | 19 | 20 | 21 | 22 | 23 | 24 | 25 | 26 | 27 | 28 | 29 | 30 | 31 | 32 | 33 | 34 | 35 | 36 |
|---|---|---|---|---|---|---|---|---|---|---|---|---|---|---|---|---|---|---|---|---|---|---|---|---|---|---|---|---|---|---|---|---|---|---|---|---|
| Pupils are introduced to the division of decimal numbers by one-digit whole number, initially, in practical contexts involving measures and money. They recognise division calculations as the inverse of multiplication. | | | | | | | | | | | • | | | | | | | | | | | | | | | | | | | | | | | | | |
| Pupils also develop their skills of rounding and estimating as a means of predicting and checking the order of magnitude of their answers to decimal calculations. This includes rounding answers to a specified degree of accuracy and checking the reasonableness of their answers. | | | | | | | | | | | • | | | | | | | | | | | | | | | | | | | | | | | | | |

*Stretch and Challenge Issue*

## Ratio and proportion

| | 1 | 2 | 3 | 4 | 5 | 6 | 7 | 8 | 9 | 10 | 11 | 12 | 13 | 14 | 15 | 16 | 17 | 18 | 19 | 20 | 21 | 22 | 23 | 24 | 25 | 26 | 27 | 28 | 29 | 30 | 31 | 32 | 33 | 34 | 35 | 36 |
|---|---|---|---|---|---|---|---|---|---|---|---|---|---|---|---|---|---|---|---|---|---|---|---|---|---|---|---|---|---|---|---|---|---|---|---|---|
| solve problems involving the relative sizes of two quantities where missing values can be found by using integer multiplication and division facts | • | | | | | | | | | | | | • | • | • | | | | | | | | | | | | | | | | | | | | | |
| solve problems involving the calculation of percentages [for example, of measures, and such as 15% of 360] and the use of percentages for comparison | • | | | | | | • | | | | | • | • | • | • | • | • | | | | | | | | | | | | | | | | | • | | • |
| solve problems involving similar shapes where the scale factor is known or can be found | | | | | | | | | | | | | | • | | • | | | | | | | | | | | | | | | | | | | | |
| solve problems involving unequal sharing and grouping using knowledge of fractions and multiples. | • | | | | | | | | | | | | • | • | • | | | | | | | | | | | | | | | | | | | | | |

## Notes and guidance (non-statutory)

| | 1 | 2 | 3 | 4 | 5 | 6 | 7 | 8 | 9 | 10 | 11 | 12 | 13 | 14 | 15 | 16 | 17 | 18 | 19 | 20 | 21 | 22 | 23 | 24 | 25 | 26 | 27 | 28 | 29 | 30 | 31 | 32 | 33 | 34 | 35 | 36 |
|---|---|---|---|---|---|---|---|---|---|---|---|---|---|---|---|---|---|---|---|---|---|---|---|---|---|---|---|---|---|---|---|---|---|---|---|---|
| Pupils recognise proportionality in contexts when the relations between quantities are in the same ratio (for example, similar shapes and recipes). | • | | | | | | | | | | | | • | • | • | | • | | | | | | | | | | | | | | | | | | | |
| Pupils link percentages or 360° to calculating angles of pie charts. | | | | | | | | | | | | • | | | | | | | | | | | | | | | | | | | | | | • | | • |
| Pupils should consolidate their understanding of ratio when comparing quantities, sizes and scale drawings by solving a variety of problems. They might use the notation *a:b* to record their work. | | | | | | | | | | | | | • | • | • | | | | | | | | | | | | | | | | | | | | | |
| Pupils solve problems involving unequal quantities, for example, 'for every egg you need three spoonfuls of flour', $\frac{3}{5}$ of the class are boys'. These problems are the foundation for later formal approaches to ratio and proportion. | | | | | | | | | | | | | • | • | • | | | | | | | | | | | | | | | | | | | | | |

*Stretch and Challenge Issue*

| | 1 | 2 | 3 | 4 | 5 | 6 | 7 | 8 | 9 | 10 | 11 | 12 | 13 | 14 | 15 | 16 | 17 | 18 | 19 | 20 | 21 | 22 | 23 | 24 | 25 | 26 | 27 | 28 | 29 | 30 | 31 | 32 | 33 | 34 | 35 | 36 |
|---|---|---|---|---|---|---|---|---|---|----|----|----|----|----|----|----|----|----|----|----|----|----|----|----|----|----|----|----|----|----|----|----|----|----|----|----|
| **Algebra** | | | | | | | | | | | | | | | | | | | | | | | | | | | | | | | | | | | | |
| • use simple formulae | | | | | | | | • | | | | | | | | | • | | • | • | • | • | • | • | • | • | | | | | | • | • | | | |
| • generate and describe linear number sequences | | | | | | | | | | | | | | | | | • | | | | | | | | | | | | | | | | | | | |
| • express missing number problems algebraically | | | | | | | | • | | | | | | | | | | • | | | | | | | | | | | | | | | | | | |
| • find pairs of numbers that satisfy an equation with two unknowns | | • | | | | | | | | | | | | | | | | | | | | | | | | | | | | | | | | | | |
| • enumerate possibilities of combinations of two variables | | | | | | | | | | | | | | | | | • | | | | | | | | | | | | | | | | | | | |

### Notes and guidance (non-statutory)

Pupils should be introduced to the use of symbols and letters to represent variables and unknowns in mathematical situations that they already understand, such as:

  – missing numbers, lengths, coordinates and angles
  – formulae in mathematics and science
  – equivalent expressions (for example, $a + b = b + a$)
  – generalisations of number patterns
  – number puzzles (for example, what two numbers can add up to).

| | 1 | 2 | 3 | 4 | 5 | 6 | 7 | 8 | 9 | 10 | 11 | 12 | 13 | 14 | 15 | 16 | 17 | 18 | 19 | 20 | 21 | 22 | 23 | 24 | 25 | 26 | 27 | 28 | 29 | 30 | 31 | 32 | 33 | 34 | 35 | 36 |
|---|---|---|---|---|---|---|---|---|---|----|----|----|----|----|----|----|----|----|----|----|----|----|----|----|----|----|----|----|----|----|----|----|----|----|----|----|
| Notes and guidance | | • | | | | | | • | | | | | | | | | • | • | • | • | • | • | • | • | • | • | | | | | | • | • | | | |

*Stretch and Challenge Issue*

## Measurement

| | 1 | 2 | 3 | 4 | 5 | 6 | 7 | 8 | 9 | 10 | 11 | 12 | 13 | 14 | 15 | 16 | 17 | 18 | 19 | 20 | 21 | 22 | 23 | 24 | 25 | 26 | 27 | 28 | 29 | 30 | 31 | 32 | 33 | 34 | 35 | 36 |
|---|---|---|---|---|---|---|---|---|---|---|---|---|---|---|---|---|---|---|---|---|---|---|---|---|---|---|---|---|---|---|---|---|---|---|---|---|
| solve problems involving the calculation and conversion of units of measure, using decimal notation up to three decimal places where appropriate | | | | | | | | | | | • | | | | | | | • | • | • | • | | • | • | • | • | | | | | | | | | | |
| use, read, write and convert between standard units, converting measurements of length, mass, volume and time from a smaller unit of measure to a larger unit, and vice versa, using decimal notation up to three decimal places | | | | | | | | | | | • | | | | | | | • | • | • | • | | • | • | | | | | | | | | | | | |
| convert between miles and kilometres | | | | | | | | | | | | | | | | | | | | | | | | • | | | | | | | | | | | | |
| recognise that shapes with the same areas can have different perimeters and vice versa | | | | | | | | | | | | | | | | | | | | | | • | | | | | | | | | | | | | | |
| recognise when it is possible to use formulae for area and volume of shapes | | | | | | | | | | | | | | | | | | | | | • | | • | | | | | | | | | | | | | |
| calculate the area of parallelograms and triangles | | | | | | | | | | | | | | | | | | | | | | | • | | | | | | | | | | | | | |
| calculate, estimate and compare volume of cubes and cuboids using standard units, including cubic centimetres (cm³) and cubic metres (m³), and extending to other units [for example, mm³ and km³] | | | | | | | | | | | | | | | | | | | | | • | | | | | | | | | | | | | | | |

## Notes and guidance (non-statutory)

| | 1 | 2 | 3 | 4 | 5 | 6 | 7 | 8 | 9 | 10 | 11 | 12 | 13 | 14 | 15 | 16 | 17 | 18 | 19 | 20 | 21 | 22 | 23 | 24 | 25 | 26 | 27 | 28 | 29 | 30 | 31 | 32 | 33 | 34 | 35 | 36 |
|---|---|---|---|---|---|---|---|---|---|---|---|---|---|---|---|---|---|---|---|---|---|---|---|---|---|---|---|---|---|---|---|---|---|---|---|---|
| Pupils connect conversion (for example, from kilometres to miles) to a graphical representation as preparation for understanding linear/proportional graphs. | | | | | | | | | | | | | | | | | | | | | | | | | | | | | | | | | | | • | |
| They know approximate conversions and are able to tell if an answer is sensible. | | | | | | | | | | | | | | | | | | | • | • | | | | • | | | | | | | | | | | • | |
| Using the number line, pupils use, add and subtract positive and negative integers for measures such as temperature. | | • | | | | | | | | | | | | | | | | | | | | | | | | | | | | | | | | | | |

Stretch and Challenge Issue

## Notes and guidance (non-statutory) Continued

| | 1 | 2 | 3 | 4 | 5 | 6 | 7 | 8 | 9 | 10 | 11 | 12 | 13 | 14 | 15 | 16 | 17 | 18 | 19 | 20 | 21 | 22 | 23 | 24 | 25 | 26 | 27 | 28 | 29 | 30 | 31 | 32 | 33 | 34 | 35 | 36 |
|---|---|---|---|---|---|---|---|---|---|---|---|---|---|---|---|---|---|---|---|---|---|---|---|---|---|---|---|---|---|---|---|---|---|---|---|---|
| They relate the area of rectangles to parallelograms and triangles, for example, by dissection, and calculate their areas, understanding and using the formulae (in words or symbols) to do this. | | | | | | | | | | | | | | | | | | | | | | | ● | | | | | | | | | | | | | |
| Pupils could be introduced to compound units for speed, such as miles per hour, and apply their knowledge in science or other subjects as appropriate. | | | | | | | | | | | | | | | | | | ● | | ● | | | | | | | | | | | | | | | | ● |

*Stretch and Challenge Issue*

## Geometry – Properties of shapes

| | 1 | 2 | 3 | 4 | 5 | 6 | 7 | 8 | 9 | 10 | 11 | 12 | 13 | 14 | 15 | 16 | 17 | 18 | 19 | 20 | 21 | 22 | 23 | 24 | 25 | 26 | 27 | 28 | 29 | 30 | 31 | 32 | 33 | 34 | 35 | 36 |
|---|---|---|---|---|---|---|---|---|---|---|---|---|---|---|---|---|---|---|---|---|---|---|---|---|---|---|---|---|---|---|---|---|---|---|---|---|
| • draw 2-D shapes using given dimensions and angles | | | | | | | | | | | | | | | | | | | | | | | | | | ● | | ● | ● | ● | ● | ● | ● | | | |
| • recognise, describe and build simple 3-D shapes, including making nets | | | | | | | | | | | | | | | | | | | | | | | | | | | ● | | | | | | | | | |
| • compare and classify geometric shapes based on their properties and sizes and find unknown angles in any triangles, quadrilaterals, and regular polygons | | | | | | | | | | | | | | | | | | | | | | | | | | ● | | ● | | ● | | ● | | | | |
| • illustrate and name parts of circles, including radius, diameter and circumference and know that the diameter is twice the radius | | | | | | | | | | | | | | | | | | | | | ● | | | | | ● | | ● | ● | ● | ● | | | | | |
| • recognise angles where they meet at a point, are on a straight line, or are vertically opposite, and find missing angles | | | | | | | | | | | | | | | | | | | | | | | | | | | | ● | | | | | | | | |

## Notes and guidance (non-statutory)

| | 1 | 2 | 3 | 4 | 5 | 6 | 7 | 8 | 9 | 10 | 11 | 12 | 13 | 14 | 15 | 16 | 17 | 18 | 19 | 20 | 21 | 22 | 23 | 24 | 25 | 26 | 27 | 28 | 29 | 30 | 31 | 32 | 33 | 34 | 35 | 36 |
|---|---|---|---|---|---|---|---|---|---|---|---|---|---|---|---|---|---|---|---|---|---|---|---|---|---|---|---|---|---|---|---|---|---|---|---|---|
| Pupils draw shapes and nets accurately, using measuring tools and conventional markings and labels for lines and angles. | | | | | | | | | | | | | | | | | | | | | | | | | | ● | | ● | ● | ● | ● | ● | ● | | | |
| Pupils describe the properties of shapes and explain how unknown angles and lengths can be derived from known measurements. | | | | | | | | | | | | | | | | | | | | | | | | | ● | ● | ● | | | | | | | | | |
| These relationships might be expressed algebraically for example, $d = 2 \times r$, $a = 180 - (b + c)$. | | | | | | | | | | | | | | | | | | | | | | | | | | ● | | ● | | | | | | | | |

*Stretch and Challenge Issue*

## Geometry – Position and direction

| | 1 | 2 | 3 | 4 | 5 | 6 | 7 | 8 | 9 | 10 | 11 | 12 | 13 | 14 | 15 | 16 | 17 | 18 | 19 | 20 | 21 | 22 | 23 | 24 | 25 | 26 | 27 | 28 | 29 | 30 | 31 | 32 | 33 | 34 | 35 | 36 |
|---|---|---|---|---|---|---|---|---|---|---|---|---|---|---|---|---|---|---|---|---|---|---|---|---|---|---|---|---|---|---|---|---|---|---|---|---|
| describe positions on the full coordinate grid (all four quadrants) | | | | | | | | | | | | | | | | | | | | | | | | | | | | | | • | • | | | | | |
| draw and translate simple shapes on the coordinate plane, and reflect them in the axes | | | | | | | | | | | | | | | | | | | | | | | | | | | | | | • | • | | | | | |

### Notes and guidance (non-statutory)

Pupils draw and label a pair of axes in all four quadrants with equal scaling. This extends their knowledge of one quadrant to all four quadrants, including the use of negative numbers.

| | 1 | 2 | 3 | 4 | 5 | 6 | 7 | 8 | 9 | 10 | 11 | 12 | 13 | 14 | 15 | 16 | 17 | 18 | 19 | 20 | 21 | 22 | 23 | 24 | 25 | 26 | 27 | 28 | 29 | 30 | 31 | 32 | 33 | 34 | 35 | 36 |
|---|---|---|---|---|---|---|---|---|---|---|---|---|---|---|---|---|---|---|---|---|---|---|---|---|---|---|---|---|---|---|---|---|---|---|---|---|
| | | | | | | | | | | | | | | | | | | | | | | | | | | | | | | • | • | | | | | |

Pupils draw and label rectangles (including squares), parallelograms and rhombuses, specified by coordinates in the four quadrants, predicting missing coordinates using the properties of shapes. These might be expressed algebraically for example, translating vertex $(a, b)$ to $(a - 2, b + 3)$; $(a, b)$ and $(a + d, b + d)$ being opposite vertices of a square of side $d$.

| | 1 | 2 | 3 | 4 | 5 | 6 | 7 | 8 | 9 | 10 | 11 | 12 | 13 | 14 | 15 | 16 | 17 | 18 | 19 | 20 | 21 | 22 | 23 | 24 | 25 | 26 | 27 | 28 | 29 | 30 | 31 | 32 | 33 | 34 | 35 | 36 |
|---|---|---|---|---|---|---|---|---|---|---|---|---|---|---|---|---|---|---|---|---|---|---|---|---|---|---|---|---|---|---|---|---|---|---|---|---|
| | | | | | | | | | | | | | | | | | | | | | | | | | | | | | | • | • | | | | | |

## Statistics

| | 1 | 2 | 3 | 4 | 5 | 6 | 7 | 8 | 9 | 10 | 11 | 12 | 13 | 14 | 15 | 16 | 17 | 18 | 19 | 20 | 21 | 22 | 23 | 24 | 25 | 26 | 27 | 28 | 29 | 30 | 31 | 32 | 33 | 34 | 35 | 36 |
|---|---|---|---|---|---|---|---|---|---|---|---|---|---|---|---|---|---|---|---|---|---|---|---|---|---|---|---|---|---|---|---|---|---|---|---|---|
| interpret and construct pie charts and line graphs and use these to solve problems | | | • | | | | | | | | • | | | | | | | | | | | | | | | | | | | | • | | • | • | • | • |
| calculate and interpret the mean as an average | | | | | | | | | | | | | | | | | | | | | | | | | | | | | | | | | • | | | |

### Notes and guidance (non-statutory)

Pupils connect their work on angles, fractions and percentages to the interpretation of pie charts.

| | 1 | 2 | 3 | 4 | 5 | 6 | 7 | 8 | 9 | 10 | 11 | 12 | 13 | 14 | 15 | 16 | 17 | 18 | 19 | 20 | 21 | 22 | 23 | 24 | 25 | 26 | 27 | 28 | 29 | 30 | 31 | 32 | 33 | 34 | 35 | 36 |
|---|---|---|---|---|---|---|---|---|---|---|---|---|---|---|---|---|---|---|---|---|---|---|---|---|---|---|---|---|---|---|---|---|---|---|---|---|
| | | | | | | | | | | | • | | | | | | | | | | | | | | | | | | | | | | • | • | | • |

Pupils both encounter and draw graphs relating two variables, arising from their own enquiry and in other subjects.

| | 1 | 2 | 3 | 4 | 5 | 6 | 7 | 8 | 9 | 10 | 11 | 12 | 13 | 14 | 15 | 16 | 17 | 18 | 19 | 20 | 21 | 22 | 23 | 24 | 25 | 26 | 27 | 28 | 29 | 30 | 31 | 32 | 33 | 34 | 35 | 36 |
|---|---|---|---|---|---|---|---|---|---|---|---|---|---|---|---|---|---|---|---|---|---|---|---|---|---|---|---|---|---|---|---|---|---|---|---|---|
| | | | | | | | | | | | | | | | | | | | | | | | | | | | | • | | | | | • | • | • | |

They should connect conversion from kilometres to miles in measurement to its graphical representation.

Pupils know when it is appropriate to find the mean of a data set.

| | 1 | 2 | 3 | 4 | 5 | 6 | 7 | 8 | 9 | 10 | 11 | 12 | 13 | 14 | 15 | 16 | 17 | 18 | 19 | 20 | 21 | 22 | 23 | 24 | 25 | 26 | 27 | 28 | 29 | 30 | 31 | 32 | 33 | 34 | 35 | 36 |
|---|---|---|---|---|---|---|---|---|---|---|---|---|---|---|---|---|---|---|---|---|---|---|---|---|---|---|---|---|---|---|---|---|---|---|---|---|
| | | | | | | | | | | | | | | | | | | | | | | | | | | | | | | | | | | | • | |

## Cross-curricular links to the National Curriculum Programme of Study

Cross-curricular link and *Stretch and Challenge* Feature

| Subject | Feature | 1 | 2 | 3 | 4 | 5 | 6 | 7 | 8 | 9 | 10 | 11 | 12 | 13 | 14 | 15 | 16 | 17 | 18 |
|---|---|---|---|---|---|---|---|---|---|---|---|---|---|---|---|---|---|---|---|
| Links with home | At Home | | • | | | | • | | | | | • | | | | • | • | | |
| Links to money | Money Matters | • | | | | • | | • | | | • | • | • | • | • | • | | | • |
| Physical Education | Sports Update | | | | | | | | • | | | | | | | • | • | • | |
| Design & Technology | Construct | | | | | | | | | | | | | | | | | | |
| Art & Design /Music | The Arts Roundup | | | • | | | | | | • | | | | • | | • | | | |
| History | In the Past / Famous Mathematicians | | | • | • | | | • | | • | • | | | | | • | | • | |
| Geography | Around the World | • | • | | • | • | • | • | | | | • | | • | • | | | | |
| Computing | Technology Today | • | • | | | | | | | | | | • | | | | | | |
| Science | Focus on Science | | • | | | • | • | | | | | | • | • | | | | | |
| English | The Language of Maths | • | | • | | | | • | | | | • | • | | • | • | • | | |
| Mathematics | Let's Investigate | • | • | • | • | • | • | • | • | • | • | • | • | | • | • | • | | |
| Mathematics | The Puzzler | • | | • | • | • | • | | • | • | | • | • | • | • | | • | | |
| Mathematics | Looking for Patterns | | • | • | • | • | • | • | • | • | | • | | | • | • | | • | |
| Mathematics | What's the Problem? | | | | • | | | | • | • | | | • | • | • | • | • | | |

| Issue | Topic | Domain(s) |
|---|---|---|
| 1 | Number | Number: – Number and place value |
| 2 | Negative numbers | Number: – Number and place value |
| 3 | Addition | Number: – Addition, subtraction, multiplication and division |
| 4 | Subtraction | Number: – Addition, subtraction, multiplication and division |
| 5 | Multiplication | Number: – Addition, subtraction, multiplication and division |
| 6 | Division | Number: – Addition, subtraction, multiplication and division |
| 7 | Mixed operations | Number: – Addition, subtraction, multiplication and division |
| 8 | Mixed operations and algebra | Number: – Addition, subtraction, multiplication and division |
| 9 | Fractions | Number: – Fractions, (including decimals and percentages) |
| 10 | Fractions | Number: – Fractions, (including decimals and percentages) |
| 11 | Decimals | Number: – Fractions, (including decimals and percentages) |
| 12 | Percentages | Number: – Fractions, (including decimals and percentages) |
| 13 | Percentages | Number: – Fractions, (including decimals and percentages) |
| 14 | Ratio and proportion | Ratio and proportion |
| 15 | Ratio and proportion | Ratio and proportion |
| 16 | Ratio and proportion | Ratio and proportion |
| 17 | Algebra | Algebra |
| 18 | Algebra – The Financial Issue | Algebra |

Cross-curricular link and *Stretch and Challenge* Feature

| Category | Feature | 19 Length | 20 Mass | 21 Volume and capacity | 22 Time | 23 Area | 24 Perimeter | 25 Measurement | 26 2-D shapes | 27 3-D shapes | 28 Movement and angle | 29 Reflections | 30 Translations | 31 Geometry | 32 Geometry | 33 Geometry | 34 Statistics | 35 Statistics | 36 Statistics |
|---|---|---|---|---|---|---|---|---|---|---|---|---|---|---|---|---|---|---|---|
| Links with home | At Home | • | • | • | | • | | | | | • | • | | | | | | • | |
| Links to money | Money Matters | • | | | | | | | | | | | | | | | | | |
| Physical Education | Sports Update | • | | • | • | • | | • | | • | • | • | | | | | | • | • |
| Design & Technology | Construct | • | | | | | • | | | • | • | • | • | • | • | • | | | • |
| Art & Design / Music | The Arts Roundup | | | | | | | | | | • | • | • | | | • | • | | |
| History | In the Past / Famous Mathematicians | | | • | | • | | • | • | • | • | • | | | • | • | • | | |
| Geography | Around the World | • | • | • | | | | • | • | | • | • | | • | • | • | | • | • |
| Computing | Technology Today | | | | | | | | | | • | | | | | • | | | |
| Science | Focus on Science | • | • | • | • | | | • | | | • | | | | | | • | • | • |
| English | The Language of Maths | • | • | • | | | • | | | | | | | | | • | • | | • |
| Mathematics | Let's Investigate | • | • | • | • | • | • | • | • | • | • | • | • | • | • | • | • | • | |
| Mathematics | The Puzzler | | | | • | • | | | • | • | • | • | | | • | • | • | • | |
| Mathematics | Looking for Patterns | | • | | • | • | • | | | | • | • | • | | | • | | | |
| Mathematics | What's the Problem? | | • | | | • | • | | • | | | | | | | • | | | |

| Domain(s) | Topic | Issue |
|---|---|---|
| Measurement | Length | 19 |
| | Mass | 20 |
| | Volume and capacity | 21 |
| | Time | 22 |
| | Area | 23 |
| | Perimeter | 24 |
| | Measurement | 25 |
| Geometry: – Properties of shapes | 2-D shapes | 26 |
| | 3-D shapes | 27 |
| Geometry: – Position and direction | Movement and angle | 28 |
| | Reflections | 29 |
| | Translations | 30 |
| Geometry: – Properties of shapes | Geometry | 31 |
| | Geometry | 32 |
| – Position and direction | Geometry | 33 |
| Statistics | Statistics | 34 |
| | Statistics | 35 |
| | Statistics | 36 |

## Resources used in *Stretch and Challenge 6*

A fundamental skill of mathematics is knowing what resources to use and when it is appropriate to use them. It is for this reason that many of the activities in *Stretch and Challenge* give no indication to the children as to which resources to use. Although the teacher's notes that accompany each activity include a list of resources, children should be encouraged to work out for themselves what they will need to use to successfully complete an activity.

It is assumed that for each activity children will have ready access to pencil and paper, and any other resources that are specifically mentioned in an activity, for example, computers or other Resource sheets. However, all other equipment should be left for the children to locate and use as and when they see is appropriate.

A list of all the resources children are likely to need in *Stretch and Challenge 6* is given below.

| Resource | *Stretch and Challenge* Issue | | | | | | | | | | | | | | | | | |
|---|---|---|---|---|---|---|---|---|---|---|---|---|---|---|---|---|---|---|
| | 1 | 2 | 3 | 4 | 5 | 6 | 7 | 8 | 9 | 10 | 11 | 12 | 13 | 14 | 15 | 16 | 17 | 18 |
| pencil and paper | • | • | • | • | • | • | • | • | • | • | • | • | • | • | • | • | • | • |
| Resource sheets | 2,3 | 2,3,5 | 2,3 | 2,3 | 2,3 | 2,3 | 2,3 | 2,3 | 2,3 | 2,3 | 2,3,5 | 2,3 | 2,3 | 2,3 | 2,3,4 | 2,3 | 2,3 | 2,3 |
| computer | | • | | | | | | | | | | | | | | | | |
| computer with Internet access | • | | | | • | | | | | | • | • | | • | • | • | • | |
| data handling software | | | | | | | | | | | | • | | | | | | |
| ruler | | • | • | | • | | | • | | | • | • | | | | | | |
| calculator | | • | • | • | • | • | • | • | | | • | • | • | • | • | | • | • |
| bowl of ice and thermometer | | • | | | | | | | | | | | | | | | | |
| empty frozen food packages | | • | | | | | | | | | | | | | | | | |
| fraction wall | | | | | | | • | | | | | | | | | | | |
| selection of newspapers / magazines / catalogues | | | | | | | | | | | • | • | | | | | | |
| material for making a poster, e.g. card, felt-tip pens … | | | | | | | | | | | • | | | | | • | | |
| cheques from a range of different banks | | | | | | | | | | | • | | | | | | | |
| pair of compasses | | | | | | | | | | | | • | | | | | | |
| protractor | | | | | | | | | | | | • | | | | | | |
| recipe books | | | | | | | | | | | | | | | • | • | | |
| set of dominoes | | | • | | | | | | | | | | | | • | | | |
| map of the local area and a contrasting area | | | | | | | | | | | | | • | | | | | |
| child's reading book | | | | | | | | | | | | | | • | | | | |
| two 1, 2, 3, 1, 2, 3 dice | | | | | | | | | | | | | | • | | | | |
| local telephone directory | | | | | | | | | | | | | | | • | | | |
| pack of playing cards | | | | | | | | | | | | | | | • | | | |
| access to different sized children's classroom chairs | | | | | | | | | | | | | | | • | | | |
| measuring equipment | | | | | | | | | | | | | | | • | | | |
| 2 sheets of A4 paper | | | | | | | | | | | | | | | • | | | |
| coloured pencils | | | | | | | | | | | | | | | • | | | |

| Resource | Stretch and Challenge Issue | | | | | | | | | | | | | | | | | |
|---|---|---|---|---|---|---|---|---|---|---|---|---|---|---|---|---|---|---|
| | 19 | 20 | 21 | 22 | 23 | 24 | 25 | 26 | 27 | 28 | 29 | 30 | 31 | 32 | 33 | 34 | 35 | 36 |
| pencil and paper | • | • | • | • | • | • | • | • | • | • | • | • | • | • | • | • | • | • |
| Resource sheets | 2,3,5 | 2,3,5 | 2,3 | 2,3 | 2,3,8 | 2,3,5,8 | 2,3,5 | 2,3,6 | 2,3 | 2,3,5,6,8–11 | 2,3,6 | 2,3,6,8,9 | 2,3,5,8–10 | 2,3,5,6,8 | 2,3,5–11 | 2,3,5 | 2,3,5 | 2,3,5 |
| computer with Internet access | • | • | • | | | • | • | | | • | • | • | • | • | • | • | • | • |
| data handling software | | | | | | | | | | | | | | | | • | • | • |
| ruler | • | • | | | • | • | • | • | • | • | • | • | • | • | • | • | • | • |
| calculator | • | • | • | • | • | | • | • | | | | | | | | • | • | • |
| pair of compasses | • | | | | | | | | | • | • | | • | | • | • | | • |
| protractor | | | | | | | | | | • | | | | | | • | | • |
| scissors | | | | | • | | | • | | | | • | • | | | | | |
| collection of different polyhedrons | | | | | | | | • | | | | | | | | | | |
| straws and joiners and / or commercially produced skeletal construction kit | | | | | | | | • | | | | | | | | | | |
| six paper squares (per child), ideally each a different colour | | | | | | | | • | | | | | | | | | | |
| interlocking cubes | | | | | | | | • | | | | | | | | | | |
| cardboard | | | | | | | | • | | | | • | | | | | | |
| 1–6 dice | | | | | | | | • | | | | | | | | | | |
| postcards, travel brochures, books, magazines and wallpaper samples showing examples of reflective symmetry | | | | | | | | | | | • | | | | | | | |
| camera | | | | | | | | | | | • | | • | | | | | |
| coloured pencils | | | | | | | | • | | | • | • | • | | • | | | |
| sticky tape | | | | | | | | | | | | • | | | | | | |
| geoboard and elastic bands | | | | | • | • | | | | | | • | | | | | | |
| map of the local area | | | | | | | | | | | | | | • | | | | |
| floor robot, magnetic / orienteering compass; coin, 1–6 dice, 1–8 digit cards; random number generator, e.g. number spinner or similar; torch | | | | | | | | | | • | | | | | | | | |
| chessboard | | | | | | | | | | • | | | | | • | | | |
| tape measure | • | | | • | | | | • | | • | | | | | | | | • |
| trundle wheel | • | | | | • | | | | | | | | | | | | | |
| selection of maps showing different scales | • | | | | | | | | | | | | | | | | | |
| material for making a poster e.g. card, felt-tip pens … | | • | • | | | | | | | | | | | • | | | | |
| selection of food packages | | • | | | | | | | | | | | | | | | • | |
| collection of cylinders; 100 ml can; sand or rice; measuring cylinder with scale in cubic centimetres; water; collection of small solid objects | | | • | | | | | | | | | | | | | | | |
| time / clock interactive teaching tool; digital clock; mirror | | | | • | | | | | | | | | | | | | | |
| stopwatch | | | | • | | | | | | | | | | | | | | • |
| newspapers | | | | | • | | | | | | | | | | | • | • | • |
| range of measuring equipment | | | | | • | | | | | | | | | | | | | |
| world atlas or globe | | | | | | • | • | | | | | | | | | | | |
| road atlas | | | | | | | • | | | | | | | | | | | |
| matchsticks | | | | | | • | | • | | | | | | | | | | |
| string | | | | | | | • | | | | | | | | | | | |
| electricity bill | | | | | | | | | | | | | | | | | | • |
| set square | | | | | | | | • | | | | | | | | | | |
| at least six circular objects, all different sizes | | | | | | | | • | | | | | | | | | | |

# The Maths Herald

Name:

Date:

## The Language of Maths

Our number system is based on the number 10. It is called the *decimal numeral system* and has 10 as its base. That is why is it referred to as a *base 10* number system.

However number systems can be based on other numbers.

The *ternary numeral system* has 3 as its base. So it is referred to as *base 3*.

The table on the right shows the numbers 1 to 12 written in both base 10 (decimal) and base 3 (ternary).

Can you work out what the numbers 13 to 20 are in base 3?

Investigate different based numeral systems.

What are the numbers 1 to 20 written in these bases?

| base 10 | 1 | 2 | 3 | 4 | 5 | 6 |
|---|---|---|---|---|---|---|
| base 3 | 1 | 2 | 10 | 11 | 12 | 20 |

| base 10 | 7 | 8 | 9 | 10 | 11 | 12 |
|---|---|---|---|---|---|---|
| base 3 | 21 | 22 | 100 | 101 | 102 | 110 |

## Technology Today

The *binary numeral system* is the number system used in computing.

Investigate the binary numeral system.

© HarperCollins *Publishers* 2016

---

## Around the World

Look at the flags of different countries.

Using fractions, decimals and/or percentages, write a sentence describing the proportion of the different colours used in each flag.

Germany

France

Switzerland

Czech republic

Denmark

Italy

## The Puzzler

What mathematical symbol can you place between the numbers 1 and 2 to make a number greater than 1, but less than 2?

× < %
÷ □ +
= π ≠ >
≥ √ ○ £

## The Language of Maths

Counting is an important and fundamental skill not only in mathematics, but also in so many different aspects of life. When you started to add, subtract, multiply and divide, you did so using the skills of counting.

Often counting needs to be accurate, for example, when using money, when taking the class register, finding out how many school dinners there are.

But sometimes the numbers involved are just too large to get a precise number.

irrational number

Write about how you would get an approximate number for each of these:

- pebbles on a beach
- grains of sand in a sand pit
- hairs on your head
- stars in the sky.

# Technology Today

In a division calculation, a remainder can be expressed in different ways, for example as a fraction, a decimal or a whole number. In computing, the *modulo* operation finds the remainder of division of 1 number by another number.

Given 2 positive numbers, x (dividend) and y (divisor), x modulo y (abbreviated as x mod y) can be thought of as the remainder of the division of x by y.

Look at these examples involving modulo 3:

**Example 1**

7 mod 3 = 1

because 7 ÷ 3 leaves a remainder of 1

**Example 2**

9 mod 3 = 0

because 9 ÷ 3 leaves a remainder of 0

**Example 3**

14 mod 3 = 2

because 14 ÷ 3 leaves a remainder of 2

Choose other numbers between 1 and 20 and calculate their value in modulo 3.

Choose a set of 10 numbers between 1 and 20. Calculate the value of each of these numbers in modulo 4 and modulo 5.

Look at the values of each number in mod 3, mod 4 and mod 5. What do you notice?

## Let's Investigate

This triangular pattern of numbers is referred to as *Pascal's Triangle*.

What is the rule?

Write the next 2 rows of Pascal's Triangle.

Now rewrite Pascal's Triangle replacing each of the numbers with its value in modulo 3 (see  Technology Today activity).

Investigate the different patterns that arise.

Can you predict what the next 2 rows of Pascal's Triangle will be written in modulo 3 values?

```
          1
        1   1
      1   2   1
    1   3   3   1
  1   4   6   4   1
1   5  10  10   5   1
```

---

# Around the World

Most people, in very different jobs, rely on the use of whole numbers, fractions, decimals, percentages and / or ratio and proportion in order to be able to do their jobs properly.

Make 5 lists.

For each list, write down which jobs in particular use that type of number. How do they use the numbers? Why are they so important to what they do?

Which jobs belong to more than 1 list?

> 1 whole numbers
> 2 fractions
> 3 decimals
> 4 percentages
> 5 ratio and proportion

# Money Matters

In 1992, the Australian government decided to withdraw the use of the 1¢ and 2¢ coins from circulation.

The smallest monetary unit now used in Australia is the 5¢ coin.

What would be the implications of removing all 1p and 2p coins from circulation in the UK?

Make 2 lists: 1 list detailing how it would affect businesses, the other list how it would affect consumers.

# Around the World

A census is an official count or survey of a population, where various details are recorded.

In 2010, China, the country with the most people in the world, conducted a census.

Find out what the Chinese census surveyed.

Write a report about some of the results of the census.

© HarperCollins*Publishers* 2016

# The Maths Herald

Name:

Date:

## Let's Investigate

| 1 | 3 | 5 | 7 | 9 | -1 | -3 | -5 | -7 | -9 |
|---|---|---|---|---|----|----|----|----|----|
| 2 | 4 | 6 | 8 | 10 | -2 | -4 | -6 | -8 | -10 |

Choose any 3 numbers. Using some or all of these numbers, investigate how close to zero you can get. If you're able to make zero, record your calculation on a number line.

For example,

Choosing the numbers  -2  -5  7  can give -5 + 7 + -2

What about choosing 4 numbers?

## Focus on Science

For this experiment you need a bowl of ice and a thermometer.

Measure and record the temperature of the bowl of ice.

After 15 minutes, once again measure and record the temperature of the ice.

Keep doing this every 15 minutes for 5 hours.

Record the results in a chart or graph.

Write a short report about your results.

---

## Around the World

Inari is an area in northern Finland.

### Location of Finland

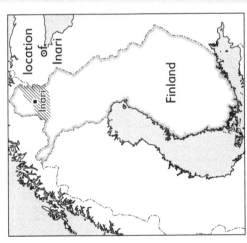

Iceland · Russia · Norway · Sweden · Finland · Estonia · Latvia · Lithuania · Denmark · Great Britain · Germany · Poland

The line graph below shows the maximum and minimum average daily temperature in Inari.

Temperature (Celsius)

20 · 10 · 0 · -10

Jan Feb Mar Apr May Jun Jul Aug Sep Oct Nov Dec

location of Inari

Finland

Write a report detailing the seasonal differences in temperature in Inari. Describe in your report the average temperature for each season and how this compares with the yearly average.

## Looking for Patterns

Using only these numbers, write down all the pairs of numbers that have a difference of 0·2.

| -0·3 | 0 | -0·5 | 0·2 | -0·1 | -0·4 | 0·1 | -0·2 |
|------|---|------|-----|------|------|-----|------|

## Let's Investigate

Look at this equation:

$a + b = 12$

If $a$ and $b$ stand for either a positive or negative whole number, investigate possible values for $a$ and $b$.

What about for these equations?

$a - b = 15$

$a + b = {}^-8$

$a - b = {}^-16$

## Technology Today

Look at each of these calculations.

7 + ⁻3    ⁻4 + 7    ⁻6 + 9

10 – ⁻6    ⁻12 – 5    ⁻16 – ⁻14

8 + ⁻3 + 7 + 9 + ⁻4

⁻7 + 4 – ⁻8 + 11

⁻10 – ⁻5 + 7 + ⁻9

Design a poster that gives a set of instructions showing how to use a calculator to find sums and differences of combinations of positive and negative numbers. Be sure to provide examples.

## At Home

Investigate frozen foods at home or at the supermarket.

All frozen foods have a recommended temperature at which they should be kept frozen.

Is this temperature the same for all types of frozen goods, for example, vegetables, ice cream, meat and seafood?

Does the suggested recommended temperature vary depending on the recommended 'use by' date?

What else can you find out about frozen foods?

---

## Around the World

Antarctica is Earth's southernmost continent. It is, on average, the coldest, driest and windiest continent.

This table shows the average minimum and record minimum temperatures in degrees Celsius on Stonington Island, Antarctica.

| | J | F | M | A | M | J | J | A | S | O | N | D |
|---|---|---|---|---|---|---|---|---|---|---|---|---|
| Average minimum (°C) | ⁻3 | ⁻4 | ⁻8 | ⁻10 | ⁻14 | ⁻17 | ⁻16 | ⁻16 | ⁻19 | ⁻16 | ⁻9 | ⁻3 |
| Record minimum (°C) | ⁻12 | ⁻11 | ⁻35 | ⁻27 | ⁻36 | ⁻37 | ⁻36 | ⁻37 | ⁻39 | ⁻29 | ⁻20 | ⁻13 |

Draw 1 line graph showing both the average minimum and record minimum temperatures on Stonington Island, Antarctica.

Write a report about the average minimum and record minimum temperatures on Stonington Island.

## Looking for Patterns

Fill in the missing numbers in each of these sequences:

37, □, 13, 1, □, ⁻23, □, ⁻59, □, ⁻83

□, □, ⁻25, □, ⁻9, ⁻1, □, 15, □

150, □, 10, □, ⁻200, ⁻270, □

□, ⁻117, ⁻80, □, ⁻6, □, 68, □

What is the rule for each sequence?

Make up 2 number sequences of your own involving negative numbers.

# The Maths Herald

S&C Volume 6

Name:

Date:

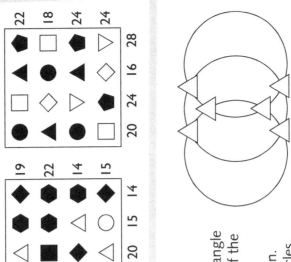

## Looking for Patterns

In each of these grids, shapes have replaced digits. Work out the value of each shape.

## The Puzzler

Write a different number in each triangle so that the 4 triangles on any one of the 3 circles add up to 30.

Invent a similar problem of your own. Instead of using interconnecting circles, what about trying rectangles or a different polygon.

## The Puzzler

The sum of 9 consecutive odd numbers is 225.

What are the numbers?

Write about how you discovered what the numbers are.

## The Puzzler

This is a 3 × 3 magic square.

Complete the magic square using only prime numbers.

The sum of each column, row and diagonal is 111 – this is the magic number.

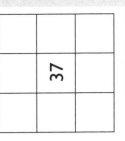

37

---

## Looking for Patterns

$6 + 7 = 13$    $8 + 9 = 17$    $4 + 5 = 9$

What do you notice about the numbers that have been added together to produce each of the answers?

What other answers can you get by adding pairs of numbers like these?

What answers can you *not* get by adding pairs of numbers like these?

What answers can you get by adding 3 numbers like these together?

What about 4 numbers like this?

What about 5 numbers?

What patterns do you notice?

Choosing a number, for example 18, can you decide whether or not the number can be written in 1 or more of these ways?

## Let's Investigate

Arrange 9 dominoes so that the sum of the dots is the same in each horizontal and vertical continuous line.

How many different arrangements can you find?

## The Puzzler

Complete this August calendar so that the sum of the Saturday dates is a multiple of 15.

| AUGUST | | | | | | |
|---|---|---|---|---|---|---|
| M | T | W | T | F | S | S |
| | | | | | | |

Complete this September calendar so that the sum of 1 of the full weeks is a multiple of 23.

Write down how you did it.

| SEPTEMBER | | | | | | |
|---|---|---|---|---|---|---|
| M | T | W | T | F | S | S |
| | | | | | | |

# The Language of Maths

A *tautonym* is a word that has 2 or more identical parts. For example, DODO, PAPA.

To work out a *numerical tautonym*, we first give each letter a value that is equal to its numerical position in the alphabet, so A = 1, B = 2, C = 3, ... Z = 26).

A *numerical tautonym* is a word which, when split into 2 or more equal parts and the letter values of each part added, has the same total for each part.

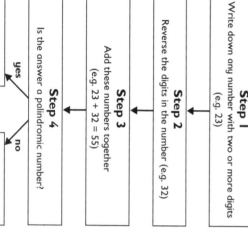

For example, the word 'WALL' can be split in half: the letters W and A total 24 (23 + 1), and the letters L and L also total 24 (12 + 12). The 2 parts have the same total. Therefore, 'WALL' is a numerical tautonym.

Can you find other 4-letter numerical tautonyms?

Can you think of any 6-letter numerical tautonyms?

What about 8-letter numerical tautonyms?

---

## Let's Investigate

A *palindrome* is a word, phrase or number that reads the same backwards as forwards. For example, 'MADAM', 'NURSES RUN', 575, 2002.

The steps on the right show how to make a palindromic whole number.

Does this work in exactly the same way for decimal numbers?

Give examples to justify your conclusions.

**Step 1**
Write down any number with two or more digits
(e.g. 23)

↓

**Step 2**
Reverse the digits in the number (e.g. 32)

↓

**Step 3**
Add these numbers together
(e.g. 23 + 32 = 55)

↓

**Step 4**
Is the answer a palindromic number?

— yes → Stop

— no → Repeat Steps 2, 3 and 4

---

## Famous Mathematicians

This triangular pattern of numbers was discovered in 1653 by a French mathematician named Blaise Pascal.

What is the rule?

Investigate other rules for producing triangles of numbers.

```
            1
          1   1
        1   2   1
      1   3   3   1
    1   4   6   4   1
  1   5   10  10  5   1
```

---

## Let's Investigate

Look at this set of 5 numbers:

$$\{1, 2, 5, 7, 8\}$$

14 can be made by adding together some of the numbers (7 + 5 + 2).

Using a digit only once in a calculation, can you make 10? 16? 20?

Which numbers less than 20 can't be made?

Make a set of 5 numbers that will make every number from 1 to 21 and none over 21.

---

## The Arts Roundup

Morcella Manor is holding an open-air concert.

When they opened the gates, 200 people entered the grounds.

During each hour after that, the number of people who entered the grounds was 200 more than the number already in the grounds.

At 9:00 p.m. when the concert began, there were 6200 people in the grounds.

At what time did Morcella Manor open the gates?

Write down how you worked out the answer.

S&C Volume 6

# The Maths Herald

Name: _____  Date: _____

## Around the World

The Yoruba people are one of the largest ethnic groups in West Africa, mostly in Nigeria. The Yoruba number system is based on the number 20 (*vigesimal*). Wherever possible, it uses subtraction to express numbers.

According to the Yoruba system, the numbers 11 to 14 are written by adding to 10 (i.e. 11 = 10 + 1, 12 = 10 + 2, ...).

However, the numbers 15 to 19 are written by subtracting from 20 (i.e. 15 = 20 – 5, 16 = 20 – 4, ...).

Similar to the numbers 11 to 19, the numbers 21 to 24 are written by adding to 20, and the numbers 25 to 29 are written by subtracting from 30.

Each number after 30 is written as a multiple of 20 plus or minus tens and units. This pattern is repeated for numbers up to 200, then the system becomes irregular.

## Let's Investigate

3 and 5 is a pair of consecutive primes that have a difference of 2.

Find other pairs of consecutive primes less than 100 that have a difference of 2.

What about pairs of consecutive primes less than 100 that have a difference of 4?

For example:
$33 = (20 \times 2) - 10 + 3$
$45 = (20 \times 3) - 10 - 5$
$71 = (20 \times 4) - 10 + 1$
$107 = (20 \times 6) - 10 - 3$

Can you find all the numbers 1–100 using the Yoruba number system?

Try using subtraction rather than addition wherever possible.

What about all the numbers to 200?

---

## Let's Investigate

Here is another method for subtracting pairs of numbers.

**Step 1:** Subtract each digit of the minuend (the number from which the subtrahend is to be subtracted) from 9.

**Step 2:** Add the answer to the subtrahend (the number to be subtracted).

**Step 3:** Subtract each digit of the answer from 9. The result is the answer.

```
    845
  – 577

  8 (9–8) 4 (9–4) 5 (9–5)
      1       5       4

    154
  + 577
    731

  7 (9–7) 3 (9–3) 1 (9–1)
      2       6       8
```

Using combinations of 3-digit and 4-digit numbers investigate whether this method always works.

Does this method work for decimals?

Provide examples to justify your reasoning.

Do you like this method? Is it a method that you might regularly use? Explain why or why not.

## What's the Problem?

mathematical constant

867 – 635          7362 – 4073

£57.66 – £34.71     £687.34 – £199.99

If you were to answer each of these subtraction calculations which method would you use? Would it be either of the Let's Investigate methods mentioned in this issue, or would it be a different method? Would you use the same method for all 4 calculations? Justify your reasoning for using particular methods.

## Famous Mathematicians

D.R. Kaprekar (1905–1986) was an Indian mathematician.

He discovered this interesting mathematical constant.

**Step 1:** Choose a 3-digit number (but not one with the same digits).

**Step 2:** Rearrange the digits to make the smallest 3-digit number possible. Then find the difference between these 2 numbers.

**Step 3:** Rearrange the digits in the answer to make the largest and smallest numbers possible. Then find the difference between these 2 numbers.

Repeat **Step 3** until you get the same calculation repeating itself.

Starting with the number 738 there are 3 subtraction calculations needed before the calculation starts repeating itself.

What is the largest number of subtraction calculations needed before the calculation starts repeating itself? Choose different 3-digit numbers to find out.

What happens if you start with a 4-digit number?

```
  738
– 378
  360
```

```
  630
–  36
  594
```

```
  954
– 459
  495
```

738 ✓ 444 ✗

## Looking for Patterns

Write a prime number in each shape so that the answer is zero.

The numbers in the circles are consecutive prime numbers.

How many different calculations can you make?

□ – ○ – ○ – ○ = 0

Once again write a prime number in each shape so that the answer is zero.

However, this time the numbers in the circles are *not* consecutive prime numbers.

How many different calculations can you make?

□ – ○ – ○ – ○ = 0

---

## The Puzzler

Find a 1-digit number where the difference between its square and square root is 14.

Find a 2-digit number where the difference between its square and square root is 1290.

## The Puzzler

Write a subtraction calculation where each of the 3 numbers (*minuend*, *subtrahend* and *difference*) contains each of the 9 digits, 1 to 9.

□□□
□□□
□□□

–

## Let's Investigate

Look at this method for subtracting pairs of numbers.

**Step 1:** Subtract each digit of the subtrahend (the number to be subtracted) from 9.

```
  583
– 396
```

```
  9      9      6
(9↓3)  (9↓9)  (9↓6)
  6      0      3
```

**Step 2:** Add the answer to the minuend (the number from which the subtrahend was subtracted).

```
  583
+ 603
 1186
```

**Step 3:** Look at the answer. Cross out the most significant digit (the digit with the largest place value) and add it to the 'new' number. The result is the answer.

```
↗186
```

186 + 1 = 187

Using combinations of 3-digit and 4-digit numbers investigate whether this method always works.

Does this method work for decimals?

Provide examples to justify your reasoning.

Do you like this method? Is it a method that you might regularly use? Explain why or why not.

# The Maths Herald

Name:

Date:

## Money Matters

The thickness of a £1 coin is just over 3 mm.

Lucinda wants to buy a new mobile phone costing £174.

If Lucinda was to build a tower of £1 coins, how high in centimetres would it have to be to pay for the phone?

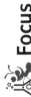

## The Puzzler

$41 \times 51 = 2091$

Use this to help you calculate $41 \times 52$.

What about $42 \times 52$?

What did you do?

$17 \times 202 = 3434$

Use this to help you calculate $34 \times 202$.

What about $34 \times 404$?

What did you do?

## The Puzzler

$n!$ means $n \times (n-1) \times (n-2) \times \ldots \times 2 \times 1$

So, $3!$ means $3 \times 2 \times 1 = 6$

What is $4!$ ?

What about: $4! \times 2$

$(4 \times 2)!$

## Focus on Science

Light travels 299 792 km each second.

It takes the light of the Sun 8 minutes and 9 seconds to reach Earth. How far is the Earth from the Sun?

Light from the Sun takes 3 minutes and 13 seconds to reach Mercury, its nearest planet. How far is Mercury from the Sun?

The Sun's light takes 6 minutes and 1 second to reach Venus, its second nearest planet. How far is Venus from the Sun?

---

## Looking for Patterns

A *power* tells us how many of the same number are multiplied together.

$6 \times 6$ is shortened to $6^2$, where 2 is the power.

We say: "6 to the power of 2" or "6 squared".

$$6^2 = 6 \times 6$$
$$= 36$$

$6 \times 6 \times 6$ is shortened to $6^3$, where 3 is the power.

We say: "6 to the power of 3".

$$6^3 = 6 \times 6 \times 6$$
$$= 216$$

$6^2$ and $6^3$ are both examples of index notation.

Look at these calculations involving index notation.

$6^2 \times 6^3 = (6 \times 6) \times (6 \times 6 \times 6)$

$= 6 \times 6 \times 6 \times 6 \times 6$

$= 6^5$

$= 7776$

$6^5 \div 6^3 = (6 \times 6 \times 6 \times 6 \times 6) \div (6 \times 6 \times 6)$

$= 6 \times 6$

$= 6^2$

$= 36$

What is the rule for multiplying and dividing numbers in index form?

Check your rule using a calculator.

Write several more examples similar to those above.

## Let's Investigate

The numbers 57 and 63 are both 3 away from the same multiple of 10, i.e. 60.

57 is three less than 60, and 63 is three more than 60.

Look at this method for multiplying pairs of numbers that have the same difference from the same multiple of 10.

$$57 \times 63 = (60 - 3)\,(60 + 3)$$
$$= 60^2 - 3^2$$
$$= 3600 - 9$$
$$= 3591$$

Investigate this method by choosing pairs of 2-digit numbers that have the same difference for the same multiple of 10, e.g. 88 and 92, 36 and 44.

Does this method work when multiplying similar pairs of 3-digit numbers?

What about similar pairs of 4-digit numbers?

Be sure to justify your conclusions with examples.

## Around the World

Both the Chinese and Hindus invented a clever way of multiplying numbers.

Look at the 2 examples below.

438 × 7

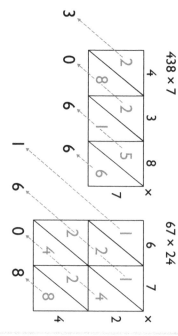

67 × 24

Use this method to work out the answers to the following calculations.

83 × 76          537 × 49

886 × 356          73.9 × 34.6

## Let's Investigate

Using *only* the digits 2, 3, 5 or 7, how many different multiplication calculations can you make?

**Rules:**

- You can use some or all of the digits.
- You can use each digit more than once in a calculation.
- The digits must form the 2 numbers being multiplied together as well as the answer.

Here is one: 5 × 7 = 35

factorial

---

## Looking for Patterns

Replace each star ( ☆ ) with a digit.

```
        ☆  ☆
×       ☆  ☆
——————————————
        3  3  6
   2    8  8  0
——————————————
   3    2  1  6
```

```
        ☆  ☆
×       ☆  7
——————————————
     ☆  ☆  5
        ☆  ☆
           4
```

For each calculation, write a statement explaining how you worked out what digits the stars represented.

## Let's Investigate

Use the digits 1, 2, 3, 4 and 5 only once to make 2 or more numbers.

For example:

125 and 34          or          15 and 34 and 2

Multiply these 2 numbers together.

For example:

125 × 34 = 4250     or     15 × 34 × 2 = 1020

Using other combinations of the digits 1 to 5, what is the greatest product you can make?

## Looking for Patterns

**Step 1:** Write the digits 1 to 9 in order, leaving out the number 8, to form an 8-digit number.

12 345 679

**Step 2:** Choose any 1-digit number.

7

**Step 3:** Multiply the digit by 9.

7 × 9 = 63

**Step 4:** Multiply the product by 12 345 679.

63 × 12 345 679 = ☐

What do you notice?

Repeat choosing different 1-digit numbers.

Can you predict what the answers will be for each of the 9 digits?

Predict what will happen if you do this using other numbers up to and including 18.

Investigate.

Were your predictions correct?

© HarperCollins*Publishers* 2016

# The Maths Herald

Name:

Date:

| Planet | Average distance from Sun (km) |
|---|---|
| Mercury | 58 million |
| Venus | 108 million |
| Earth | 150 million |
| Mars | 228 million |
| Jupiter | 778 million |
| Saturn | 1·4 billion |
| Uranus | 2·9 billion |
| Neptune | 4·4 billion |

## Focus on Science

Light travels at 299 792 km per second.

Calculate the approximate time it takes light to travel from the Sun to each of the planets.

Write about how you calculated your approximations.

## Let's Investigate

Investigate whether the following statement is true or false.

When you reverse the digits of any 2-digit number to make a new 2-digit number and find the total of the 2 numbers, your answer is always divisible by 11.

What happens if you use pairs of 3-digit, 4-digit or larger numbers?

TRUE or FALSE?

## The Puzzler

1, 2, 3, 4, 5

$\times$ $\div$

Using each of the above digits and operations only once, what is the smallest whole number you can make?

---

## The Puzzler

What is the smallest 2-digit number (x) that leaves a remainder (r) when it is divided by 2, 3, 4, 5 or 6, but *not* 7?

$x \div 2 = $ ☐ r?

$x \div 3 = $ ☐ r?

$x \div 4 = $ ☐ r?

$x \div 5 = $ ☐ r?

$x \div 6 = $ ☐ r?

Write a puzzle similar to this of your own.

## Looking for Patterns

Write a digit in each box to complete the following calculations.

Clue: Each of the products share the same 2-digit factor (☐☐).

☐☐ $\times$ ☐☐ = 1972

☐☐ $\times$ ☐☐ = 816

☐☐ $\times$ ☐☐ = 2686

☐☐ $\times$ ☐☐ = 2244

## At Home

Remember, the term *population density* refers to how many people there are for each unit of area.

To work out human population density, we divide the population of a region by the area of that region.

What is the *approximate* human population density of your neighbourhood?

What do you need to know to be able to calculate this?

You will probably need to make several assumptions. What are they?

What are your assumptions based on?

# Around the World

*Population density* is the term used to describe how many people there are for each unit of area.

To work out the worldwide human population density, we divide the world's population by the Earth's total area.

Find out which countries have the greatest and smallest population densities.

So, if the world's population is 7·4 billion, and Earth's total area (including land and water) is 510 million square kilometers, then the worldwide human population density is 7·4 billion ÷ 510 million = 14·5 people per km². If only the Earth's land area of 150 million km² is taken into account, then human population density increases to 49·3 people per km².

Look at the figures below. Use them to calculate the population density for the different countries, rounded to the nearest person.

| Country | Population | Area (km²) |
| --- | --- | --- |
| Australia | 24 062 755 | 7 682 300 |
| India | 1 288 290 000 | 3 287 240 |
| Jamaica | 2 723 246 | 10 991 |
| United Kingdom | 65 097 000 | 243 610 |
| United States | 323 379 000 | 9 826 675 |

dividend

## The Puzzler

How do the population densities of each of these countries compare with the worldwide human population density figures?

0 1 2 3 4 5 6 7 8 9

Using each of the digits 0 to 9 only once, it is possible to make 2 one-digit numbers and 4 two-digit numbers that are all multiples of 3. What are the 6 numbers?

It is also possible to make 3 one-digit numbers, 2 two-digit numbers and 1 three-digit number that are all multiples of 3. What are these 6 numbers?

2

---

## The Puzzler

You can make a puzzle very similar to the one on the left.

Here's how to begin.

Write down any 3-digit number.    527

Write it down again to create a 6-digit number.    527 527

Divide this number by 7.    75 361

Divide the answer by 11.    6851

Divide this answer by 13.    ☐

What do you notice?

Write down any 2-digit number.    68

Write the number twice more to create a 6-digit number.    686 868

Divide this number by ○.    ☐

Divide the answer by ◇.    ☐

Divide this answer by △.    ☐

What is the rest of the puzzle?

Can you explain why this happens?

## Looking for Patterns

We know that all numbers ending in 0, 2, 4, 6 and 8 are divisible by 2.

We can say that this is a *divisibility test* for 2.

We also know these tests of divisibility:

- If a number ends in 0 or 5, then it is divisible by 5.
- If a number ends in 0, then the number is divisible by 10.

Write divisibility tests for 3, 4, 6, 8 and 9.

Can you write divisibility tests for 7, 11 and 12?

Provide proof that your tests work by giving examples.

© HarperCollins*Publishers* 2016

3

## The Language of Maths

7 × 7 can be written as $7^2$ and is read as *seven squared* or *seven to the power of 2*.

4 × 4 × 4 can be written as $4^3$ and is read as *four cubed* or *four to the power of 3*.

The *power* or *index* is 2.

The *power* or *index* is 3.

$7^2 = 49$

$4^3 = 64$

Find the value of each of the following:

3⁵   5³   2⁷   8⁵   7⁴

## Money Matters

A percentage of the money that people earn is paid to the government in the form of *income tax*. This money is collected by the government and is used to build and maintain roads, schools, hospitals and other public facilities, and to pay the salaries of government employees such as nurses, teachers and the police.

A part of a person's income is tax free. This is called an *allowance*. After this money has been deducted the remaining income is taxable. The rate of tax is determined by the government. Below is the personal allowance that all tax payers in the UK are allowed, as well as the different rates of income tax.

| Personal allowance |
| --- |
| £11 000 |

| Band | Taxable income | Rate |
| --- | --- | --- |
| Basic rate | £0 – £32 000 | 20% |
| Higher rate | £32 001 – £150 000 | 40% |
| Additional rate | Over £150 000 | 45% |

*Example:*

Calculate the income tax payable for someone who earns £48 000 per year.

£48 000 – £11 000 = £37 000 (earnings – personal allowance = taxable income)

Amount of tax due on £37 000 = (£32 000 × 20%) + (£5000 × 40%)

(taxable income = basic rate + higher rate. Note: £37 000 – £32 000 = £5000)

Total income tax = £6400 + £2000 = £8400 (£32 000 × 20%) + (£5000 × 40%)

Use the tables above to calculate the income tax payable by someone earning:

£56 000 per year   £82 000 per year   £195 000 per year

# The Maths Herald

Name:                    Date:

## Let's Investigate

The *square root* is a number that when multiplied by itself gives the stated number. √ is the abbreviation for square root.

$\sqrt{49} = 7$

So, the square root of 49 is 7, because 7 × 7 = 49.

A square root is the opposite of a square number. $7^2 = 7 × 7 = 49$

One way to calculate the square root is to divide the number by prime numbers in order to reduce the number to 1.

*Example 1*

$\sqrt{484} =$   $\sqrt{484} = 484 ÷ 2$
$= 242 ÷ 2$
$= 121 ÷ 11$
$= 11 ÷ 11 = 1$

So, 484 = 2 × 2 × 11 × 11
= (2 × 11) × (2 × 11)
= 22 × 22

$\sqrt{484} = 22$

*Example 2*

$\sqrt{729} =$   $\sqrt{729} = 729 ÷ 3$
$= 243 ÷ 3$
$= 81 ÷ 3$
$= 27 ÷ 3$
$= 9 ÷ 3$
$= 3 ÷ 3 = 1$

So, 729 = 3 × 3 × 3 × 3 × 3 × 3
= (3 × 3 × 3) × (3 × 3 × 3)
= 27 × 27

$\sqrt{727} = 27$

Use the prime number method to find the square root of these numbers.

$\sqrt{576}$  $\sqrt{676}$  $\sqrt{841}$
$\sqrt{961}$  $\sqrt{1225}$  $\sqrt{1444}$

## Looking for Patterns

Which pair of 2-digit numbers has:
- a total of 89?
- and a difference of 35?
- and a product of 1674?

Which pair of 3-digit numbers has:
- a total of 799?
- and a difference of 247?
- and a product of 144 348?

Write about how you worked out what the pairs of numbers are.

Make up a similar problem of your own for a friend to solve.

## Famous Mathematicians

Heron of Alexandria was a Greek mathematician and engineer who lived about 75 AD. He discovered a formula for finding square roots.

Heron's method for finding the square root of a number

**Step 1.** Make an approximation of the square root.

**Step 2.** Divide the number you are trying to find the square root of by your approximation.

**Step 3.** Add the answer to your approximation.

**Step 4.** Find the average of this number by dividing it by 2.

To get a more accurate answer repeat Steps 2 to 4.

Use Heron's method to find the approximate square root of each of these numbers. Give your answers to 2 decimal places.

$\sqrt{28}$     $\sqrt{39}$     $\sqrt{46}$     $\sqrt{88}$     $\sqrt{73}$     $\sqrt{62}$

*Example*

$\sqrt{53} \approx$

**Step 1.** 7
(because $7 \times 7 = 49$)

**Step 2.** $53 \div 7 = 7\frac{4}{7}$

**Step 3.** $7\frac{4}{7} + 7 = 14\frac{4}{7}$
$= \frac{102}{7}$

**Step 4.** $\frac{102}{7} \div 2 = \frac{102}{14}$
$= 7.28$

## Money Matters

You are going to make 180 cupcakes for the school fair.

How much of each ingredient will you need?

What will be the approximate cost to make 180 cupcakes?

If you sell all the cupcakes at 75p each, how much money will you take?

How much profit will you make?

**Cupcakes** (*makes 24*)

| | |
|---|---|
| 110 g butter | |
| 110 g sugar | |
| 2 drops vanilla essence | |
| 2 large eggs | |
| 110 g self-raising flour | |
| 1 teaspoon baking powder | |

| | |
|---|---|
| 250 g butter | £1.10 |
| 1 kg sugar | 95p |
| 28 ml vanilla essence | £1.20 |
| 6 large eggs | £1.20 |
| 1 kg self-raising flour | £1.50 |
| 170 g baking powder | 85p |

## Around the World

Look at this Chinese method for finding square roots which involves subtracting odd numbers.

*Chinese method for finding the square root of a number*

**Step 1:** Subtract 1 from the number.

**Step 2:** Subtract 3 from the difference.

**Step 3:** Subtract 5 from the difference.

**Step 4:** Subtract 7 from the difference.

**Steps 5 to ?:** Continue the pattern until you reach 0. Count the number of steps. That is the square root.

Use the Chinese method to find the square root of each of these numbers.

$\sqrt{289}$     $\sqrt{576}$     $\sqrt{361}$     $\sqrt{529}$     $\sqrt{961}$     $\sqrt{784}$

*Example*

$\sqrt{64}$

$$\begin{array}{r} 64 \\ -\ 1 \\ \hline 63 \\ -\ 3 \\ \hline 60 \\ -\ 5 \\ \hline 55 \\ -\ 7 \\ \hline 48 \\ -\ 9 \\ \hline 39 \\ -11 \\ \hline 28 \\ -13 \\ \hline 15 \\ -15 \\ \hline 0 \end{array}$$

So $\sqrt{64} = 8$

## Let's Investigate

Write down 5 different 3-digit numbers.

Work out the square root of each of the numbers using any of the following methods:

- the prime number method
- Heron's method
- the Chinese method.

Then check your answer using a calculator.

What are the limitations of this method?

Which method do you prefer to use? Why?

S&C Volume 6

# The Maths Herald

Name:

Date:

## Sports Update

There are 10 teams in the Morcella Football League.

During the season, every team plays every other team twice (once at home and once away).

How many matches are played altogether throughout the season?

Write a formula for finding the total number of games played for any number of teams.

## Sports Update

The Shoalhaven Tennis Club is organising a singles elimination tournament. An elimination tournament means that if you lose the match you are out of the tournament.

In the under-8 girls' tournament there are 12 entrants.

How many matches are played altogether in the under-8 girls' tournament?

Write a formula for finding the total number of matches played for any number of entrants.

## Let's Investigate

Start with a 2-digit number.

Square each digit and add the answers.

$$89 \longrightarrow \begin{array}{c} 8^2 = 64 \\ 9^2 = 81 \end{array} \longrightarrow 145 \longrightarrow \begin{array}{c} 1^2 = 1 \\ 4^2 = 16 \\ 5^2 = 25 \end{array} \longrightarrow 42 \longrightarrow \begin{array}{c} 4^2 = 16 \\ 2^2 = 4 \end{array} \longrightarrow 20 \longrightarrow \begin{array}{c} 2^2 = 4 \\ 0^2 = 0 \end{array} \longrightarrow 4$$

Keep doing this until the answer is a 1-digit number.

Investigate doing this for different 2-digit numbers.

What if you started with 3-digit numbers?

---

## Looking for Patterns

Algebra is where letters and other symbols represent numbers in a formula or equation. Mathematicians and scientists use algebra to explain complex concepts.

- Think of a number.
- Add 3.
- Double it.
- Add 2.
- Halve it.
- Subtract your original number.

What number do you get? Do this 3 more times. What do you notice?

This number trick can be explained using algebra.

- Think of a number.    Make $n$ the number you think of.
    - Add 3.     $n + 3$
- Double it.    $2n + 6$
    - Add 2.    $2n + 8$
    - Halve it.    $\dfrac{n + 4}{4}$
- Subtract your original number.

Use algebra to explain this number trick.

- Think of a number.
- Add 5.
- Multiply the result by 2.
- Subtract 4.
- Halve it.
- Subtract your original number.

Try making up some number tricks of your own. Make sure you can explain how it works using algebra.

## What's the Problem?

In each of these calculations, the grey digits are in the correct place. The black digits are not.

Move the black digits so that each of the calculations is correct.

$$78 + 5 = 56 \qquad 67 - 6 = 84$$
$$38 \times 2 = 892 \qquad 171 \div 6 = 12$$
$$74 + 51 = 386 \qquad 98 - 54 = 710$$
$$32 \times 24 = 231 \qquad 264 \div 68 = 81$$

Now write down how you worked out where the digits belonged.

## The Puzzler

The product of each pair of oval numbers is in the rectangle between them. Complete the puzzles.

slide rule

4

# Sports Update

Calories measure the energy value of food.

The first table shows the recommended daily intake of calories for boys, girls, men and women.

To stay the same weight, you need to use the same amount of calories that you consume.

Referring to the second table, design 4 different daily programmes (1 each for a girl, boy, man, woman), which are designed to use approximately the same amount of calories as the recommended daily intake of calories.

Take into consideration normal daily calorific usage, for example walking, as well as a period of exercise.

Are your programmes realistic? If not, modify them so that they are. Be prepared to justify your modifications.

| Age | Recommended daily intake of calories |
| --- | --- |
| girls under the age of 18 | between 1000 and 2600 |
| boys under the age of 18 | between 1000 and 3200 |
| females aged 31–50 | between 1800 and 2200 |
| males aged 31–50 | between 2200 and 3000 |

| Calories used in 30 minutes | |
| --- | --- |
| walking normally | 83 |
| walking the dog | 123 |
| walking briskly | 142 |
| running | 282 |
| aerobics | 211 |
| cricket | 178 |
| swimming | 211 |
| tennis | 246 |
| cycling | 280 |
| football | 292 |
| cleaning the house | 123 |
| gardening | 176 |
| dancing | 158 |
| sleeping | -25 |
| sitting | -30 |

---

# Let's Investigate

If a calculation involves more than 1 operation then the calculation must be done in the following order.

| 1st | B | BRACKETS | ( ) | Example 1 |
| --- | --- | --- | --- | --- |
| | | | | $(8 \times 7) - 13$ |
| 2nd | O | OF | power of, e.g. $4^2$ | $= 56 - 13$ |
| | | | | $= 43$ |
| 3rd | D | DIVISION | ÷ | |
| 4th | M | MULTIPLICATION | × | Example 2 |
| | | | | $(9 \times 4) - (24 \div 6)$ |
| 5th | A | ADDITION | + | $= 36 - 4$ |
| 6th | S | SUBTRACTION | – | $= 32$ |

Using only the digits 2, 4, 5, 6, 7 and 9, make each of the numbers below. Can you find different ways to make each of these numbers? Don't forget to use brackets!

41    59    87    93    120

# Let's Investigate

In an algebraic expression, letters are often used as substitutes for numbers.

If $a = 5$, $b = 7$ and $c = 10$, investigate what answers you get from the following algebraic expressions.

$(a + b) - c$        $a + b + c$

$a + (b - c)$        $a - (b + c)$

$(a - b) + c$        $(a + b) \times c$

$a \times (b - c)$        $(a - b) \times c$

$(a \times b) - c$        $(a - b) \times c$

# What's the Problem?

In an algebraic expression, if a number is written as 3a it means 3 × a, and if a number is written as $\frac{a}{3}$ it means a ÷ 3.

Find the value of the following expressions if $c = 5$ and $d = 8$.

$3c - d + 24 =$

$34 + 5(d - c) =$

$4d - 84 + 8c + 68 =$

$12(d + c) - 7(d - c) =$

$\frac{40}{d} - \frac{15}{c} =$

$6(4c - 2d) + 6d - 6c =$

# The Maths Herald

Name:

Date:

## Famous Mathematicians

Euclid was a Greek mathematician who lived from about 330 to 275 BC.

He discovered a method for finding the highest common factor (HCF). This is known as "Euclid's Algorithm".

Use Euclid's Algorithm to reduce these fractions to their simplest terms.

$$\frac{162}{189} \quad \frac{68}{153} \quad \frac{65}{91} \quad \frac{38}{95} \quad \frac{72}{135} \quad \frac{424}{477}$$

### Euclid's Algorithm

1. Divide the larger number (dividend) by the smaller number (divisor).

2. If there is a remainder, divide this into the divisor.

3. Continue dividing the divisor by the remainder until the remainder is 0.

4. The final divisor is the HCF.

## The Puzzler

Cut this pie into quarters, so that each piece contains 2 cherries and no cherry is cut.

## The Puzzler

Arrange all the digits 1 to 9 to make a fraction that is equivalent to $\frac{1}{3}$

□ □ □
□ □ □
□ □ □

non-unitary fraction

1

---

## Looking for Patterns

On Monday, Mrs Rollo took the weekly school assembly.

At the end of the assembly she told 1 more than half of all the children in the hall to walk quietly back to their classrooms.

Once these children had left the hall, she told 1 more than half of all the children that were remaining to go back to their class.

Once these children had left the hall, once again she told 1 more than half of all the remaining children to go back to their class. She did this 3 more times.

At the end, there was only 1 child remaining in the hall.

How many children were in the hall at the start of the assembly?

## What's the Problem?

Approximately, what fraction of your life so far, have you spent:

● asleep?
● eating?
● in school?

Choose another aspect of your life and work out approximately what fraction of your life so far, you have spent doing it.

# Looking for Patterns

Ordering a set of decimals is easy. But fractions aren't so easy.

A man called John Farey investigated sequences of proper fractions in order of size – they are called 'Farey Sequences'.

The first 3 Farey sequences (Fn) are:

$$F_1 = \frac{0}{1}, \frac{1}{1}$$
$$F_2 = \frac{0}{1}, \frac{1}{2}, \frac{1}{1}$$
$$F_3 = \frac{0}{1}, \frac{1}{3}, \frac{1}{2}, \frac{2}{3}, \frac{1}{1}$$

Notice the following:

- In $F_1$ the denominators are all 1, in $F_2$ the denominators are either 1 or 2, and in $F_3$ the denominators are 1, 2 or 3.
- The series all start with $\frac{0}{1}$ and end with $\frac{1}{1}$ and the fractions are in ascending size.
- The fractions that have been added to each new sequence all the same denominator:

$$F_1 = \frac{1}{1}$$
$$F_2 = \frac{0}{1}, \frac{1}{1}$$
$$F_3 = \frac{0}{1}, \frac{1}{3}, \frac{1}{2}, \frac{2}{3}, \frac{1}{1}$$

Write down $F_4$.

Which additional fractions are in $F_4$ which weren't in $F_3$?

Write all the fractions in $F_5$ and $F_6$.

There is a formula for checking the order of fractions in a Farey sequence. This is done by calculating each entry in terms of the previous 2 entries.

If $\frac{a}{b}$ and $\frac{c}{d}$ are the 2 known consecutive fractions, and $\frac{x}{y}$ is the next fraction, then

$$\frac{c}{d} = \frac{(a + x)}{(b + y)}$$

For example:

$$F_3 = \frac{0}{1}, \frac{1}{3}, \frac{1}{2}, \frac{2}{3}, \frac{1}{1}$$

So
$$\frac{a}{b} = \frac{0}{1}$$
$$\frac{c}{d} = \frac{1}{3}$$
$$\frac{x}{y} = \frac{1}{2}$$
$$\frac{1}{3} = \frac{(0 + 1)}{(1 + 2)} \quad \frac{1}{3} = \frac{1}{3}$$

Check your sequences using the formula.

# What's the Problem?

Taylah and Cloe are sisters. They each get less than £7 pocket money each week.

- Is it possible for half of Taylah's pocket money to be less than a third of Cloe's?

- If half of Taylah's pocket money is less than a third of Cloe's, suggest 2 possible amounts of pocket money for each sister.

- If half of Taylah's pocket money is equal to a third of Cloe's, suggest what pocket money they might each be getting.

# Let's Investigate

Choose any 4 numbers less than 10. Using these numbers write as many fractions as you can with 1-digit numerators and denominators.

- How many different fractions can you make?

- Which is the smallest fraction?
- Which fractions are less than 1?
- Which fractions are equal to 1?
- Which is the largest fraction?
- Which fractions are greater than 1?
- Write the fractions in order of size.

- Organise your fractions into groups. What criteria have you used?

- How else could you group them?

Investigate fractions for other sets of 4 numbers.

# The Arts Roundup

One-eighth of The Reggio Opera Company are technicians. Two-thirds are singers. The other 5 members are musicians.

- How many technicians are there?
- How many singers are there?
- How many people are there altogether in The Reggio Opera Company?

# The Maths Herald

S&C Volume 6

Name:

Date:

## Money Matters

Mrs Farringdon has 2 children – Lucy and Melinda. She has just given each of them their pocket money. However, she has made a mistake and hasn't given each of them the same amount as she normally does.

So Lucy and Melinda have decided to fix it so that they each receive the £6 as they normally do.

This is what they do:

- Lucy gives Melinda twice as much money as Melinda has already.
- Melinda gives Lucy a third of her money.
- Lucy then gives Melinda the same amount of money as Melinda already has.

Now the girls each have the same amount of pocket money.

How much pocket money did Mrs Farringdon give Lucy and Melinda by mistake?

## Let's Investigate

This diagram shows $\frac{1}{2}$ of a $\frac{1}{2}$:

$$\frac{1}{2} \times \frac{1}{2} = \frac{1}{4}$$

This diagram shows $\frac{1}{4}$ of a $\frac{1}{2}$:

$$\frac{1}{4} \times \frac{1}{2} = \frac{1}{8}$$

Look at the 2 examples below which show how to multiply a fraction by a fraction. Explain how the method works.

*Example 1*

$$\frac{2}{3} \times \frac{3}{4}$$
$$= \frac{\cancel{2}^{1}}{3} \times \frac{3}{\cancel{4}_{2}}$$
$$= \frac{3}{6} = \frac{1}{2}$$

*Example 2*

$$\frac{7}{12} \times \frac{4}{9}$$
$$= \frac{7}{\cancel{12}_{3}} \times \frac{\cancel{4}^{1}}{9}$$
$$= \frac{7}{27}$$

Use your method for multiplying a fraction by a fraction to answer these questions.

$$\frac{3}{5} \times \frac{5}{6} \qquad \frac{1}{4} \times \frac{7}{8}$$

$$\frac{2}{3} \times \frac{5}{6} \qquad \frac{5}{8} \times \frac{6}{7}$$

Can you use your method to answer this question?

$$\frac{5}{6} \times \frac{1}{4} \times \frac{3}{8}$$

---

## Let's Investigate

It is easy to subtract fractions if they have the *same denominator*. We just subtract the numerators and reduce the fraction to its simplest terms.

*Example 1* $\frac{9}{10} - \frac{3}{10} = \frac{6}{10} = \frac{3}{5}$

*Example 2* $\frac{7}{9} - \frac{5}{9} = \frac{2}{9}$

If we are subtracting fractions that have *different denominators* we:

1. find a common denominator (using what we know about LCM to find the lowest common denominator)

2. convert each fraction to an equivalent fraction with the common denominator

3. subtract the numerators to find the numerator of our answer

4. write the numerator over the common denominator

5. reduce the fraction to its simplest terms.

*Example 3*

$\frac{6}{7} - \frac{2}{3}$ (LCM of 7 and 3 is 21)

$= \frac{18}{21} - \frac{14}{21}$ $\left(\frac{6}{7} = \frac{18}{21} \text{ and } \frac{2}{3} = \frac{14}{21}\right)$

$= \frac{4}{21}$

*Example 4*

$\frac{4}{6} - \frac{2}{9}$ (LCM of 6 and 9 is 18)

$= \frac{12}{18} - \frac{4}{18}$ $\left(\frac{4}{6} = \frac{12}{18} \text{ and } \frac{2}{9} = \frac{4}{18}\right)$

$= \frac{8}{18} = \frac{4}{9}$

Choose pairs of fractions of your own and investigate subtracting fractions. Start with simple fractions, such as $\frac{1}{2}$, $\frac{1}{4}$ and $\frac{3}{4}$.

What about subtracting pairs of mixed numbers such as $3\frac{2}{5}$ and $2\frac{4}{7}$?

## Let's Investigate

To multiply a mixed number by a mixed number:

1. Change both mixed numbers into improper fractions.

2. If possible, simplify the numerators and the denominators by cancelling.

3. Multiply the numerators to get the numerator answer.

4. Multiply the denominators to get the denominator answer.

5. Reduce the answer to its simplest terms and change an improper fraction to a mixed number.

$$3\frac{3}{5} \times 2\frac{2}{3}$$

$$= \frac{\cancel{18}^{6}}{5} \times \frac{8}{\cancel{3}_{1}}$$

$$= \frac{48}{5}$$

$$= 9\frac{3}{5}$$

Choose pairs of mixed numbers of your own and investigate multiplying pairs of mixed numbers.

# Around the World

Endwinter Road is $62\frac{1}{2}$ miles long. It starts at Endwinter Manor in the west, passing through Endwinter Worthing and Endwinter Havering, and ending at Endwinter Grantham in the east.

The distance between Endwinter Manor and Endwinter Worthing is the same as that from Endwinter Havering to Endwinter Grantham and one-third of that from Endwinter Worthing to Endwinter Havering.

How far is Endwinter Havering from Endwinter Grantham?

# The Puzzler

Complete the number chains by writing the mixed numbers that belong in the squares.

**START**

$3\frac{1}{2}$ + □ − $3\frac{1}{4}$ + □ − $2\frac{3}{4}$ = 3  **FINISH**

**START**

□ + $4\frac{2}{5}$ + □ − $1\frac{4}{5}$ − □ = $6\frac{1}{2}$  **FINISH**

# Let's Investigate

Draw diagrams to represent each of these fraction statements.

$$\frac{3}{4} - \frac{1}{4} = \frac{1}{2}$$
$$\frac{1}{2} \text{ of } \frac{1}{4} = \frac{1}{4}$$
$$2 \times \frac{1}{2} = 1$$
$$\frac{4}{4} = 1$$

---

# Money Matters

Greg went shopping. He spent £6 more than half of his money in the supermarket. His dry cleaning cost him one-third of what he had left, plus £4 more. He spent £14 at the florist. This was half of his remaining money. How much money did Greg start with?

---

# In the Past

Apart from $\frac{2}{3}$, the Ancient Egyptians only wrote fractions with a numerator of 1 (unitary or unit fractions).

They wrote fractions as a sum of different unitary fractions.

So, for example, $\frac{3}{4}$ might have been written as $\frac{1}{2} + \frac{1}{4}$.

How might the Ancient Egyptians have written fractions with a numerator of 2, i.e. $\frac{2}{n}$, such as $\frac{2}{5}$ or $\frac{2}{7}$?

If you can, try and write them as the sum of just 2 different unitary fractions.

Explore fractions with different numerators such as $\frac{3}{n}, \frac{4}{n}, \frac{5}{n}, \dots$ and consider how the Ancient Egyptians would have represented these as sums with the least number of unitary fractions.

# Let's Investigate

It is easy to add fractions if they have the same denominator. We just add the numerators and reduce the fraction to its simplest terms.

**Example 1**
$$\frac{3}{5} + \frac{4}{5} = \frac{7}{5} = 1\frac{2}{5}$$

**Example 2**
$$\frac{3}{8} + \frac{1}{8} = \frac{4}{8} = \frac{1}{2}$$

If we are adding fractions that have *different* denominators we:

1. find a common denominator (using what we know about LCM to find the lowest common denominator)
2. convert each fraction to an equivalent fraction with the common denominator
3. add the numerators to find the numerator of our answer
4. write the numerator over the common denominator
5. reduce the fraction to its simplest terms.

**Example 3**
$$\frac{2}{3} + \frac{3}{5} \quad \text{(LCM of 3 and 5 is 15)}$$
$$= \frac{10}{15} + \frac{9}{15} \quad \left(\frac{2}{3} = \frac{10}{15} \text{ and } \frac{3}{5} = \frac{9}{15}\right)$$
$$= \frac{19}{15}$$
$$= 1\frac{4}{15}$$

**Example 4**
$$\frac{6}{7} + \frac{3}{14} \quad \text{(LCM of 7 and 14 is 14)}$$
$$= \frac{12}{14} + \frac{3}{14} \quad \left(\frac{6}{7} = \frac{12}{14}\right)$$
$$= \frac{15}{14}$$
$$= 1\frac{1}{14}$$

Choose pairs of fractions of your own and investigate adding fractions. Start with simple fractions, such as $\frac{1}{2}, \frac{1}{4}$ and $\frac{3}{4}$.

What about adding pairs of mixed numbers such as $3\frac{2}{5}$ and $2\frac{4}{7}$?

2  3

# The Maths Herald

Name:

Date:

## Let's Investigate

Choose any 4 digits less than 10.

Write as many decimals as you can using 2, 3 or 4 of these digits.

- Write the decimals in order of size.
- Arrange all your decimals into 3 different groups. What criteria did you choose?
- How else could you group all your decimals?

Investigate decimals for other sets of 4 digits.

## Money Matters

When goods are imported or exported their prices are affected by exchange rates.

What are exchange rates?

What is the exchange rate today between the British pound and other major currencies?

Compare these exchange rates with the exchange rates for last week. Are they the same? If not, how are they different?

What does all this mean for the price of imported and exported goods?

## Let's Investigate

$\frac{1}{2}$ is a *unitary* or *unit* fraction (meaning it has a numerator of 1).

0·5 is $\frac{1}{2}$ expressed as a decimal.

When converted to a decimal $\frac{1}{2}$ *terminates.*

$\frac{1}{6}$ is another unitary fraction.

When $\frac{1}{6}$ is converted to a decimal it is 0·1666666 …

When converted to a decimal the fraction $\frac{1}{6}$ *recurs* (it goes on and on – it does not terminate).

Using a calculator, investigate unitary fractions where the decimal terminates.

Can you find all the terminating fractions from $\frac{1}{2}$ to $\frac{1}{100}$?

## The Puzzler

Samir has put a total of £10 into 5 envelopes.

Envelopes A and B together have a total of £5.20. Envelopes B and C have a total of £4.30; envelopes C and D a total of £3.40; and envelopes D and E have a total of £3.

How much money is each envelope?

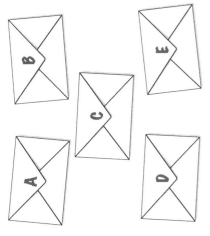

## The Puzzler

Arrange each of these numbers so that the sum of each column, row and diagonal is the same. What is the common total?

| | | | |
|---|---|---|---|
| | | | |
| | | | |
| | | | |
| | | | |

0·1  0·2  0·3

0·4  0·5  0·6  0·7

0·8  0·9  1  1·1

1·2  1·3  1·4

1·5  1·6

## Money Matters

One of the ways that we pay for the goods and services that we want is by using cash – notes and coins.

Another method of payment that people use are cheques.

Look at some cheques from different banks. How are they the same? How do they differ? What are the things that all cheques have on them?

Imagine your school has formed a bank. What name will you give your bank? Design your bank's cheque book.

---

## The Language of Maths

# D E C I M A L

What does the word 'decimal' actually mean?

---

### At Home

Look for any examples of decimals at home.

Organise your examples into three lists:

- Numbers with 1 decimal place
- Numbers with 2 decimal places
- Numbers with 3 or more decimal places

What is a cheque? How do cheques work?
What are the advantages and disadvantages of cheques over other methods of payment?

---

### Let's Investigate

0·2   0·2   0·2   0·2   0·2

Only using 4 0·2s or fewer, make as many other numbers as you possibly can.

Here are some examples:

$0·8 = (0·2 ÷ 0·2) – 0·2$   $0·04 = 0·2 × 0·2$   $1·4 = (0·2 + 0·2) + (0·2 ÷ 0·2)$

Make your answers as varied as you can.
What about using these numbers: 0·2, 2, 2·2, 22?
What if you started with a digit other than 2?

---

### Looking for Patterns

One of the most common uses and applications of decimals is when measuring.

For example:

$235 cm = 2·35 m$    $14 cm 8 mm = 14·8 cm$

$1600 g = 1·6 kg$    $1500 ml = 1·5 l$

To convert metres into centimetres we multiply by 100

e.g. $2·5 m × 100 = 250 cm$

To convert centimetres into metres we divide by 100

e.g. $650 cm ÷ 100 = 6·5 m$

Design a poster explaining how to convert between different metric units for length, mass and capacity. Be sure to include at least 1 example for each.

---

### The Language of Maths

centimetre
milligram        millimetre

These are words we commonly use to describe measures.
What do the prefixes 'centi' and 'milli' mean?
What about the prefix 'deci'?

decimetre
centigram        centilitre
decilitre

What do each of these measures equal?

# The Maths Herald

Name:

Date:

## The Puzzler

In a magic square the sum of each column, row and diagonal is the same – this is the magic number (or percent).

Complete the magic square.

What is the magic percent?

Make up a magic percent square of your own.

| 70% | | |
|---|---|---|
| | 10% | |
| | | 40% |

## Let's Investigate

Write down all the different things that you do on a normal weekday.

Can you group these activities into different categories?

Over the course of 1 day, keep a detailed log of the things that you do in each of these categories.

Let's suppose that 1 whole day, 24 hours, is 100%.

Work out what percent of your day is spent on each of the categories.

Then draw a pie chart to represent your day.

How would this compare to a Saturday or Sunday? Investigate!

## Focus on Science

What is a humidity meter?

What does RH% refer to?

What does it mean?

---

## Money Matters

When shops have sales, they often publicise the discount as a percentage.

Why do you think this is?

What are the 'normal' percentage discounts that shops offer?

Again, why do you think this is?

## Technology Today

Hector and Gomez are twins. Except on Sundays, they spend every afternoon playing their favourite computer game – Solar Seize. Below are their scores for last week.

58 out of 80 means that on Monday Hector played a total of 80 games and won 58.

- On which day did Hector win the highest percentage of games?
- On which day did Hector win the lowest percentage of games?
- On which day did Gomez win the highest percentage of games?
- On which day did Gomez win the lowest percentage of games?

| Hector | |
|---|---|
| Monday | 58 out of 80 |
| Tuesday | 22 out of 50 |
| Wednesday | 7 out of 20 |
| Thursday | 6 out of 10 |
| Friday | 49 out of 60 |
| Saturday | 31 out of 40 |

| Gomez | |
|---|---|
| Monday | 25 out of 40 |
| Tuesday | 45 out of 60 |
| Wednesday | 12 out of 20 |
| Thursday | 7 out of 10 |
| Friday | 60 out of 80 |
| Saturday | 24 out of 50 |

# The Language of Maths

The words *deposit* or *down payment* refer to an amount of money that is paid as a first instalment that secures the purchase of something you wish to buy later. The *balance* is the amount of money that is paid later when you actually take ownership of the thing you are buying.

In most cases a deposit is required on large purchases such as a holiday, a car or a house and is a percentage of the full price.

Limited Edition
Butter Box
£9998
FARDS LATEST
MODEL
Only 5% Deposit
Required

Investigate deposits. What other purchases allow a deposit? What percentage of the full amount is required as a deposit? What are the other conditions of the deposit?

## Let's Investigate

What percent of your class are boys? What percent are girls?

Use percentages to make 8 other comparisons between all the children in your class.

Think about interesting things to make comparisons about.

Don't just compare 2 groups within the class, like boys and girls.

Try making comparisons between 3, 4 or more groups.

## Money Matters

What do the letters VAT stand for? What does this mean? How does it work?

What is the current rate of VAT in the UK?

How do you calculate the VAT on goods and services?

Choose some items in a magazine or catalogue that *do not* have VAT added. Calculate the new price of each item once VAT has been added.

If something already includes VAT, what is the calculation required to find the price before VAT?

Choose some items in a magazine or catalogue that already have VAT added. Calculate the price of each item before VAT was added.

## Money Matters

Many countries in Europe also have systems similar to VAT (although they are not referred to as VAT).

Investigate the current rates of VAT in different countries in Europe.

Illustrate through various examples the difference in Euros (€) you would pay for a range of goods and services bought in different countries throughout Europe.

# The Language of Maths

Write a percentage for each sector of the pie chart.

Make your percentages as accurate as possible.

What might this pie chart be representing? Write a key to explain the chart.

## Money Matters

Percentages are often used in the financial pages of a newspaper.

Look through several newspapers and cut out any references to percentages.

Find out what these percentages mean.

S&C Volume 6

# The Maths Herald

Name:

Date:

## Money Matters

When a price is increased, a certain amount is added to the original price. This is called an *increment* of the original price. This is often expressed as a percentage of the original price.

To calculate the percentage increase, divide the increment by the original price and then multiply by 100%.

$$\text{Percentage increase} = \frac{\text{increment}}{\text{original price}} \times 100\%$$

When a price is decreased, a certain amount is taken off the original price. This is called a *discount* of the original price. This is often expressed as a percentage of the original price.

To calculate the percentage decrease, divide the discount by the original price and then multiply by 100%.

$$\text{Percentage decrease} = \frac{\text{discount}}{\text{original price}} \times 100\%$$

Work out the percentage increase or decrease of each of the following.

During a sale the price of a pair of shoes has been discounted from £60 to £42. What is the percentage discount?

In the past 5 years, the price of installing a new washing machine has increased from £150 to £225. How much of a percentage increase is this?

The price of a monthly train ticket has increased from £280 to £322. By what percent has the price increased?

2 years ago Tim bought a new LCD television for £800. Now the same television costs £640. By what percent has the cost of the television fallen?

Look through newspapers and magazines to find the prices of a range of different items.

Imagine that you are the retailer. You decide to offer a discount on some of the products, and raise the prices on others. What percentage discount or increment will you put on each product? What will this mean to the price of each product? As a retailer, what types of products are good for offering a discount on? What types of products are good for including a price increase? Why?

---

## Focus on Science

The Earth is 149 596 208 km from the Sun.

Mercury is only 57 859 856 km from the Sun. Approximately what percentage of the Earth's distance from the Sun is Mercury's distance from the Sun?

Venus is 108 224 912 km from the Sun. Approximately how far is Venus from the Sun as a percentage of the Earth's distance from the Sun?

## What's the Problem?

The land area of the Earth is 148 300 000 km² and this is approximately 30% of the Earth's surface. Approximately what is the total surface area of the Earth?

What surface area of the Earth is covered by water?

## The Puzzler

Complete each of these statements in at least 2 different ways.

5 is ◯ % of ☐

12 is ◯ % of ☐

18 is ◯ % of ☐

55 is ◯ % of ☐

percentage points

## The Arts Roundup

An orchestra consists of 40 male and 30 female musicians.

16 of the male musicians and 40% of the female musicians also belong to other smaller ensembles. What percentage of the orchestra members also perform with smaller ensembles?

# Money Matters

Some businesses need people to help them sell their goods. These people are known as dealers, salespeople or agents. Sometimes these people are not paid a regular salary. Instead, they are paid a percentage of the value of the goods that they sell. This type of payment is called a *commission*.

To calculate a commission in pounds:

Percentage of the commission × value of goods sold

To calculate a commission as a percentage: $\dfrac{\text{commission received}}{\text{value of goods sold}} \times 100\%$

*Example 1*

An agent received £750 commission on £15 000 worth of goods sold. What was the agent's commission as a percentage?

Commission received: £750
Value of goods sold: £15 000

$= \dfrac{£750}{£15\ 000} \times 100\%$

$= 5\%$

*Example 2*

A salesman was paid 7% commission on all the goods he sold. If he sold £92 000 worth of goods, how much commission did he receive?

Value of goods sold: £92 000
Percentage of the commission: 7%

$= 7\% \times £92\ 000$

$= \dfrac{7}{100} \times £92\ 000$

$= £6440$

Complete this table.

| Agent | Value of goods sold | Commission as a percentage | Commission in pounds |
|---|---|---|---|
| D Rogers | £34 000 | 6% | |
| M Quincy | £194 000 | | £9700 |
| A Leech | £29 500 | | £2360 |
| W Ali | £67 800 | 4% | |
| C T Adams | £45 350 | 3% | |

Imagine that all 5 agents work for the same company. Who is the company's best agent? Why? Who is their worst agent? Why?

---

# Around the World

Consult a map of your town or the local area.

Calculate the approximate percentage of land that is allocated to:

- housing
- sporting and recreational areas, and open spaces
- commerce and industry
- other uses.

Compare your figures with other towns. Write about how you arrived at your approximations.

## Focus on Science

Your skin is the largest organ of the body.

The average adult has approximately 2000 cm² of skin. The average teenager approximately 1500 cm² and a child about 800 cm².

The diagram on the right shows what percentage of the body's total surface area of skin covers different parts of the body.

Use this information to calculate the surface area of the different body parts for an adult, a teenager and a child.

**9%**
Head and neck

**18%**
Both arms and hands

**37%**
Torso

**36%**
Both legs and feet

## Focus on Science

The human adult has 32 teeth.

There are 4 different kinds of teeth:

molars: 6 pairs
incisors: 4 pairs
bicuspids: 4 pairs
canines: 2 pairs

What percentage of an adult's teeth are:

- molars?
- incisors?
- bicuspids?
- canines?

# The Maths Herald

Name:

Date:

## 🌍 Around the World

The pyramids at Giza, in Egypt, were built approximately 4500 years ago. For over 4000 years the Great Pyramid, the largest of the 3, was the tallest monument in the world. It is still the largest stone monument ever built.

All 3 pyramids are the shape of a square-based pyramid.

When they were built, the ratio of the bases of the pyramids to their heights was 8 : 5.

The Great Pyramid of Khufu          Width of base 230 m

The Pyramid of Khafre          Width of base 214 m

The Pyramid of Menkare          Width of base 105 m

Work out the heights of each of the pyramids.

---

## 🔍 Let's Investigate

If you roll a pair of 1, 2, 3, 1, 2, 3 dice, the sum of the 2 dice can be 2, 3, 4, 5 or 6.

Roll a pair of 1, 2, 3, 1, 2, 3 dice 45 times and note how many times you get each total.

What is the most frequent total?

What is the least frequent total?

What is the approximate ratio of the most frequent total to the least frequent total?

## 💰 Money Matters

I have £5.60 in coins.

These are the ratios of the coins I have:

- For every 50p I have two 10p.
- For every two 5p I have a 50p.
- For every two 10p I have three 20p.

What coins do I have?

## 🐜 Looking for Patterns

A bag has red, green, blue and yellow counters in it.

The ratio of red counters to green counters is 6 : 5.

The ratio of green counters to blue counters is 5 : 4.

The ratio of blue counters to yellow counters is 8 : 5.

There are between 40 and 80 counters in the bag.

How many of each colour of counter is in the bag?

# Money Matters

If you go on holiday to the USA you will need to change some UK pounds (£) into US dollars ($) to spend while you are there.

The ratio between the pound and the US dollar varies from day to day, but is approximately 5 : 8.

In other words £5 will buy you $8.

Work out how many dollars each of these people got when they changed their pounds into dollars.

NEW YORK

- Peter changed £100.
- Aslan changed £50.
- Silvia changed £140.
- Tommi changed £175.
- Rada changed £320.

Some of them didn't spend all of their dollars while they were in America.

- Silvia returned with $72.
- Tommi returned with $116.
- Rada returned with $162.

When they returned they changed their dollars back into pounds.

How many pounds did they get?

---

# What's the Problem?

What is the ratio of starfish to shells in the bucket?

What fraction of the contents of the bucket are shells?

What proportion of the contents are starfish?

Now draw 6 fish in the bucket.

What is the ratio of fish to starfish?

What proportion of the contents of the bucket are starfish now?

---

# The Language of Maths

The letter 'e' is the most frequently used letter in the English language.

Open your favourite book on any page that is full of text.

Count the number of letter 'e's on it.

Now count the number of letter 'd's there are.

What is the approximate ratio of 'e's to 'd's?

If you opened your book at another page and did the same thing, would you expect the ratio to be the same?

Why or why not?

Try this out and see if you are right.

---

# Let's Investigate

There are 8 main planets in our Solar System. They all *orbit* around the Sun. Generally, the farther a planet is from the Sun the longer it takes to orbit it. The Earth is the third planet from the Sun and takes 365 days to orbit it.

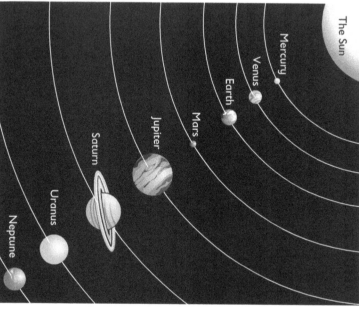

Investigate how long the other planets in our Solar System take to orbit the Sun.

What is the approximate ratio of the time that each planet takes to orbit the Sun, to the time the Earth takes?

# The Maths Herald

Name:

Date:

---

## The Arts Roundup

Using the Resource sheet, draw a simple picture in the small 4 × 4 square.

Now using the large 4 × 4 grid, enlarge your picture.

By what ratio have you enlarged your picture?

---

## At Home

You will need a recipe book for this activity.

Plan a 3-course meal for 10 people.

Make a list of all the ingredients you will need for each course, and the precise quantities of each ingredient.

Once you have done this, find out an approximate cost for the meal.

---

## Let's Investigate

Approximately what proportion of the surnames in the local telephone directory begin with the letter C?

What about the letter J?

What is the most common letter for surnames to begin with?

What is the least common letter?

Write about how you arrived at each of your approximations.

---

## Looking for Patterns

Martine takes 5 strides to walk as far as Johannes walks in 4 strides.

Each of Johannes's strides is 30 centimetres.

If Martine takes 18 strides how many centimetres has she walked?

---

## In the Past

The Ancient Greeks called rectangles where the ratio of the length of the longer side to the length of the shorter side was approximately 1·6 to 1 *golden rectangles*.

Find examples of rectangles in school and at home, e.g. windows, table tops, sheets of paper …

Are any of the rectangles golden rectangles?

The ratio 1·6 to 1 is often referred to as the *golden ratio*.

$\boxed{\phantom{xx}}$ 1·6

$\boxed{\phantom{xx}}$ 1

When different body measurements are compared they often approximate the golden ratio.

Measure 2 different body parts, e.g. the length of your arm from shoulder to fingertips, and the length from your fingertips to your elbow. Is the ratio the golden ratio?

Can you find 2 body parts that are?

---

## Let's Investigate

Take a sheet of A4 paper and by continually folding and cutting the sheet, produce 6 smaller paper sizes – A5, A6, A7, A8, A9, A10.

Take another sheet of A4 paper and place this alongside the 6 other paper sizes in order smallest to largest.

Measure the length and width of each of the 7 sheets of paper. What do you notice about them? What are the ratios?

---

## Let's Investigate

The ratio of Strip B to Strip E is 2 : 5.

What other pairs of strips have a ratio of 2 : 5?

The ratio of Strip C to Strip F is 3 : 6 or 1 : 2.

What other pairs of strips have a ratio of 1 : 2?

Pick 2 different strips and write the ratios.

Can you find other pairs of strips with the same ratio?

Repeat with other pairs of strips.

A B C D E F G H I J

scale factor

## Sports Update

Every morning Lance and Fabio go running for the same amount of time.

Lance is able to run 6 miles in the time that it takes Fabio to run 4·5 miles.

If, by the end of a week, Lance has run a total of 39 miles. How far has Fabio run?

## The Language of Maths

The ratio of grey circles to black circles in these 2 diagrams is 2 : 3.

Draw 2 different diagrams to show each of the following. Use different colours.

- The ratio of red circles to blue circles is 1 : 5.
- The ratio of green circles to yellow circles is 4 : 7.
- The ratio of red circles to black circles is 2 : 1 : 3.
- The proportion of the circles that are red is $\frac{2}{3}$.
- The proportion of the circles that are green is $\frac{3}{5}$.

For the diagrams you drew in the first 3 questions above, write a description of what proportion of each diagram has red, blue, green, yellow or black circles.

For the diagrams you drew in the last 2 questions above, describe the ratio.

## What's the Problem?

Write a word problem with:

- a ratio of 2 : 5 and a total amount of £112
- a ratio of 5 : 8 where the smaller amount is 30
- a proportion of 25% and a total amount of £24
- a proportion of $\frac{6}{7}$ where the larger amount is 35.

---

## Let's Investigate

Using 1 of the chairs that the children in your class sit on, measure the following:

- the length of the chair leg
- the height of the back of the chair
- the width of the chair seat
- the depth of the chair seat.

What are the ratios between these 4 different measurements?

Are the ratios the same for the chairs in the Foundation Stage, Key Stage 1 and in Year 6? What about your teacher's chair?

Width of the seat

Height of the back of the chair

Depth of the seat

Length of the chair leg

## Let's Investigate

Look at a set of dominoes with all the dominoes with a blank side removed.

$4 \times 3 = 12$

Multiply together the number of dots on each side.

- What is the ratio of even products to odd products?
- What proportion of the products is odd?
- What proportion of the products is even?

What if you found the total number of dots on each side?

What is the total number of dots on each side?

## The Language of Maths

This is the name of a village in Wales. It is the longest place name in Europe and one of the longest place names in the world.

Llanfairpwllgwyngyllgogerychwyrndrobwllllantysiliogogogoch

- What is the ratio of vowels to consonants?
- What is the ratio of the letter l to the letter o?
- What proportion of the letters are vowels?
- What proportion of the letters are g?

How else can you describe the name using the language of ratio and proportion?

# The Maths Herald

Name:

Date:

## At Home

Make a list of all the members of your extended family.

What proportion of your family is female?

What is the ratio of males to females in your family?

Write 3 more statements about your extended family. Describe your family using the vocabulary of ratio and/or proportion.

## The Puzzler

Which drink tastes stronger:

7 parts orange juice mixed with 3 parts water

*or*

8 parts orange juice mixed with 4 parts water?

How did you work it out?

## The Language of Maths

Solve these problems involving inverse proportion:

- It takes 12 hours for 8 men to construct a fence around a sporting field. How long would it take 6 men?
- 4 friends go on a trek. They take 5 containers of water with them which lasts them for 9 days. How long would the same amount of water last them if 6 friends had gone on the trek?
- Walking at 5 kph, it takes Dipo 45 minutes to walk home from school. How long would it take him if he walked at 6 kph?

---

## What's the Problem?

On average, how many children a day in your school have school dinners?

Imagine that you are the school cook.

Below are a list of the ingredients needed to make a main dish and a dessert.

Calculate how much of each ingredient you would need to use to cater for all the school dinners.

Show all your working.

### Courgette Tart
*(For 6 people)*

365 g courgette
1 large onion
$\frac{3}{4}$ cup grated cheese
1 cup self-raising flour
$\frac{1}{2}$ cup oil
5 eggs
pinch each of salt and pepper

### Banana Cake
*(For 8 people)*

125 g butter
175 g soft brown sugar
2 eggs
280 g plain flour
1 tsp bicarbonate of soda
pinch of salt
125 ml milk
3 medium ripe bananas
1 tsp vanilla extract
75 g walnuts

## The Language of Maths

What is ratio?
What is proportion?
How are they related?
What words and symbols are associated with ratio and proportion?
Design a poster showing what ratio and proportion mean.
Provide different examples on your poster.

$$a : b = b : a$$

## What's the Problem?

All the guest rooms at the Harriet Hotel are being refurbished. There are a total of 120 rooms, all of which are identical. It took 12 men 5 days to lay new carpet in 60 of the rooms.

- How many men would be needed to lay carpet in all 120 rooms in 8 days?

- How many days would it take 16 men to lay carpet in all 120 rooms?

Explain in writing how you worked out the answer to each of the problems.

## What's the Problem?

Once a month the remote town of Wombat Village is visited by the mobile library unit.

The mobile library carries books, CDs and DVDs for people to borrow.

This month altogether the library has a total of 1976 books, CDs and DVDs.

The ratio of the number of books to CDs to DVDs is 5 : 1 : 2.

How many books, CDs and DVDs does the unit have this month?

## Sports Update

Nawra Rovers are playing at home to Berry Rangers.

7 out of every 8 people in the stadium are Nawra Rovers supporters.

Of the Nawra Rovers supporters, 1 out of every 9 people are season ticket holders.

There are a total of 91 Nawra Rovers season ticket holders watching the match.

How many people are in the stadium?

---

## Let's Investigate

Your class is going to have a party.

Here is the shopping list.

Work out how much of each item you need to buy.

Be as accurate as possible – you don't want to be short of anything, and you want to have as little waste as possible.

Think carefully about:

- the quantities that each person is likely to need

- those items that will need sharing between everyone in the class.

Once you have calculated how much of each item you will need to buy, work out an approximate costing for each of the items. Then work out the approximate total bill for the party and the cost per person.

sweets
soft drink
cake
crisps
fruit
mini pizzas
chicken wings
paper cups
paper plates
napkins

## Let's Investigate

Find a recipe that sounds tasty.

Choose one that has around 8 to 10 ingredients.

How many people is the recipe for?

Rewrite the quantities of each ingredient needed for a different number of people.

Rewrite the quantities of each ingredient needed for another different number of people.

# The Maths Herald

Name:                                    Date:

## Famous Mathematicians

Pythagoras was a Greek philosopher (569–500 BC). He made many important discoveries in mathematics, particularly in geometry.

Pythagoras also showed how whole numbers could be represented as geometric shapes.

A *square number* can be represented by dots in a square pattern.

These are the first 4 *square numbers*:

1st     2nd     3rd     4th

A *triangular number* can be represented by dots in a triangular pattern.

These are the first 4 *triangular numbers*:

1st     2nd     3rd     4th

An *oblong number* can be represented by dots in a rectangular pattern, where 1 side is longer than the other.

These are the first 4 *oblong numbers*:

1st     2nd     3rd     4th

formula

Can you work out what the 5th to 10th square, triangular and oblong numbers are?

What about the 50th square, triangular and oblong numbers?

Can you work out a rule for finding any square, triangular or oblong number?

---

## Looking for Patterns

Look at these rows of greenhouses.

In the first row there is only 1 greenhouse – with a total of 5 sides.

In the second row there are 2 greenhouses – with a total of 9 sides.

In the third row there are 3 greenhouses – with a total of 13 sides.

How many sides would there be for a row of 10 greenhouses?

Write a formula for finding the number of sides for a row of any number of greenhouses.

## Looking for Patterns

What are the next 2 numbers in this sequence?

6, 24, 60, 120, 210, …

Explain in words the rule for the sequence. Write a formula for finding any number in the sequence.

## Looking for Patterns

Which of these sequences will be the first to reach 1000 or more?

A = 1, 4, 9, 16, 25, …

B = 1, 3, 6, 10, 15, …

C = 0, 1, 1, 2, 3, …

D = 1, 2, 4, 8, 16, …

How did you work it out?

Which term in each sequence is the first to reach 1000 or more?

What is the rule or name of each of these sequences?

## Sports Update

**4–3**

The final score of a football match was 4 – 3.

How many different possible half-time scores could there have been?

What are they?

If you know the final score of a football match, what is the rule for calculating how many possible half-time scores there could have been?

## Famous Mathematicians

Pythagoras was able to show many different number relationships using shapes.

Draw dot arrays to show these relationships.

*The sum of 2 consecutive triangular numbers is a square number.*

*8 times a triangular number plus 1 is a square number.*

*The sum of 2 even numbers equals an even number.*

*2 times a triangular number is an oblong number.*

*The sum of 2 odd numbers equals an even number.*

*The sum of an even number and an odd number equals an odd number.*

## Famous Mathematicians

Carl Gauss was a German mathematician who lived from 1777 to 1855. He was particularly interested in the theory of numbers.

Gauss found a *formula* for finding the total of any set of *consecutive* counting numbers starting from 1.

Look at the table on the right to help you discover the formula.

Can you use the letter 'n' to help you write your formula?

Look at the numbers in the third column. What do you notice about them?

Use your formula to work out the total of the first 100 numbers:

$1 + 2 + 3 + 4 + 5 \ldots + 100 = ?$

| Counting numbers | Number in set ($n$) | Total |
|---|---|---|
| 1 | 1 | 1 |
| 1 + 2 | 2 | 3 |
| 1 + 2 + 3 | 3 | 6 |
| 1 + 2 + 3 + 4 | 4 | 10 |
| 1 + 2 + 3 + 4 + 5 | | |
| 1 + 2 + 3 + 4 + 5 + 6 | | |
| 1 + 2 + 3 + 4 + 5 + 6 + 7 | | |
| 1 + 2 + 3 + 4 + 5 + 6 + 7 + 8 | | |
| 1 + 2 + 3 + 4 + 5 + 6 + 7 + 8 + 9 | | |
| 1 + 2 + 3 + 4 + 5 + 6 + 7 + 8 + 9 + 10 | | |

## Famous Mathematicians

Leonardo Pisano Bogollo was born in Pisa in Italy around 1170 AD. He was also known as Leonardo of Pisa and more commonly was called Fibonacci. He is said to have been the greatest European mathematician of the Middle Ages.

Fibonacci was interested in how numbers occur in patterns in nature.

One of his most famous problems involved rabbits. Fibonacci assumed that:

- a male (M) and a female (F) rabbit can start reproducing at 1 month old
- a pair of rabbits will create another pair of rabbits every month: 1 male and 1 female.

He wanted to know how many pairs of rabbits there would be at the end of the year. Fibonacci knew that in real life this problem would probably not happen. However, he was interested in the numbers and the patterns that occurred.

The following table shows what Fibonacci discovered.

| Month | Rabbits | Pairs |
|---|---|---|
| 1 | $MF^1$ — First pair of rabbits. They are not yet a month old and therefore are too young to reproduce. | 1 |
| 2 | $MF^1$ — First pair of rabbits are now a month old and are therefore able to reproduce. | 1 |
| 3 | $MF^1 \rightarrow MF^2$ — First pair $MF^1$ reproduce pair: $MF^2$ | 2 |
| 4 | $MF^1 \rightarrow MF^2$, $MF^2 \rightarrow MF^3$ — Pair $MF^1$ reproduce another pair: $MF^3$. Pair $MF^2$ are too young to reproduce. | 3 |
| 5 | $MF^1 \rightarrow MF^2$, $MF^2 \rightarrow MF^3$, $MF^3 \rightarrow MF^4$, $MF^5$ — Pair $MF^1$ reproduce another pair: $MF^4$. Pair $MF^2$ reproduce pair: $MF^5$. Pair $MF^3$ are too young to reproduce. | 5 |
| 6 | $MF^1$, $MF^2$, $MF^3$, $MF^4$, $MF^5$, $MF^6$, $MF^7$, $MF^8$ — Pair $MF^1$ reproduce another pair: $MF^6$. Pair $MF^2$ reproduce another pair: $MF^7$. Pair $MF^3$ reproduce pair: $MF^8$. Pairs $MF^4$ and $MF^5$ are too young to reproduce. | 8 |

Using the information in the table, can you work out how many rabbits there would be at the end of the year?

## Looking for Patterns

Look at the number of pairs in the table in the *Famous Mathematicians* activity above.

What pattern do you notice?

This pattern is referred to as the *Fibonacci sequence*.

Apply the rule to write the first 20 numbers of the Fibonacci sequence.

# The Maths Herald

S&C Volume 6

Name:          Date:

## Money Matters

When you put, or *deposit*, a certain amount of money into a bank it is called the *principal*. The bank pays you interest on this money. The amount of interest you get depends on the rate that the bank is paying. The interest is usually paid as a percentage per year or *per annum* (p.a.).

Often, people put their money into a *fixed term deposit*. This means they deposit a fixed sum of money, or principal (P), at a fixed rate of interest (R) for a fixed length of time (T). The amount of interest earned on a fixed term deposit is called *simple interest* (I).

To calculate simple interest you use the following formula:

$$I = \frac{PRT}{100}$$

The *amount* (A) is the sum of the principal and the interest earned. To calculate the amount you use the following formula: $A = P + I$.

*Example*

Calculate the interest a person will earn if they deposit £5000 for a period of 4 years at a rate of 3% per annum.

$P = £5000, R = 3\%, T = 4$ years

$$= \frac{5000 \times 3 \times 4}{100}$$

$$= \frac{60\,000}{100} = £600$$

$P = £5000, I = £600$

$£5000 + £600 = £5600$

$= £5600$

What will be the amount at the end of the 4 years?

Use the simple interest formula to calculate the simple interest for each of the following people.

**Name:** Mr J Brown
**Principal:** £2000
**Rate:** 3% per annum
**Time:** 2 years

**Name:** Mr T Kanu
**Principal:** £12 000
**Rate:** 6% per annum
**Time:** 3 years

**Name:** Mrs A Williams
**Principal:** £4000
**Rate:** 5% per annum
**Time:** 4 years

**Name:** Mrs B Andersen
**Principal:** £30 500
**Rate:** 6·5% per annum
**Time:** 5 years

*continued on page 2*

© HarperCollins *Publishers* 2016

---

*Continued from page 3*

When a company makes a profit, the shareholders receive a share in the profits as well. These are called a *dividend*. Dividends are calculated as a percentage of the nominal value of the shares.

*Example 1*

A company issues 4000 shares with a nominal value of £5 per share and sells them for a market price of £4.20 a share.

**a.** What is the total nominal value of shares?

$4000 × £5$

Total nominal value = £20 000

**b.** What is the total market price of shares?

$4000 × £4.20$

Total market value = £16 800

**c.** Are the shares sold below par, at par or above par?

The shares are sold below par.

**d.** What is the difference between the nominal value and the market price?

£20 000 – £16 800

The difference between the nominal value and the market price = £3200.

*Example 2*

A shareholder has 600 shares in a company. If the company offers 6% dividend on shares with a nominal value of £8 per share, how much money does the investor receive?

Dividend on 1 share

$= 6\% × £8 = £0.48$

Dividend on 600 shares

$= 600 × £0.48 = £288$

- A company sells 10 000 shares with a nominal value of £2 at par. How much money is raised?

- Fatima has 1200 shares in a company. They have a nominal value of £4 each and pay a dividend of 2·75%. How much is the total dividend she gets?

- Tayo has 500 shares in a company. The shares pay a dividend of 3·5% and she receives £350. What is the nominal value of each share?

- 1000 shares, each with a nominal value of £30, pay a dividend of 5·5%. What is the total dividend?

- A company sells 15 000 shares, with a nominal value of £25 each, at £5 above par. What is the total amount of money that it raises?

economics

*continued from page 1*

Use the amount formula to calculate the total amount each of the 4 people will receive at the end of their fixed term.

Look in a newspaper for details on savings.

## Money Matters

Sometimes companies or individuals borrow money from banks or other financial institutions. The money borrowed is called a *loan*, which must be paid back over a given period of time. The bank or other financial institution charge *interest* (I) on the money that is borrowed. The rate of interest (R) often depends on how much money is being borrowed (P) and for how long (T).

In most cases, when a bank or other financial institution lends money, they require that the borrower repays a fixed amount of the loan each month, as well as the interest, until the total amount of the loan has been repaid. The time it takes to repay the loan in this way is called the *life of the loan* (T).

To calculate the amount of interest you pay over the life of the loan, use the following formula:

$$I = \left(\frac{PRT}{100}\right) \div 2$$

The total *amount* (A) is the sum of the principal and the interest paid.

*continued on page 3*

What are the different options that are on offer? Which do you think is the most favourable option?

If someone had £10 000 to save, which option would you suggest they take? Why?

To calculate the amount use the following formula: A = P + I.
To calculate the amount of money paid each month (M), you divide the total amount (A) by the number of monthly repayments. Use the following formula:

$$M = \frac{A}{T \times 12}$$

*Example*

A man borrows £15 000 for 5 years at a rate of 4% per annum.

**a.** What is the amount of interest he will pay over the life of the loan?

$$P = £15\,000, \ R = 4\%, \ T = 5 \text{ years}$$
$$= \frac{(15\,000 \times 4 \times 5)}{100} \div 2$$
$$= \frac{300\,000}{100} \div 2$$
$$= 3000 \div 2$$
$$= £1500$$

**b.** What is the total amount he will have to pay?

$$P = £15\,000, \ I = £1500$$
$$= £15\,000 + £1500$$
$$= £16\,500$$

*continued on page 3*

---

*continued from page 2*

**c.** How much money will he need to pay back each month?

$$A = £16\,500, \ T = 5 \text{ years}$$
$$= \frac{£16\,500}{5 \times 12}$$
$$= \frac{£16\,500}{60}$$
$$= £275$$

For each of the following, calculate:

**a.** the amount of interest to be paid over the life of the loan

**b.** the total amount to be paid back over the life of the loan

**c.** how much money will need to be paid back each month.

| Name of borrower: | Mr Charles |
| --- | --- |
| Principal being borrowed: | £93 000 |
| Rate of interest: | 4% |
| Life of the loan: | 2 years |

| Name of borrower: | Net Works |
| --- | --- |
| Principal being borrowed: | £1 500 000 |
| Rate of interest: | 9% |
| Life of the loan: | 25 years |

| Name of borrower: | Mr & Mrs Lee |
| --- | --- |
| Principal being borrowed: | £360 000 |
| Rate of interest: | 6% |
| Life of the loan: | 12 years |

| Name of borrower: | Crystal Pools |
| --- | --- |
| Principal being borrowed: | £900 000 |
| Rate of interest: | 7% |
| Life of the loan: | 20 years |

Look for details of loan offers in a newspaper.

What are the different options that are on offer? Which do you think is the most favourable option?

If someone needed to borrow £50 000, which option would you suggest they take? Why?

## Money Matters

Many companies raise money by issuing *shares* in their company.

These shares can be bought by anyone who then becomes part owners in the company. People who buy shares in a company are called *investors* or *shareholders*.

When a company issues shares they set a price for each share which is called the *nominal value* or *face value*.

The price that each share is sold for is called the *market price*. This may be the same as the nominal value or above or below it.

If a share is sold for the nominal value it is said to be at *par*.

If a share is sold above the nominal value it is said to be above par or at a *premium*.

If a share is sold below the nominal value it is said to be below par or at a *discount*.

*continued on page 4*

S&C Volume 6

# The Maths Herald

Name:

Date:

## 🐜 Construct

Just as most maps are drawn to scale, so too are different plans. Plans are drawn for whole buildings, individual rooms, pieces of machinery or furniture, or anything where it is not possible to have a life-size drawing.

Draw a simple plan of your classroom including the most important features, e.g. desks, whiteboard, cupboards, door, …

Measure these features and record them on your plan.

Now work out a scale for your plan and draw another plan of your classroom to scale.

Draw a simple plan of a piece of furniture in your classroom, e.g. desk or cupboard.

Measure all its features and record them on your plan.

Now work out a scale for your plan and draw another plan of the piece of furniture to scale.

## 🌍 Around the World

Usually a map cannot be drawn life-size. It has to fit onto a piece of paper. So in most cases maps are drawn to scale.

Something that is actually 5 km away may be drawn as 1 cm away on a map. In this case 1 cm represents 5 km. The scale is 1 cm : 5 km.

Using a map that has a scale on it, compare the distances between different landmarks.

Try and be as accurate as possible with your measurements.

---

## 🎵 The Language of Maths

*20,000 Leagues Under the Sea* is a classic science-fiction novel by French writer Jules Verne published in 1869. It tells the story of Captain Nemo and his submarine Nautilus.

What is a league?

What is it equivalent to?

What may be an alternative title for *20,000 Leagues Under the Sea*?

## 🏠 At Home

Estimate the distance from school to your home. Write down how you arrived at this estimate.

Now write down how you could most accurately measure this distance.

Can you do it? If so, do it!

## 🌍 Around the World

The distance around the equator is 40 000 km or approximately 25 000 miles. Estimate how long it would take to travel round the equator.

What is your estimation based on? Write a report to justify your estimation.

## 💰 Money Matters

10p coins are placed one on top of the other to make a tower.

What would be the value of a 1 kilometre tower of 10p coins?

# Focus on Science

The diameter of the Earth is approximately 13 000 km.

The diameter of Pluto is approximately 2000 km and the diameter of the Sun approximately 1 400 000 km.

For example, you may decide to draw the Earth with a diameter of 13 mm and Pluto with a diameter of 2 mm.

Find out the approximate diameters of all the planets in the solar system and draw them to the same scale.

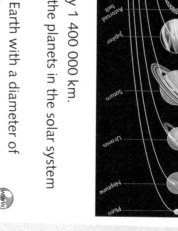

# Around the World

The horizon is the line at which the Earth's surface and the sky appear to meet.

How far away is the horizon if you were standing on the seashore?

Use these formulas to find out:

$d$ = distance to the horizon

An approximate formula when measuring in kilometres and metres is:

$$d = \sqrt{12 \cdot 7h}$$

$h$ = your height above sea level

An approximate formula when measuring in miles and feet is:

$$d = \sqrt{1 \cdot 50h}$$

nanometre

Measure your height from ground to eye level. Then calculate how far the horizon appears to you.

Choose some friends and find out how far the horizon appears to them.

Why not try this out for someone at home (or your teacher)!

---

# Let's Investigate

Each step on an ordinary flight of stairs has a vertical *riser* which is the height of the step, and a horizontal *tread*, which is the depth of the step that you walk on.

Investigate the dimensions used for playing different sports such as:

- football
- rugby union
- basketball
- cricket
- tennis
- baseball

Draw a diagram showing the shape and dimensions for a sport of your choice.

Make sure that your diagram is to scale.

# Sports Update

Most sports are played on areas of a particular shape and with specific dimensions.

The *slope* or *pitch* of the stairs is the total rise divided by the total *run*. It is sometimes called the *rake* of the stairs. The *pitch line* is the imaginary line along the tip of the treads.

Investigate different staircases.

- What is the height of an average riser?
- What is the depth of an average tread?
- Is there a ratio between the height of the riser and the depth of the tread?
- What is the average slope of a staircase?

Pitch line

Riser height

Tread depth

Run

Rise

# Let's Investigate

Give 8 children in your class a slip of paper.

Ask them to write their name on the paper and draw a line they estimate to be 10 cm long.

Collect the slips of paper and measure each line to the nearest millimetre and record the results.

What was the percentage error for each child?

From the results, do most children tend to overestimate or underestimate short lengths?

# The Maths Herald

S&C Volume 6

Name:

Date:

## Around the World

Throughout many parts of the world traders buy and sell raw materials or primary agricultural products such as wheat (flour), sugar, rice, tea and coffee. These are called *commodities*.

The table below shows the number of sacks of flour that 8 different traders bought and the average mass of each sack of flour. Use the information in the table to answer the questions.

| Trader | A | B | C | D | E | F | G | H |
|---|---|---|---|---|---|---|---|---|
| Number of sacks of flour bought | 5 | 8 | 3 | 4 | 7 | 6 | 4 | 5 |
| Average mass of sack (kg) | 240 | 160 | 280 | 200 | 180 | 220 | 225 | 250 |

- Altogether, how much flour did Trader E buy in kg?
- Who bought more flour: Trader A or Trader B? How much more flour did they buy?
- Which trader bought $\frac{3}{4}$ of the total amount of flour as Trader A?
- Which trader bought a total of $1\frac{1}{4}$ tonnes of flour?
- Which 2 traders together bought a total of 2160 kg?
- Which trader bought the least amount of flour? How much flour was this?
- Which trader bought the most amount of flour? How much flour was this?
- Write the total amount of flour that each trader bought, starting with the trader that bought the least.

## Around the World

Which countries are the biggest producers of these different commodities:

- wheat
- rice
- coffee?
- sugar
- tea

How much do they produce each year? How is it measured?

Draw a table, graph or chart showing the world's top producers of wheat, sugar, rice, tea and coffee. Write a report of what you have found out.

---

## At Home

Most packaged food is sold by mass. For example, pasta, nuts, dried beans. Even fruit and vegetables are often sold in packets according to their mass.

Investigate the approximate number of different food items that are equivalent to 1 kilogram.

What, for example, is the average number of oranges you get for a kilogram? What about pasta shells, potatoes, carrots … ?

Remember, you are only after an approximate number, and the average. Write a report about what you found out and how you went about it.

## What's the Problem?

If someone has a mass 63 kg, what is their approximate mass in stones and pounds?

*Hint*

You need to know about the relationship between the imperial measures (stones and pounds) and their metric equivalent.

Write an explanation of how you worked out the answer.

## What's the Problem?

If someone has a mass 12 st 8 lb, what is their approximate mass in kilograms?

*Hint*

You need to know about the relationship between the imperial measures (stones and pound) and their metric equivalent.

Write an explanation of how you worked out the answer.

# Looking for Patterns

In each of these problems, the first 2 sets of scales balance. Work out how many ○ s are needed to balance the third set.

**Puzzle 1**

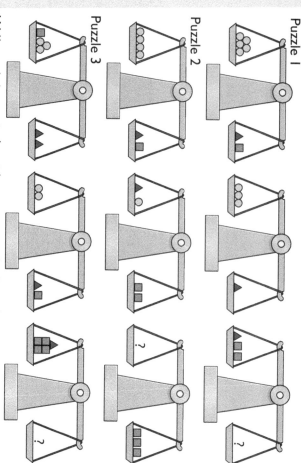

**Puzzle 2**

**Puzzle 3**

Now make up a similar problem of your own.

Write a statement about how you worked out how many ○ s were needed to balance the third sets of scales.

# The Language of Maths

Design a poster describing the difference between mass and weight.

inference

# Focus on Science

A cube 1 m × 1 m × 1 m (1 cubic metre / 1 m³) filled with water has a mass of 1000 kg. Investigate the mass of each of the following:

- balsa wood
- gold
- lead
- pine wood
- silver
- aluminium

---

# Focus on Science

Every time you jump, you experience gravity – it pulls you back down to the ground. Without gravity, you'd float off into the atmosphere, along with all of the other matter on Earth.

All the planets in the solar system have different gravitational pulls.

As a result, you would weigh more on some planets and less on others. Find out your approximate weight on each of the planets, by multiplying your Earth weight by these gravity factors.

| Planet | Gravity Factor |
|---|---|
| Mercury | 0·38 |
| Venus | 0·88 |
| Earth | 1 |
| Mars | 0·38 |
| Jupiter | 2·53 |
| Saturn | 1·19 |
| Uranus | 0·91 |
| Neptune | 1·13 |

Find the Earth weight of other objects and then calculate their approximate weight on each of the other planets.

# Let's Investigate

What is the mass and volume of rubbish that your class produces in a week? How much of this rubbish is recycled?

What are you going to have to do to find out?

Present your information using tables, graphs and / or charts.

What inferences can you make from your investigation about the following?

- the amount of rubbish your class produces in a term / year
- the amount of rubbish that is produced by the entire school in a week / term / year
- the amount of rubbish that is recycled by your class, and the entire school, each term / year
- on average, how much rubbish each person in the school produces in a term / year.

# The Maths Herald

Name:

Date:

## Around the World

### Around the World

*Volume* is the amount of space that something occupies.

Look at the cuboid on the right.

Its dimensions are 10·2 cm × 2·8 cm × 4·6 cm.

Its volume is 131·376 cm³.

To find the volume of any cube or cuboid we multiply the length by the width by the height.

We can write this as:

volume of a cuboid = length × width × height

or  = l × w × h

or  = lwh

Knowing the exact volume is extremely important to freight companies that transport parcels all round the world. Calculate the volume of each of these parcels.

10·2 cm
4·6 cm
2·8 cm

A — 210 mm, 208 mm, 235 mm

B — 15 m, 9 m, 7·6 m

C — 7 cm, 6·7 m, 4·3 cm

D — 4·5 m, 4·5 m

E — 578 mm, 227 mm, 382 mm

A rectangular parcel has a volume of 462 000 cm³.

Its height is 80 cm. What might be the other dimensions of the parcel?

© HarperCollins *Publishers* 2016

---

## Famous Mathematicians

Sometimes we need to find the volume of irregular solids for which there is no mathematical formula we can use.

Archimedes, a Greek mathematician, physicist, engineer and astronomer was born in Sicily in 287 BC. It is said that one day he got into a full bath and the water overflowed. When he realised that the volume of water that had overflowed was equal to the volume of his body, he jumped out and ran through the streets shouting 'Eureka!'

We can use a measuring cylinder like the one shown above to measure the volume of irregular solids. The markings on the measuring cylinder are in cubic centimetres (cm³).

volume of solid shape = total volume of − volume of
immersed in water    water and solid   water

### Activity

1. Pour some water into a measuring cylinder and record the water-level mark.

2. Place the solid object into the water and record the new water-level mark.

3. The increase in height of the water-level is the volume of the solid object.

Follow steps 1–3 above for each of the solid objects. Record your results in a table stating the following information:

- name of solid object
- volume of water

- volume of water and solid object
- volume of solid

**You need:**
- measuring cylinder
- water
- collection of small solid objects, e.g. small stone, coin, ball of modelling clay

## Let's Investigate

What is the volume of your classroom?

Which classroom in your school is the largest by volume? What is its volume?

Which classroom in your school is the smallest by volume? What is its volume?

Which are the largest and smallest rooms by volume in your school? What are their volumes?

# Let's Investigate

A *prism* is a 3-D shape with its 2 ends the same size and shape and parallel to each other. A prism is the same size and shape all the way through its length.

It does not get wider or narrower.

Look at these prisms.

triangular prism

cylinder

If you cut across these prisms, you will get 2 smaller prisms.

Such a cut across a shape is called a *cross-section*.

The shape of a cross-section of a triangular prism is a triangle.

cross-section

cross-section

The shape of a cross-section of a cylinder is a circle.

To find the volume of any prism we use the formula:

volume of a prism = area of cross-section × length

So to find the volume of a cylinder the formula is:

volume = area of circle × length

$$V = \pi r^2 \times l \;(\text{or } V = \pi r^2 l)$$

*Hint:*

Remember pi (π) is the ratio of a circle's circumference to its diameter. It is approximately 3·14.

So to find the volume of a triangular prism the formula is:

volume = area of triangle × length

$$V = \tfrac{1}{2} bh \times l \;(\text{or } V = \tfrac{1}{2} bhl)$$

Calculate the volume of these prisms.

**A**

5 cm
7 cm

**B**

10 cm
32 cm

**C**

9 cm
5 cm
4 cm
14 cm

**D**

5 cm
12 cm

---

## At Home

Gather together a collection of cylinders.

Using the formula from Let's Investigate on page 2 calculate the volume of each cylinder.

## Sports Update

This is the formula for finding the volume of a sphere.

$$\tfrac{4}{3}\pi r^3$$

If these are the radii for different sporting balls, what are the volumes of the balls to the nearest 1 cm³?

Volleyball

13 cm

Tennis ball

3 cm

Cricket ball

5 cm

Basketball

12 cm

## Focus on Science

Try the following experiment to compare the volume of a cone with the volume of a cylinder, both having the same radius and height.

Make a paper cone that just fits inside a can (100 ml can size is best).

Using sand or rice, find out how many conesful fill the can.

So, how does the volume of a cone compare with that of a cylinder, both with the same radius and height?

paper cylinder

can

## The Language of Maths

Design a poster describing the difference between volume and capacity.

S&C Volume 6

# The Maths Herald

Name:                                    Date:

## Looking for Patterns

Carleton St Peter has a church clock with 2 bells – a high-pitched bell and a low-pitched bell.

The low-pitched bell strikes the number of hours at each quarter hour using the 12-hour clock.

The high-pitched bell strikes at quarter past, half past and quarter to the hour – 1 strike for quarter past the hour, 2 strikes for half past and 3 strikes for quarter to the hour. For example, at 4:30 p.m. the low-pitched bell strikes 4 times and the high-pitched bell strikes twice.

How many strikes do each of the bells make in a 24-hour day?

## The Puzzler

The hour hand of a clock is pointing to 29 minutes past the hour.

What is the minute hand pointing to?

## Let's Investigate

This is how each of the 10 digits appears on a digital clock.

0 123456 789

horology

Imagine that a 12-hour digital clock was placed in front of a mirror, so that for example, 2 looks like 5 and vice-versa.

At what times would the reflection show the same as the digital clock itself?

What about if it were a 24-hour digital clock?

© HarperCollins Publishers 2016

---

## Let's Investigate

On what day of the week were you born? Don't know? Use this formula known as Zeller's Rule to find out (unless you were born before 1760 – sorry!).

$$f = k + \left[\frac{13 \times m - 1}{5}\right] + D + \left[\frac{D}{4}\right] + \left[\frac{C}{4}\right] - 2 \times C$$

$f$ = day of the week in which the person was born

$k$ = day of the month in which the person was born

$m$ = month in which the person was born

$D$ = the last 2 digits of the year in which the person was born

$C$ = the first 2 digits of the year in which the person was born

The following rules also apply to the formula:

**Rule 1:** Round down each number inside the brackets [ ].

For example, 2·7 rounds down to 2.

**Rule 2:** Months have to be counted specially for Zeller's Rule: March is 1, April is 2, and so on. Which means January is 11 and February is 12. (This makes the formula simpler, because on leap years February 29 is counted as the last day of the year.) Because of this rule, January and February are always counted as the 11th and 12th months of the *previous* year. Using the date 29 January 2002, for example, $m = 11$ and $D = 01$ (the last two digits of the year previous to 2002).

What is your date of birth?

Use the formula above to get a day of the week number ($f$).

Once you have calculated the day of the week number ($f$) here's what to do to find out on which day of the week you were born.

*Step 1*: Divide the day of the week number ($f$) by 7: $\frac{f}{7}$.

**Rules:**

- Use pencil and paper to do the division calculation so that the remainder is expressed as a whole number and not a decimal.
- If the remainder is negative, add 7.

*Step 2*: The remainder you get from the division calculation is the day of the week (0 = Sunday, 1 = Monday, 2 = Tuesday...)

On which day of the week were you born?

Find out the year, month and date in which 10 people were born.

They can be friends, family members or famous people. However, they must have been born after 1760 and not in a leap year.

Use the formula to find out on which day of the week each person was born.

| FEBRUARY | | | | | | |
|---|---|---|---|---|---|---|
| M | T | W | T | F | S | S |
| | | | | 1 | 2 | 3 |
| 7 | 8 | 9 | 10 | 11 | 12 | 13 |
| 14 | 15 | 16 | 17 | 18 | 19 | 20 |
| 21 | 22 | 23 | 24 | 25 | 26 | 27 |
| 28 | | | | | | |

# Sports Update

The marathon is a race of 42·195 km. It commemorates the run made by Pheidippides from Marathon to Athens in 490 BC to announce the victory of the Greeks over the invading Persians.

Many cities throughout the world run their own marathon event every year. The marathon is also one of the most important events in the Olympics.

This table shows the male and female marathon world record holders.

| Name | Nationality | Location of marathon | Year | Time (h:min:s) |
| --- | --- | --- | --- | --- |
| Dennis Kimetto | Kenya | Berlin, Germany | 2014 | 2:02:57 |
| Paula Radcliffe | UK | London, UK | 2003 | 2:15:25 |

The 100-metre race is one of the world's most famous athletic events.

This table shows the male and female 100-metre world record holders.

| Name | Nationality | Location of race | Year | Time (s) |
| --- | --- | --- | --- | --- |
| Usain Bolt | Jamaica | Berlin, Germany | 2009 | 9:58 |
| Florence Griffith Joyner | USA | Indianapolis, USA | 1988 | 10:49 |

Imagine if both the male and female 100-metre record holders were able to run the marathon at the same speed as they ran 100 metres. Calculate, in hours and minutes, how long it would take each of them to complete the 42·195 km race.

## An activity for two

You need:
- tape measure
- some friends
- stopwatch
- pencil and paper

1. Use the tape measure to measure out a distance of 100 metres. Mark a 'Start' line and a 'Finish' line on the ground.
2. Using the stopwatch, time how long it takes each person to run 100 metres. Record your results in a table.
3. When you have recorded the results, discuss them with your partner.
4. Decide how best to represent the data – perhaps as a table, line graph or bar chart.
5. When you have represented the data, write 5 statements about your results.
6. Compare your results with the results of the male and female 100-metre world record holders.

---

# Focus on Science

Speed is how fast someone or something moves. It is often measured in *kilometres per hour* (km/h) or *metres per second* (m/s).

If you run on average 7 km/h, you run 7 kilometres in every hour.

In 2 hours you would travel 14 km (2 h × 7 km).

In 3 hours you would travel 21 km (3 h × 7 km).

In $\frac{1}{2}$ hour you would travel 3·5 km ($\frac{1}{2}$ h × 7 km).

When travelling, it is very difficult to keep exactly the same speed all the time. When we talk about speed, we normally mean the *average speed*.

To find the average speed someone or something travels at, we divide the total distance travelled by the total amount of time taken:

$$\text{average speed} = \frac{\text{total distance travelled}}{\text{total time taken}}$$

If the average speed and the total time taken are known, we can find the total distance travelled by:

$$\text{total distance travelled} = \text{average speed} \times \text{total time taken}$$

In the same way, if the average speed and the total distance travelled are known, we can find the total time taken by:

$$\text{total time taken} = \frac{\text{total distance travelled}}{\text{average speed}}$$

- Barry drives 525 km on business. The journey takes him 7 hours. What is Barry's average speed?
- A man cycles 7·5 km in half an hour.
  How far could he cycle in $3\frac{1}{2}$ hours at this speed?
  How long would it take him to cycle 60 km at this speed?
- Copy and complete the table.

| Total distance travelled | Total time taken | Average speed |
| --- | --- | --- |
| 60 km | 4 h | 40 km/h |
| 315 km | 30 min | 90 km/h |
| 93 km | $7\frac{3}{4}$ h | |
| 21 km | | 5 km/h |

## The Puzzler

Write down today's date, and the time it is right now to the nearest second!

How many months, days, hours, minutes and seconds until the start of your birthday?

S&C Volume 6

# The Maths Herald

Name:

Date:

## Looking for Patterns

This is area *a*.

This is area *b*.

This is *a* + *b*.

What is the area of this shape?

What are the areas of these shapes?

Draw some different shapes with areas which are 2*a* + *b*.

---

## The Puzzler

- If the area of tangram piece C is 1 square unit, what are the areas of all of the other pieces?
- What is the area of the whole tangram puzzle?

## Sports Update

22 cm

A football measures 22 cm across.

Design a method for working out the approximate total surface area of the football.

## At Home

Choose 2 pages from a daily newspaper that have both news and advertisements.

- Look at these same 2 pages in the paper every day for 4 days.
- Work out how much of the area of each page is news and how much is adverts.
- Do these areas change from day to day?
- On the fourth day, work out the 4-day average for both news and advertisements. Write about anything you notice.

# In the Past

Tutankhamun is the most famous of all ancient Egyptian pharaohs. little was known about Tutankhamun until 1922 when an English archaeologist by the name of Howard Carter discovered his tomb in the Valley of the Kings.

born in c. 1341 BC and ruled Egypt from c. 1333 BC until his death in c. 1323 BC. Very Known as the 'Boy King', he was

ANNEX
←355 cm→ ←260 cm→ ←430 cm→

ANTECHAMBER
786 cm

④

BURIAL CHAMBER
414 cm
←640 cm→

③

PASSAGE
←561 cm→
166 cm
②

① Staircase

TREASURY
475 cm
←383 cm→

① First doorway

② Second doorway

③ Third doorway

④ Fourth doorway

Staircase

- Calculate the area of each of the 5 rooms in Tutankhamun's tomb. Give your answers in square metres.
- What is the total area of the tomb in square metres?
- Now using the same total area, rounded to the nearest metre, redesign Tutankhamun's tomb making sure that you include all 5 rooms.

---

# Let's Investigate

Make 2 polygons on a geoboard or draw them on squared dot paper. Use a formula or count square units inside the polygons to calculate the area of each shape.

Now use Pick's Formula to calculate the area of the 2 polygons you made.

hectare

## Pick's Formula

For any polygon made on a geoboard or graph paper, the area of the polygon is equal to the sum of the pins (or intersections) on the perimeter of the polygon, divided by 2, plus the pins (or intersections) inside the polygon, minus 1.

$$A = (p \div 2) + i - 1$$

($A$ = area, $p$ = perimeter, $i$ = interior pins)

Compare the areas you got using Pick's formula with the areas you got using a different formula or counting. What do you notice?

Try Pick's Formula using other polygons.

For what types of polygons does this formula work best?

# Let's Investigate

Using an 11 × 11 geoboard, make the largest octagon you can. What fraction of the area of the geoboard is outside the octagon?

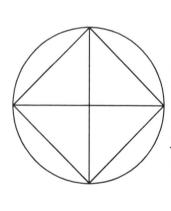

# What's the Problem?

If the diameter of the circle is 16 cm, what is the area of the square?

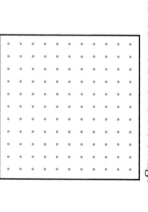

**S&C** Volume 6

# The Maths Herald

Name:

Date:

## What's the Problem?

- A square piece of paper is folded in half horizontally to form a rectangle.

If the rectangle has a perimeter of 36 cm, what is the perimeter of the square?

- A square piece of paper is folded to form 3 identical rectangles.

If the perimeter of one of the rectangles is 40 cm, what is the perimeter of the square?

## Construct

In the middle of tiling her bathroom, Alice noticed that she could remove one of the tiles without changing the overall perimeter of the tiled area.

Which tile is this?

| | | |
|---|---|---|
| B | C | D |
| E | F | A |
| G | H | I |
| | | J |

## Around the World

Draw a plan, to scale, of the land on which your school is built.

Label the dimensions of the land on your plan.

What is the school's perimeter?

## The Language of Maths

Prove or disprove the following statement.

> Shapes that are congruent have the same perimeter, and shapes that have the same perimeter are congruent.

---

## Looking for Patterns

Draw the next 2 shapes in each sequence.

Look at each of these matchstick patterns.

For each sequence:

- How many squares and matches are added each time?

- What is the formula for calculating the total number of matches used to make *n* number of squares?

- What is the formula for calculating the total number of matches around the perimeter of *n* number of squares?

Try some matchstick patterns of your own. Describe the different relationships.

## Let's Investigate

Measure and calculate the total perimeter of the plot of land that your school is on (see the Around the World activity on page 1).

Then measure and calculate the perimeter of the school building. If you have more than 1 building find the perimeters of all the buildings.

Draw to scale a simple plan that shows your measurements.

# Around the World

All countries of the world have borders. These borders are lines that officially separate 1 country from another. A border can either be a physical line such as a fence or coastline, or it can be an invisible line that exists only on maps and official records.

There is, for example, a physical line – a fence, that separates the United States from Mexico. However, in many parts of continental Europe, between France and Italy for example, apart from road signs, you would not realise that you were crossing a border from 1 country into another.

A country's borderline acts as the country's perimeter. Investigate the perimeters of different countries. Which countries have the largest perimeter? Which have the smallest? Which countries are different in shape but have a similar perimeter?

# Construct

Graham's Hotel recently installed a rectangular swimming pool. For health and safety reasons they need to put a fence around the pool and some of the surrounding land. The total area that they need to fence off is 80 square metres. If the length of the fencing on each side can only measure a whole number of metres, what are all the different lengths of fencing the hotel can use?

## Let's Investigate

- Can you make a shape on a geoboard that has a perimeter and area that are numerically equal? If you can, draw your shape on squared dot paper.

- What about making 2 different shapes on a geoboard where the 2 perimeters are the same and the 2 areas are the same? If you can, draw your shapes on squared dot paper. Can you make different pairs of shapes?

---

# What's the Problem?

Brian is putting a wallpaper frieze onto the walls around his rectangular sitting room. The perimeter of the room is 12·6 metres. If the length of the sitting room is double its width, what are the dimensions of the sitting room?

## Let's Investigate

The perimeter of each of these rectangles is less than its area. Can you draw any rectangles whose perimeters are greater than their areas?

5 cm
4 cm
perimeter = 18 cm
area = 20 cm²

8 cm
3 cm
perimeter = 22 cm
area = 24 cm²

# The Language of Maths

For each of the following shapes, write a formula or rule for working out the perimeter.

a | a
a | b | a | b
b
a | a
b | a | b
c
a | b | c
b | a | c
circumference | a

# The Maths Herald

Name:

Date:

## Famous Mathematicians

Archimedes was a Greek mathematician, physicist, engineer and astronomer, who was born in Sicily in 287 BC. Among his greatest discoveries was the *Law of the Lever*.

The centre of a see-saw, the point of balance, is called the *fulcrum*.

Imagine a see-saw 4 m long, with a child weighing 24 kg sitting 2 m from the fulcrum and a child weighing 32 kg sitting at the other end of the see-saw.

24 kg
32 kg

2 m
1·5 m

fulcrum
4 m

According to Archimedes' Law of the Lever in order for the see-saw to balance, the child weighing 32 kg will need to sit 1·5 m from the fulcrum.

Here are some measurements that, according to Archimedes' Law of the Lever, mean that the see-saw will balance.

Look at the measurements and work out a formula for Archimedes' Law of the Lever. Try using the symbols W1, D1, W2 and D2 to express your formula.

| Person 1 | | Person 2 | |
|---|---|---|---|
| Weight (W1) | Distance from fulcrum (D1) | Weight (W2) | Distance from fulcrum (D2) |
| 24 kg | 2 m | 32 kg | 1·5 m |
| 40 kg | 1 m | 20 kg | 2 m |
| 20 kg | 1·5 m | 24 kg | 1·25 m |
| 80 kg | 0·5 m | 20 kg | 2 m |
| | 2 m | 60 kg | 1·5 m |
| 70 kg | 1·25 m | 35 kg | 2 m |
| 36 kg | 2 m | 30 kg | |
| 52·5 kg | | | 1·25 m |

Now use your formula to complete the table.

## Let's Investigate

The *kilometre* is the most commonly used metric unit for expressing distances.

However, in the UK, we still use the imperial measurement *mile* to measure distance.

1 mile ≈ 1·6 kilometres

The most commonly used formula for converting miles (mi.) to kilometres (km) is:

km = mi. × 1·6

Another formula for converting miles to kilometres is:

km = mi. + $\frac{1}{2}$ mi. + $\frac{1}{10}$ mi.

*or*

km = mi. + 0·5 mi. + 0·1 mi.

Use both formulas to convert miles to kilometres.

Do both formulas give the same answer?

Which formula do you find easier? Why?

## Let's Investigate

Sad news! Your school is closing down.

It has been decided to sell the land and subdivide it into housing lots.

Calculate the total area of the plot of land your school is on, including all playing fields.

Work out how many housing lots will fit into the area of the school.

Draw, to scale, your proposal for redeveloping the land.

### Things to think about:

- What is your interpretation of the term 'housing lots'?
- What type of housing are you proposing – bungalows, semidetached, terraced, flats…?
- What type of housing is in keeping with the local area?
- What are the minimum dimensions required for each type of housing?

Write a report stating the reasoning behind all the decisions you have made.

Be prepared to justify your decisions.

## Famous Mathematicians

Galileo was born in 1564 in Italy. He made many amazing discoveries in science and mathematics.

Before Galileo, people thought that heavy objects fell faster than lighter objects. To prove that this was not true, Galileo dropped a cannonball and a pebble from the leaning Tower of Pisa. Both objects hit the ground at the same time.

Galileo discovered that there was a relationship between the time it takes an object to fall to the ground and the distance it travels during the fall. The table below shows this relationship.

Use the table to discover the formula for Galileo's discovery.

| Time of fall (seconds) | Distance (m) |
|---|---|
| 1 | 4·8 |
| 2 | 19·2 |
| 3 | 43·2 |
| 4 | 76·8 |
| 5 | 120 |

At 828 m, the world's tallest building is the Burj Khalifa in Dubai. Using your formula, work out approximately how long it would take for an object to fall from the top of the building.

## Focus on Science

*Decibel* is a unit used to measure the degree of loudness of sound. The softest sound that humans can hear is 0 decibels. The normal tone of a speaking voice is around 60 decibels. If a sound is more than about 100 decibels, humans find it very uncomfortable to listen to.

Investigate 5 different sounds. Find out what their decibel rating is.

Draw a decibel scale and show where your 5 sounds belong on the scale.

## Around the World

Using a globe and a piece of string, work out the approximate sailing distances from:

● London to New York
● London to Sydney via the Suez Canal

Choose 2 other places and work out their sailing distance.

Find out the actual sailing distances (in kilometres) between these places.

Compare these with your approximations.

---

## Let's Investigate

*Decibels* are used to measure the level of sound.

Investigate other unusual units of measure for measuring specific things.

What, for example, are each of these units of measure used for? Do they have an equivalent metric measurement? If so, what is it?

● fathom
● knot ● hand
● quintal ● furlong

What other unusual units of measure can you find? If they have an equivalent metric measurement, what is it?

## Famous Mathematicians

Joseph Lagrange was a French mathematician born in 1736. One of his greatest contributions to mathematics was his work on developing the metric system of measurement.

Make a list of all the different metric units for length, mass and volume and capacity.

Investigate the imperial unit equivalents for each of the metric units on your list.

## Around the World

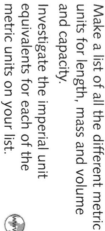

Many countries around the world, including most countries in continental Europe, use the metric system of measurement exclusively.

In the UK, we use a mixture of the imperial and metric systems.

Write a short report about the advantages and disadvantages of using just one system of measurement.

If the UK decided to convert entirely to just using the metric system, what things would need to change?

| A 46 | |
|---|---|
| Nottingham | 17 |
| Leicester | 32 |
| (M1 South) | 35 |

Richter scale

# The Maths Herald

Name:

Date:

## Let's Investigate

Look at the circles below. They show how many line segments (chords) there are in circles with 2 points, 3 points, 4 points and 5 points.

What patterns do you notice?

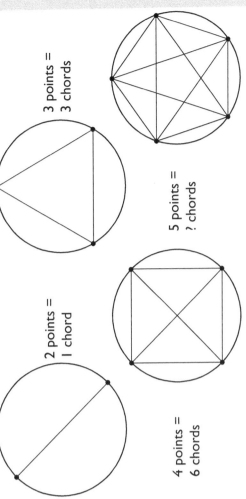

2 points =
1 chord

3 points =
3 chords

4 points =
6 chords

5 points =
? chords

How many chords are there in a circle with:

- 5 points?
- 6 points?
- 7 points?
- 8 points?

Look at the pattern in the number of chords for circles with 2, 3, 4, 5, 6, 7 and 8 points. What do you notice?

Write a formula for finding the number of chords in a circle with any number of points.

Apply your formula to find out how many chords there are in the circle with 24 points, shown here.

---

## Famous Mathematicians

Pythagoras was a Greek philosopher (569–500 BC). He made many important discoveries in mathematics, particularly in geometry. One of Pythagoras' greatest discoveries is called the *Pythagorean theorem*.

Pythagoras' theorem states that, for any right-angled triangle, the square of the length of the hypotenuse is equal to the sum of the squares of the lengths of the other 2 sides.

Pythagoras' theorem $c^2 = a^2 + b^2$

Use Pythagoras' theorem to answer the following questions.

Draw a diagram to explain each of your answers.

- You run due north for 5 miles, then due east for 12 miles. What is the shortest distance you are from your starting point?

- A 5 m ladder leans against a wall with its foot 3 m away from the wall. How far up the wall does the ladder reach?

The longest side of a right-angled triangle, the side opposite the right angle, is called the *hypotenuse* (labelled *c*).

## Sports Update

It can be said that a person doing push-ups, when in the upper position, has formed a right-angled triangle.

Draw and label right-angled triangles using the lengths in the table, which are approximates of the triangles formed by 5 people doing push-ups.

Use a scale of 1 cm to 20 cm for your triangles.

For your drawings:

- calculate the length of the ground level line
- use a ruler, pencil and set-square
- use a sharp pencil
- be as accurate as possible.

Length of arm

Body length

Ground level

| | Arm length (cm) | Body length (cm) |
|---|---|---|
| Lisa | 42 | 102 |
| Dan | 64 | 150 |
| Michelle | 36 | 84 |
| Joseph | 48 | 112 |
| Ian | 58 | 136 |

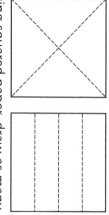

## Let's Investigate

Mathematicians have calculated that the circumference of a circle is about 3·14 or $3\frac{1}{7}$ ($\frac{22}{7}$) times the diameter. They call this number *pi* (after a letter in the Greek alphabet) and it is written: π.

Gather together a collection of at least 6 circular objects, all different sizes. For example, plates of different sizes, wastepaper basket, analogue clock, geometric circular shape.

Using a tape measure, measure the diameter and circumference of each of the objects. Record your measurements.

Now divide the circumference of each object by its diameter.

Finally find the average of all of the answers you have just calculated.

How does your average compare with the value of pi?

The *circumference* is the distance all the way round a circle: the boundary line.

The *diameter* is a straight line drawn through the centre of a circle. It divides the circle into 2 halves.

diameter

circumference

The *radius* (or 'radii' for plural) is the distance from the centre of the circle to its circumference. All radii of a circle are the same length.

radius

## Let's Investigate

A square can be cut into 4 congruent pieces in different ways.

For example:

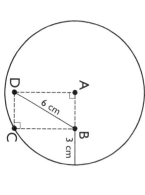

Using squared paper, draw as many different ways as you can.

## The Puzzler

What is the diameter of this circle? Write an explanation about how you worked out the answer.

A
B
C
D
6 cm
3 cm

## What's the Problem?

Remember: Pi (π) is the ratio of the circumference of a circle to its diameter and is equal to approximately 3·14.

The formula for calculating the circumference of a circle is:

$$\text{circumference} = \pi \times \text{diameter}$$

So, the diameter of a circle is:

$$\text{diameter} = \text{circumference} \div \pi$$

$$c = \pi d$$

As the diameter is twice the radius, the formula for calculating the circumference of a circle from the radius is:

$$\text{circumference} = 2\pi \times \text{radius}$$

$$c = 2\pi r$$

So, the radius of a circle is:

$$\text{radius} = \text{circumference} \div 2\pi$$

- Calculate the circumference of a circle with a diameter of 18 cm.
- Calculate the circumference of a circle with a radius of 6 cm.
- To the nearest centimetre, calculate the diameter of a circle with a circumference of 173 cm. What is its radius?

Gather together a collection of at least 6 circular objects, all different sizes. For example, plates of different sizes, wastepaper basket, analogue clock, geometric circular shape.

Using a tape measure, measure the diameter or radius of half of the objects, then calculate the circumference of each object.

Now measure the circumference of the remaining objects, then calculate the diameter and radius of each object.

congruent

## The Puzzler

Arrange 9 matchsticks like this:

- Remove 4 matches to leave 2 equilateral triangles.
- Remove 3 matches to leave 2 equilateral triangles.
- Remove 2 matches to leave 2 equilateral triangles.

Draw your result.

Now arrange 12 matchsticks like this:

- Move 4 matches to make 2 squares.
- Move 4 matches to make 3 squares.
- Move 3 matches to make 3 squares.
- Remove 2 matches to leave 2 squares.

Draw your result.

# The Maths Herald

Name:        Date:

vertex

edge

face

## Famous Mathematicians

3-D shapes are made up of faces, edges and vertices (or corners).

A *polyhedron* is a shape with four or more faces.

In the 18th century, Leonard Euler (pronounced Oiler), a Swiss mathematician, discovered a formula giving the relationship between the number of faces, edges and vertices for polyhedrons.

Complete the table to discover Euler's formula. Try to use the letters F, V and E to express your formula.

| Polyhedron | Faces (F) | Vertices (V) | Edges (E) |
|---|---|---|---|
| cube (hexahedron) | 6 | 8 | 12 |
| cuboid | 6 | 8 | 12 |
| triangular-based pyramid (tetrahedron) | | | |
| square-based pyramid | | | |
| triangular prism | | | |
| octahedron | | | |
| dodecahedron | | | |
| icosahedron | | | |

A football is not a sphere. It is actually a truncated icosahedron. It has 90 edges and is made from 32 polygons: 12 regular pentagons and 20 regular hexagons. How many vertices does a football have?

## Construct

How many different model skeletons can you make using up to 12 straws and 8 joiners in each model?

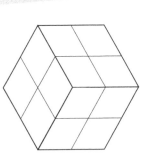

---

## The Puzzler

The digits 1 to 6 are written on the faces on a cube.
The 3 illustrations below show the cube in 3 different orientations.

This is what the cube looks like as 4 different nets.

icosidodecahedron

Write the digits in the correct places on each of the nets.

## Let's Investigate

How many different 2 × 2 × 2 cubes can you make using 4 interlocking cubes of 1 colour and 4 cubes of another colour?
Draw them.

Investigate using different numbers of each colour.

## Let's Investigate

Look at this 2 × 2 × 2 cube.

How many small cubes make up the large cube?

Imagine that the large cube was painted yellow so that it was yellow on all the outside faces. How many small cubes have:

- 3 yellow faces?
- 1 yellow face?
- 2 yellow faces?
- 0 yellow faces?

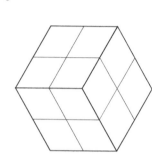

What do you notice about your answer to the first question and your answers to the second question?

Imagine a 3 × 3 × 3 cube. Answer the questions above for a cube this size.

This time imagine a 4 × 4 × 4 cube. Now answer the questions above for a cube of this size.

What similarities do you notice about all your results?

## Construct

 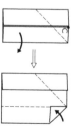

This calendar is made from 2 cubes and 3 cuboids (only 1 of the cuboids is displayed).

Between them the three cuboids have the 12 months of the year written on them. The cubes have numbers on them that can be moved around to display the correct date.

Look at the 2 cube nets below. Write digits on all the faces of both nets so that when put side by side, they will display all the numbers from 01 to 31.

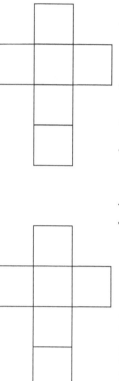

---

## Construct

Make an origami cube. You need 6 paper squares, ideally each a different colour.

**Step 1:**
Take 1 piece of paper and fold it in half to form a crease.

**Step 2:**
Open the square and fold both sides in towards the centre crease.

**Step 3:**
Make a fold from point A to point B. Then open out to step 2 again.

**Step 4:**
Fold point C under, along the diagonal fold.

**Step 5:**
Fold the left-hand flap under the right-hand flap.

**Step 6:**
Repeat steps 3, 4 and 5, but this time folding the bottom right-hand flap under the left-hand flap. You should now have 2 flaps and 2 pockets.

**Step 7:**
Make 2 additional diagonal folds.

**Step 8:**
Using the other sheets of paper repeat Steps 1 to 7, 5 more times, to give a total of 6 origami pieces.

**Step 9:**
To assemble the cube, take 2 origami pieces and insert a flap from 1 piece into the pocket of the other piece. Then insert a second flap into the other side of the same opening. Each opening in each square fits 2 flaps from other adjoining squares. Keep inserting flaps into pockets until all the sides are connected and a cube is formed.

© HarperCollinsPublishers 2016

S&C Volume 6

# The Maths Herald

Name:

Date:

## Sports Update

A British standard pool (billiards) table is 1·82 m long by 0.91 m wide. This means that it is twice as long as it is wide. It has 6 pockets: 1 in each corner and 1 halfway along the length of each side of the table.

Look at these unusual dimensions for a billiards table.

If a ball is hit from corner A at an angle of 45° to the edge of the table all its rebounds will be 45°.

For a 3 × 1 table, the ball would fall into pocket D.

For each of these tables work out which pocket the ball will fall into if it is always hit from corner A at an angle of 45°.

1

2

3

4

## Let's Investigate

If you took 3 paces forwards, turned 60°, took another 3 paces forwards and turned right 60°, and kept on doing this, this is the path you would walk.

Write instructions for other shapes.

Then give your instructions to a friend. Can they draw your shapes?

## Let's Investigate

A random trail can be generated by the toss of a coin, the roll of a 1–6 dice or choosing a card from a pack of 1–8 digit cards (reshuffled after each choice).

Coin

1–6 dice

1–8 digit cards

Heads  Tails

radian

Using different dot paper, investigate the different random paths you can make using a coin, dice and digit cards.

What about if you used a random number generating function on a computer?

## Focus on Science

Does the angle of a light source affect the length of a shadow?

Using a torch, design an experiment to find out.

Write a report on your experiment.

Show your results in a graph.

What conclusions can you draw?

## At Home

Look around your home and find as many different angles as you can.

Sort the angles you find into the following categories:

- right angles
- obtuse angles
- acute angles

## Technology Today

Look at the lists of instructions that you wrote in the  Let's Investigate activity on page 1.

Can you recreate your shapes using ICT?

## Around the World

One way of giving directions to someone is by using compass directions, for example 'head south' or 'walk in a north-easterly direction'. Another way of giving a compass direction is to give the size of the angle measured from the north as a 3-digit number that is always measured in a clockwise direction from north. Such readings are called bearings.

N — 60°

N — 210°

The first diagram on the left shows a bearing of 060°, while the second diagram shows a bearing of 210°.

Bearings are read using a magnetic compass.

How does a magnetic compass work? Find a spot in the playground. Choose 6 objects visible from this spot, and read the bearings using the compass.

## Construct

Here's how to make the same shape as a 50p coin.

1. Using a pair of compasses, draw a large circle. Make a faint point where the centre of the circle is.

2. Draw a faint line from the centre of the circle to the edge of the circle (i.e. a radius). Label the point 'A'.

3. Draw another 6 radii. All 7 radii need to be equally spaced. As there are 360° in a circle, this means that each angle needs to be about 51° (360° ÷ 7 = 51·428…°). Label the points 'B' to 'G'.

4. Place the point of the compass on point A and increase the angle of the compass to draw an arc from point D to point E.

5. Place the point of the compass on point B and draw an arc from point E to point F.

6. Repeat for points C to G.

7. Erase the circle you drew in Step 1 to see the 50p.

## The Puzzler

The game of chess has 6 different kinds of pieces: king, queen, bishop, knight, rook, and pawn. Each piece moves in its own special way. The knight is special because, unlike the other pieces, it doesn't move in a straight line. It makes L-shaped moves, jumping over anything in its way to reach an empty square on a chessboard.

For example, a knight can move 2 squares forward, then 1 square sideways, or it can move 1 square forward, then 2 squares sideways.

The Knight's Tour is a mathematical puzzle involving a knight on a chessboard. The Knight is placed on the empty board and, moving according to the rules of chess, must visit each square exactly once.

Investigate the possibilities of making knight's tours on the following boards. Record your results on squared paper.

3 × 4  4 × 5  5 × 5

6 × 6

Normal 8 × 8 chessboard

## Let's Investigate

Look at this trail.

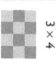

This is a 1, 2, 3… turn pattern. It is made from 1 unit of track, a clockwise turn of 90°, 2 units of track, a clockwise turn of 90°, 3 units of track, a clockwise turn of 90°, and so on.

Investigate trails using triangular dot paper.

# The Maths Herald

Name:                                   Date:

## Construct

Throughout history, architects have used reflective symmetry when designing buildings.

Look at these buildings. For each one, find examples of reflective symmetry. Be sure to look for examples in particular architectural features such as columns and windows, as well as in the building as a whole.

*Taj Mahal, Agra, India*

*St Paul's Cathedral, London, UK*

*Palace of the Winds, Jaipur, India*

*Roman temple*

Using postcards, travel brochures, books and magazines, make a collection of buildings that show reflective symmetry.

Can you find examples of reflective symmetry in your school or home?

## Around the World

The Ndebele are a tribe from Southern Africa. They are known for producing elaborate mural art to decorate their homes, using bright colours with high levels of both vertical and horizontal symmetry.

Investigate Ndebele art. Then design your own Ndebele mural.

---

## In the Past

Mosaics are pictures or designs made with small pieces of coloured material such as glass or tile stuck onto a surface. Ancient Romans, Greeks and Egyptians, and many other ancient civilisations all produced elaborate mosaics to decorate large homes and important buildings.

Look at these examples of mosaic patterns.

They all show examples of reflective symmetry.

Investigate mosaic patterns.

Draw and colour your own mosaic pattern involving symmetry.

## The Puzzler

Draw a reflection of your name in mirror lines placed at different angles relative to your name. For example:

LUCINDA

plane of symmetry

## At Home

Many wallpaper designs have examples of reflective symmetry.

Why do you think this is?

Make a collection of different symmetrical wallpaper designs.

## Around the World

The Akan are a tribe from Ghana in West Africa. They are known for carving elaborate stools from a single piece of wood.

Some Akan stools also show examples of reflective symmetry.

Find out more about Akan stools then draw a detailed design for your own stool.

## The Arts Roundup

A common feature of Islamic art is the covering of surfaces with geometric patterns.

Follow these instructions to make an Islamic pattern.

1. Use a pair of compasses to draw a circle.
2. Place the compass point anywhere on the circumference of the circle and move the pencil leg so that a mark is made on the circumference.
3. Then without changing the compass setting, move the point of the compass to the pencil mark and make another pencil mark on the circumference.
4. Do this for a total of 6 times.
5. Use a ruler to join up the points in sequence round the circle to make a hexagon.
6. Join up every second point to make an equilateral triangle.
7. Join up the other 3 points of the hexagon to make a second equilateral triangle.
8. Now look at the centre of the pattern you have created – you should see another smaller hexagon.
9. Repeat steps 6 and 7.
10. Now look at the centre of the pattern you have created – you should see an even smaller hexagon.
11. Repeat steps 6 and 7.

Follow the instructions again but this time start with the largest possible circle. How many stars can you make altogether?

When you have drawn the patterns, colour them so that they are symmetrical.

## Looking for Patterns

Make a 10 × 10 grid.

Colouring in the squares, design a pattern that shows examples of horizontal, vertical and diagonal symmetry.

You must use 6 different colours and every square on the grid must be shaded.

When you have finished, write a description of your design, stating its reflective properties.

## Sports Update

Symmetry is extremely important in the execution of figure skating moves.

Write a statement for each of these moves commenting on the symmetry involved.

Circle eight

Three

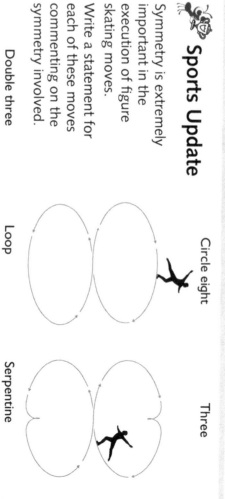

Double three

Loop

Serpentine

S&C Volume 6

# The Maths Herald

Name:

Date:

## Looking for Patterns

A tessellation is a geometric pattern that fits together without leaving any spaces.

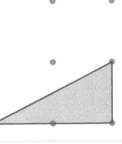

This shape has been translated to make the tessellating pattern below.

What other shapes can be translated to make good tessellating patterns?

## The Arts Roundup

The Dutch artist Maurits Escher used many tessellations in his work. He often used methods based on mathematics.

Make a tessellation using one of Escher's methods.

- Take a square and draw an interesting design along one side.
- Copy this design onto the opposite side and cut it out.

The result will be a tessellating template.

For example:

Using your template, make translations to create an interesting tessellation.

Decorate your tessellation with contrasting colours.

---

## Let's Investigate

Using squared paper, draw a 4 quadrant coordinates grid. You may wish to extend the $x$ and $y$ axes beyond ±5 as shown here: perhaps to ±10.

Draw a quadrilateral in the first quadrant of the coordinates grid. Label the shape "A".

Translate shape A in the first quadrant. Label the shape "A$^1$".

Translate shape A:

- twice in the second quadrant (labelled: A$^2$ and A$^3$)
- twice in the third quadrant (labelled: A$^4$ and A$^5$)
- twice in the fourth quadrant (labelled: A$^6$ and A$^7$).

Reproduce the 8 quadrilaterals you have drawn on the square coordinates grid onto triangular dot paper.

Write about what you notice.

Investigate further by:

- drawing other quadrilaterals and polygons
- using different grids
- using other types of transformations.

## The Puzzler

What are all the possible translations of a 1-unit by 2-unit right-angled triangle on a 3 × 3 geoboard?

What about on a 4 × 4 geoboard and a 5 × 5 geoboard?

# The Arts Roundup

Maurits Escher was a graphic artist from The Netherlands whose work was heavily influenced by mathematics. He is famous all over the world for his intricate and intriguing designs and drawings which still influence artists, songwriters and filmmakers today.

Investigate the life and work of MC Escher and comment on the mathematics involved in some of his works of art.

transformation

## Construct

Here is another method for creating tessellating patterns using translations.

- Take a square and change 2 adjacent sides by cutting out shapes. Try and pass through the corner between them.

- Using the pieces you have cut out, tape these to the opposite sides. The result will be a tessellating template.

For example:

Using your template, make translations to create an interesting tessellation.

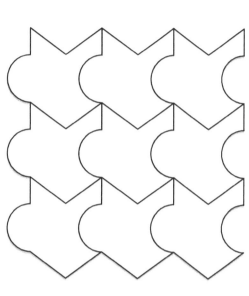

Decorate your tessellation with contrasting colours.

## In the Past

Mosaics are pictures or designs made with small pieces of coloured material such as glass or tile stuck onto a surface. Ancient Romans, Greeks and Egyptians, and many other ancient civilisations all produced elaborate mosaics to decorate large homes and important buildings.

Look at these examples of mosaic border patterns. They all show examples of translations.

Investigate mosaic border patterns.

Draw and colour your own mosaic border pattern involving translations.

## Let's Investigate

Which triangles can the shaded triangle land on exactly after 1 translation?

What about these shapes?

What about after 2 translations?

A

B

C

D

E

© HarperCollinsPublishers 2016

S&C Volume 6

# The Maths Herald

Name:

Date:

## Around the World

During Diwali celebrations, Hindu families draw colourful Rangoli designs on the floor near the entrance to their home to welcome guests.

Look at these 2 Rangoli patterns.

They both show examples of rotational symmetry.

Create your own Rangoli pattern.

Be sure to include some rotational symmetry in your pattern.

## Looking for Patterns

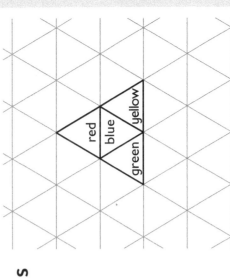

This shape has been made from isometric paper.

Use isometric paper to draw large triangles like these.

Using 4 different colours, shade each of the 4 small triangles a different colour.

Rotate your large triangle about 1 of its vertices.

Keep rotating your large triangle.

---

## Construct

For example:

1. Make a template of any odd shape and cut it out. Then draw a straight line through it – anywhere you like.

2. Draw 2 lines at 90° to each other on a sheet of paper.

3. Place the straight line of the template along 1 of the lines – with 1 end of it where the lines cross. Draw around your template.

4. Repeat on each of the 4 lines, rotating your template each time.

You may want to colour your completed pattern. Look for overlapping shapes.

Try again with a different shape or with lines at different angles, such as:

## Let's Investigate

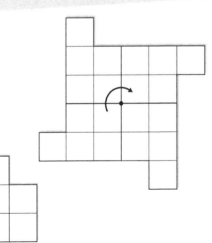

What are pentominoes?

Choose a pentomino.

Turn it through 90° about one corner.

Turn it through 90° again and again.

Investigate tessellations of the new shape.

Try with other pentominoes or tetrominoes.

## Looking for Patterns

A tessellation is a geometric pattern that fits together without leaving any spaces.

Many tessellations are produced from geometric shapes using a method known as 'half-turn' rotation.

For example:

order of symmetry

Use the half-turn rotation method to create tessellations from each of these shapes.

What other shapes can you make tessellating patterns from using the half-turn rotation method?

## Let's Investigate

All these hubcaps show examples of rotational symmetry. How?

Investigate the cars in the school car park.

Draw examples of different rotational symmetry.

Explain how each is an example of rotation.

---

## The Arts Roundup

A common Islamic pattern is based on translating a circle along and around a horizontal line.

Follow these steps to make an Islamic circular pattern.

**Step 1**

Using a ruler draw a horizontal line in the centre of the page.

**Step 2**

Make a circle with a compass point placed in the centre of the line.

**Step 3**

Use the 2 points where the circle intersects with the line to draw 2 more circles – 1 on either side of the first circle.

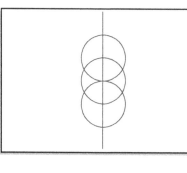

**Step 4**

Draw 4 more circles using the new points of intersection as compass points.

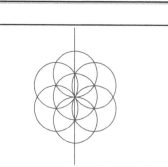

When you have drawn the patterns, colour them so that they are symmetrical.

Follow the instructions again and keep adding more circles. You will probably need to start with a smaller circle.

## Construct

A *parabola* is the name given to a particular shape of curve. The path of an object thrown in the air is a parabola.

Using 2 cm squared paper, copy this coordinates grid.

Study the diagram below. Then, using squared paper, copy it to draw your own parabola.

Using as x-axis values all the numbers from 5 to ⁻3, use the following formula to work out each of the y-axis values.

$$y = (x − 1)^2 + 1$$

Here are the first 2 pairs of coordinates.

(5,17) (4,10)

Label the coordinates of each point on your parabola.

Another way to draw a parabola is by using coordinates.

---

# The Maths Herald

Name:     Date:

## Famous Mathematicians

Maria Agnesi was an Italian mathematician born in Milan, Italy, in 1718. Agnesi was particularly interested in algebra and geometry.

"The Witch of Agnesi" is a special curve that Maria studied. The name "The Witch of Agnesi" was a misinterpretation of the translation from Italian to English but this mistranslation has stuck!

This is the formula for "The Witch of Agnesi": $y = \dfrac{a^3}{x^2 + a^2}$

A special case of "The Witch of Agnesi" curve is: $y = \dfrac{125}{x^2 + 25}$

Using 1 cm squared paper copy this coordinates grid.

Then using all the points along the x-axis, that is, ⁻10, ⁻9, ⁻8, … 0, 1, 2, …10 use the special case formula of "The Witch of Agnesi" to determine the y-axis values.

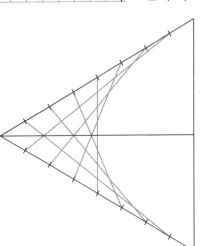

For example:

If $x = {}^-10$, then: $y = \dfrac{125}{{}^-10^2 + 25}$

NOTE: Round the y-axis values to the nearest tenth.

$$= \frac{125}{100 + 25}$$
$$= \frac{125}{125}$$
$$= 1$$

So the coordinates for this point are (⁻10, 1). Now plot the points on the graph to see the shape of the curve of "The Witch of Agnesi".

#  Construct

A maze is an area of interconnected paths that it is hard to find a way through. They are usually designed in a garden with hedges between the paths.

What makes a good maze? Write some rules for designing a good maze.

Find your way out of their maze!

Swap your maze with someone else who has designed a maze.

Design your own maze.

# Around the World

Satellite navigation systems (satnavs) are devices used for finding specific locations and getting directions to and from places. Many cars and mobile phones now have this system built in as standard features.

Find out all you can about satellite navigation systems. For example:

- Who developed them?
- Why were they developed?
- How do they work?
- How can they be used?

When you have found out as much information as you can about satnavs, design a poster to explain to others what you have found out.

---

# The Puzzler

Robert lives 5 km south west of Becky.

Louise lives 5 km north east of Becky.

Robert lives south of James.

Louise lives south east of James.

How far does James live from Louise?

# Let's Investigate

Draw a coordinates grid similar to this on dot squared paper.

Use the numbers 2, 3, 5 and 8 to make coordinates. For example: (2, 8) or (5, 5).

Use the coordinates to draw these quadrilaterals:

- parallelogram
- rhombus
- rectangle
- square
- kite
- trapezium

# Around the World

Imagine someone is coming to visit your home for the first time.

Think of a well-known landmark not far from your home.

Write a detailed set of instructions from the landmark to your home.

As well as the instructions, include a simple map for them to follow.

GPS

S&C Volume 6

# The Maths Herald

Name:

Date:

## 🐜 The Arts Roundup

Devise a design that has:

- a repeating pattern
- and a regular pentagon
- and two lines of reflective symmetry (horizontal and vertical)
- and a shape that has been rotated
- and a shape that has been translated horizontally and vertically.

Draw your design.

## ✂ Technology Today

Devise a design similar to that described in 🐜 The Arts Roundup activity above but construct it using a computer program.

## 🐜 Construct

Follow these steps.

1. Using a pair of compasses, draw a circle with a radius of 9 cm.

2. Lightly mark a point at the top of the circle and label it A.

3. Then without changing the compass setting, place the compass point on point A and lightly mark another point (point B) on the circle.

4. Place the compass point on point B and mark another point (point C).

5. Continue until you have marked 6 points on the circle (A–F).

6. Using your ruler, draw a geometric design. Here is 1 very simple design.

Make a more elaborate design of your own.

Then colour your design to show examples of reflective symmetry, rotational symmetry and translations.

## 🐜 What's the Problem?

In the game of chess, the queen is extremely useful at defending squares.

She can move in a straight line, any number of squares, in any direction, i.e. vertically, horizontally and diagonally.

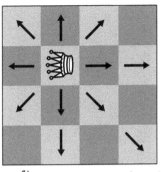

On the 4 × 4 chessboard on the right, from her position on the board, the queen is able to occupy or defend 12 out of the 16 squares.

What is the fewest number of queens you can place on a 4 × 4 chessboard so that all 16 squares are either occupied or defended? How many different solutions are there? Record your results on squared paper.

What is the fewest number of queens you can place on a 5 × 5 chessboard so that all 25 squares are either occupied or defended? How about on a 6 × 6 chessboard?

What about a full-size chessboard of 8 × 8?

surveying

## 🐜 The Language of Maths

Look carefully at this pattern.

Imagine you had to explain to someone how to draw this pattern without them seeing it.

Write a detailed set of instructions explaining what to do.

Find a friend. Don't show them this pattern. Give them your set of instructions.

Can they accurately draw the diagram?

## Around the World

Investigate reflective and rotational symmetry in flags.

Write a brief statement about each flag's symmetry.

What are some flags with no symmetry?

Canada

Jamaica

India

EU

Norway

Hong Kong

Australia

France

UK

USA

## The Puzzler

Try the Eight Queens Puzzle.

Place 8 chess queens on an 8 × 8 chessboard so that no 2 queens can attack, or capture, each other.

Record your results on squared paper.

How many different solutions can you find?

## Let's Investigate

The 2 straight lines drawn through this circle are called *chords*.

chord

The 4 shaded areas that they have created are called *segments*.

Can you draw 2 chords through

a circle so that there are only 3 segments?

How many different numbers of segments can you make by drawing 3 chords?

How about all those for 4 and 5 chords?

What patterns do you notice?

What is the maximum number of segments you can make for a particular number of chords?

Write a formula for the maximum number of segments you can make for a particular number of chords.

---

## Famous Mathematicians

These diagrams are called *networks*. Which networks can you travel without taking your finger off the paper and without retracing any line?

Leonhard Euler (1707–1783) was a Swiss mathematician.

He discovered some important rules about networks.

*Clue*

Networks can only be travelled like this if they have fewer than a certain number of odd vertices.

An *odd* vertex has an odd number of lines meeting at it.

An *even* vertex has an even number of lines meeting at it.

For each of the above networks think about the following:

- total number of vertices
- number of even vertices
- number of odd vertices
- whether can it be travelled.

Use this information to discover Euler's rules.

Now draw some of your own networks and say whether or not they can be travelled without lifting a finger or retracing any line.

# The Maths Herald

Name:  Date:

## Focus on Science

Find out the sunrise and sunset times of a place near to where you live.

Use the data for the first of the month only to draw a bar chart or graph of daylight hours.

In which month is the longest / shortest day?

What is the average length of a day?

| SUNRISE AND SUNSET | |
|---|---|
| **Birmingham** | 4:25p.m. to 8:07a.m. |
| **Bristol** | 4:32p.m. to 8:06a.m. |
| **Dublin** | 4:38p.m. to 8:29a.m. |
| **Glasgow** | 4:19p.m. to 8:33a.m. |
| **Leeds** | 4:18p.m. to 8:12a.m. |
| **London** | 4:23p.m. to 7:57a.m. |
| **Manchester** | 4:22p.m. to 8:14a.m. |
| **Newcastle** | 4:12p.m. to 8:17a.m. |

spreadsheet

## The Arts Roundup

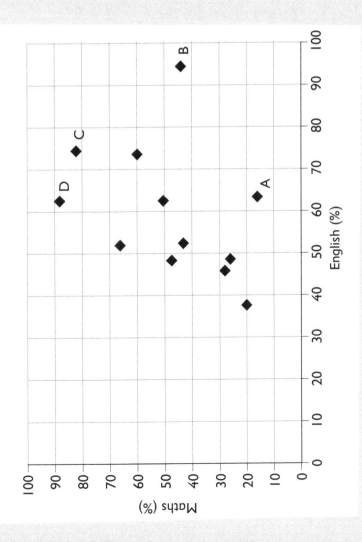

Mon  Tues  Wed  Thurs  Fri  Sat  Sun

- Oliver is the director of a week-long arts festival. Each year, after the festival, Oliver draws a graph to show the results of the festival.

  This year however, Oliver didn't fully label the graph. Use Oliver's graph to write a short description about this year's arts festival.

- Make a graph of your own similar to the one above. Partly label your graph with some information.

  Then write 3 broad questions based on the information on your graph.

  Give your graph to a friend and ask them to answer your questions and to write a further 2 or 3 statements about your graph.

  When your partner has finished, discuss their answers and statements. Do your interpretations and your friend's interpretations of the graph make sense?

---

## Looking for Patterns

A *scatter graph* is a graph that compares results in a set of data. It can also be used to look for connections or a relationship between the 2 sets of data.

Write a report explaining the results of this scatter graph. In particular comment on the results for children A, B, C and D.

*Maths (%)* — *English (%)*

(scatter graph with points labelled A, B, C, D)

## The Language of Maths

Look through a newspaper to find examples of information displayed as a graph or a table.

Re-represent the data in a pie chart.

*Hint:*

It may be helpful to convert the data in the graph or table into percentages before presenting the information in the pie chart.

# Focus on Science

What is the nearest coastal town to where you live?
Find out about the tidal times for the previous month.

Use the data to draw a bar chart or graph of low and high tides.

Can you combine the data concerning both low and high tides on the same chart or graph?

Write a report on the results.

## Let's Investigate

You will need the sports section from a newspaper for this activity.

Look for the results for a sport that you are interested in.

Ask yourself different questions about the results. Then display your results in a graph, chart or table.

If your favourite sport is football, for example, you may think about things such as:

- goals scored
- home wins
- away wins
- draws
- goal scorers
- attendance figures

### LEAGUE ONE

| | | |
|---|---|---|
| Blackpool | 0–4 | Wigan Athletic |
| Barnsley | 2–2 | Colchester United |
| Burton Albion | 2–1 | Gillingham |
| Chesterfield | 3–0 | Bury |
| Coventry City | 3–1 | Sheffield United |
| Millwall | 3–0 | Oldham Athletic |
| Rochdale | 2–2 | Swindon Town |
| Scunthorpe United | 1–0 | Port Vale |
| Shrewsbury Town | 3–4 | Peterborough United |
| Southend United | 0–1 | Bradford City |
| Crewe Alexandra | 3–1 | Doncaster Rovers |

## The Language of Maths

Look at these 3 graphs about the Lane family.

Write statements comparing the age, height and weight of the members of the Lane family.

### TODAY'S TIDES

| SEAPORT | HIGH | | LOW | |
|---|---|---|---|---|
| Virginia Beach | 06:45 a.m. | 05:55 p.m. | | |
| Nags Head | 07:00 a.m. | 06:01 p.m. | | |
| Hatteras | 07:04 a.m. | 05:58 p.m. | | |
| Wrights Beach | 08:05 a.m. | 06:03 p.m. | | |
| Myrtle Beach | 08:12 a.m. | 07:04 p.m. | | |
| Charleston | 08:25 a.m. | 07:35 p.m. | | |
| Hilton Head | 08:25 a.m. | 07:50 p.m. | | |
| Brunwick | 08:45 a.m. | 07:45 p.m. | | |
| Jacksonville | 08:50 a.m. | 07:50 p.m. | | |

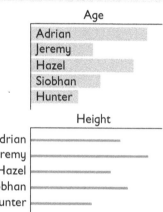

Age

Adrian
Jeremy
Hazel
Siobhan
Hunter

Height

Adrian
Jeremy
Hazel
Siobhan
Hunter

Hunter
Siobhan
Hazel
Jeremy
Adrian

Weight

---

## The Puzzler

This table shows the number of children that live in each of the flats in Rickety Towers.

Are there more flats or more children?

Write about how you worked it out.

| Number of children | Number of flats |
|---|---|
| 0 | 7 |
| 1 | 5 |
| 2 | 4 |
| 3 | 3 |
| 4 or more | 1 |

RICKETY TOWERS

## In the Past

The line graph on the right shows the average number of miles travelled by car per person from 2002 to 2012.

Write a detailed report describing the change in car use per person from 2002 to 2012.

What reasons can you give for these changes?

What conclusions can you draw?

What might the graph look like for the years 2012 to 2015? Why?

Miles travelled per person

| 7300 |
| 7200 |
| 7100 |
| 7000 |
| 6900 |
| 6800 |
| 6700 |
| 6600 |
| 6500 |
| 6400 |

2002 2003 2004 2005 2006 2007 2008 2009 2010 2011 2012
Year

Car use per person 2002 – 2012

# The Maths Herald

Name:

Date:

## Let's Investigate

Traffic lights are programmed to work differently at different times of the day. For example, a set of traffic lights near a group of shops may be programmed to turn red 30 times an hour between 8:00 a.m. and 8:00 p.m., whereas between the hours of 10:00 p.m. and 5:00 a.m. they are programmed to turn red only 15 times an hour.

What do you think are the reasons why traffic lights are programmed differently at different times of the day? Why aren't all sets of traffic lights programmed the same?

Locate an intersection near your school and collect traffic data.

Consider these questions:

- What type of data do you need to collect?
- How are you going to collect it?
- Over how long a period of time do you need to collect the data so that it is reliable?
- How are you going to present the data?

If you were planning to recommend to the local council how they should programme a set of traffic lights near your school, do you think that the mean, range, mode or median would be the most significant statistic to consider? Why?

Write your recommendations providing as much relevant statistical evidence as possible.

## Sports Update

triples ring (score = 3 × number)

doubles ring (score = 2 × number)

bullseye (score = 50)

25 ring (score = 25)

Keith has 3 dart scores with a mean of 30 and a range of 44.

His first dart scored 10.

What were his other 2 scores?

---

## Let's Investigate

Investigate whether different types of newspapers use words or sentences of different lengths.

Follow these steps:

**Step 1:** Plan

**Step 2:** Collect data

**Step 3:** Process the data

**Step 4:** Represent the data

**Step 5:** Interpret and discuss the data.

## Focus on Science

The time it takes someone to react to different stimuli can be measured in many ways.

Here is one way:

- Hold a ruler just over a person's outstretched thumb and forefinger.
- Drop the ruler at random and measure the distance it falls before the person catches it.

- Use the following formula to determine the person's reaction time:

$$t = \sqrt{\dfrac{d}{490}}$$

$t$ = time in seconds

$d$ = distance in centimetres

- Take 5 measurements and then average the 5 reaction times.

Who in your class has the fastest reactions?

primary and secondary sources

# Around the World

There are approximately 7 billion (7 000 000 000) people in the world.

It is difficult to comprehend such a large number. So imagine that the world is reduced to a village of just 100 people.

Work with a partner or in a group to make a display about the information on the right.

Show how these statistics compare with your class, your school, your local area.

Also show what these statistics mean for the entire world population.

| People in the village who: | Number (%) |
|---|---|
| are male | 50 |
| are unable to read or write | 17 |
| are under the age of 15 | 26 |
| are over the age of 64 | 8 |
| access to the Internet | 8 |
| are Asian | 60 |
| are European | 11 |
| do not have electricity | 24 |
| do not have clear safe drinking water | 13 |
| are undernourished | 15 |
| do not have a place to shelter | 23 |
| are Christian | 33 |
| are Muslim | 22 |
| are Hindu | 14 |
| speak Chinese | 12 |
| speak English | 5 |

# Let's Investigate

What is the average number of crisps in a bag of crisps?

What are you going to do to find out?

Make sure that your data methods are statistically reliable.

---

# Sports Update

At the end of a 15-game season, a basketball player calculated his statistics on his own goal shooting.

His mean score was 6. The median was 5 and the mode was 7.

What might his scores have been in each of the games?

# The Puzzler

There are 6 people in the Hughes family.

If their average age is 15, what might their ages be?

What is the average age of your family?

# Sports Update

A school football team has played a total of 5 matches so far this season.

- Their mean score is 5.
- Their mode score is 6.
- Their median score is 6.
- Their range of scores is 6.

What could their scores have been for each match?

What will the team need to score in the next match to raise the mean score to 6?

# At Home

Many different types of packaged food have printed on the packaging a notice stating the average number of servings.

What does this mean?

How do you think the manufacturers calculated this average?

What do you think they base their average on?

# The Maths Herald

Name:

Date:

## Around the World

The table below shows the average total monthly rainfall for each month of the year in Sydney, Australia.

| Average rainfall (mm) | J | F | M | A | M | J | J | A | S | O | N | D |
|---|---|---|---|---|---|---|---|---|---|---|---|---|
| | 102 | 118 | 130 | 126 | 121 | 131 | 98 | 82 | 69 | 77 | 84 | 78 |

| Summer | Dec, Jan, Feb |
|---|---|
| Autumn | Mar, Apr, May |
| Winter | June, July, Aug |
| Spring | Sep, Oct, Nov |

The table on the right shows the seasons of the year in Sydney.

The information on the amount of rain that usually falls in each season can be shown on a pie chart.

To do this, convert the fraction of the total rainfall for each season to a part of 360 degrees.

The calculation for summer is:

$$\text{Angle representing summer} = \frac{\text{total rainfall for summer}}{\text{total yearly rainfall}} \times 360°$$

$$= \frac{298}{1216} \times 360°$$

$$= 88·223\ldots$$

$$= 88° \text{ (rounded to the nearest whole degree)}$$

Use the same method to find the angles representing the total average rainfall for the other 3 seasons.

Draw a pie chart showing the average seasonal rainfall for Sydney.

What would a pie chart showing the average seasonal rainfall for London look like?

Summer 88°

---

## Around the World

Keep a record of the pollution levels in the nearest location to your school where such data is collected.

Investigate what effect factors such as wind, rain and holidays have on pollution levels.

## Sports Update

What is the distance of your average walking stride?

Construct a line conversion graph to illustrate the number of strides you take to cover a certain distance.

Check your graph's accuracy by walking and measuring the distances covered.

Construct a similar graph for someone whose walking stride is very different from yours.

## Sports Update

Find out your average walking speed in:

- metres per second
- metres per minute
- meters per hour
- kilometres per hour

Using these results, estimate how fast you run.

Then measure to find out.

How does your running speed compare with Olympic and World record holders?

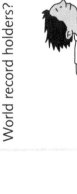

## Construct

There are 21 dots on an ordinary 1–6 dot dice.

How could you rearrange these 21 dots so that in a game of highest roll wins, your new dice will beat an ordinary 1–6 dice?

NOTE: Draws are not counted, e.g.

## The Language of Maths

Look through several newspapers to find examples of information displayed as a graph, chart or a table. For each example, write a sentence or 2 describing the main conclusions of the data.

## Focus on Science

The pie charts below show how much fuel was consumed in 1980 and 2000.

**1980**

Primary electricty 5%

Natural gas 22%

Petroleum 37%

Coal 36%

204·5 million tonnes of oil equivalent

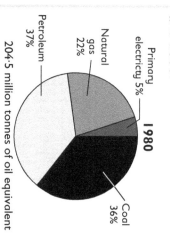

**2000**

Primary electricity 9%

Bioenergy and waste 1%

Natural gas 41%

Petroleum 33%

Coal 16%

234·8 million tonnes of oil equivalent

Source: DTI

Write a detailed report describing these changes.

Draw another pie chart predicting how much of each fuel might be consumed in 2020. Justify your predictions.

grouped frequency distribution

---

## Focus on Science

A *Watt* is a unit for measuring electric power.

1 kW (kilowatt) = 1000 watts

1 kWh (kilowatt-hour) = 1000 watts of electricity used for 1 hour

In 2014, the average electricity consumption in the UK was approximately 4100 kWh per household.

Excluding heating, average domestic electricity use can be accounted for as follows:

| Cold appliances | 17% |
|---|---|
| Cooking | 14% |
| Lighting | 16% |
| Audio visual | 13% |
| ICT | 6% |
| Washing/Drying | 14% |
| Water heating | 8% |
| Other | 12% |

Calculate how many kilowatt-hours the average household uses on each of the above categories.

Find out how many kilowatt-hours you use at home – you should find this on an electricity bill.

Calculate how many kilowatt-hours your family uses on each of the above categories.

## Sports Update

The Modified Harvard Step Test is a way of measuring levels of fitness.

*What to do:*

1. Step up and down from a chair or bench for a period of 5 minutes (300 seconds).
2. Rest for 1 minute.
3. Take your pulse rate for 30 seconds.
4. Use this formula to calculate the Fitness Factor.

$$\text{Fitness Factor} = \frac{\text{duration of exercise in seconds} \times 100}{5 \cdot 5 \times \text{pulse count}}$$

How fit is your class?

The Fitness Factor ratings are:
- below 50: poor
- 50–80: average
- 80–95: good
- above 95: excellent

Follow these steps:

**Step 1:** Plan
**Step 2:** Collect data
**Step 3:** Process the data
**Step 4:** Represent the data
**Step 5:** Interpret and discuss the data

# Teacher's notes

### Prerequisites for learning

- Count from any given number in whole-number and decimal steps, extending beyond zero when counting backwards
- Express a smaller whole number as a fraction of a larger one
- Relate fractions to their decimal representations
- Explain what each digit represents in whole numbers and decimals with up to three places
- Understand percentage as the number of parts in every 100 and express tenths and hundredths as percentages
- Solve problems involving ratio and proportion

### Resources

pencil and paper

Resource sheet 2: My notes (optional)

Resource sheet 3: Pupil self assessment booklet (optional)

computer with Internet access

## Teaching support

### Page 1

#### The Language of Maths

- Ensure that children fully understand how the numbers 1 to 12 have been written in the ternary numeral system, and are confident in using and applying this knowledge in writing the numbers 13 to 20 in base 3.
- Once you are sure that children are secure in their understanding of writing numbers in the ternary numeral system, then ask them to investigate writing the numbers 1 to 20 in other bases.
- As children will be investigating the binary numeral system in the next activity ✺ Technology Today tell them not to look at the base 2 numeral system in this activity.

#### Technology Today

- The binary system works in base 2, so instead of 10s, 100s, 1000s …the place value of these numbers works in doubles: 1, 2, 4, 8, 16, 32, 64, 128 …. If you placed these in columns as in our number system, it would look something like this:

| (128) | (64) | (32) | (16) | (8) | (4) | (2) | (1) |
|-------|------|------|------|-----|-----|-----|-----|
| 1 | 1 | 1 | 1 | 1 | 1 | 1 | 1 |

If you take the number 18, for example, it can be made from one lot of 16 and 2, so in binary it would appear as 1 0 0 1 0.

- You may wish to suggest that the children write the numbers 1 to 20 using binary notation.
- Children write several numbers as binary numerals and ask a friend to rewrite the numbers in base 10.

| Number | Binary numeral | | | | |
|--------|------|------|------|------|------|
|        | 16 | 8 | 4 | 2 | 1 |
| 1 |  |  |  |  | 1 |
| 2 |  |  |  | 1 | 0 |
| 3 |  |  |  | 1 | 1 |
| 4 |  |  | 1 | 0 | 0 |
| 5 |  |  | 1 | 0 | 1 |
| 6 |  |  | 1 | 1 | 0 |
| 7 |  |  | 1 | 1 | 1 |
| 8 |  | 1 | 0 | 0 | 0 |
| 9 |  | 1 | 0 | 0 | 1 |
| 10 |  | 1 | 0 | 1 | 0 |
| 11 |  | 1 | 0 | 1 | 1 |
| 12 |  | 1 | 1 | 0 | 0 |
| 13 |  | 1 | 1 | 0 | 1 |
| 14 |  | 1 | 1 | 1 | 0 |
| 15 |  | 1 | 1 | 1 | 1 |
| 16 | 1 | 0 | 0 | 0 | 0 |
| 17 | 1 | 0 | 0 | 0 | 1 |
| 18 | 1 | 0 | 0 | 1 | 0 |
| 19 | 1 | 0 | 0 | 1 | 1 |
| 20 | 1 | 0 | 1 | 0 | 0 |

### Page 2

#### Technology Today

- Choose other numbers between 1 and 20 and work with the children to calculate their value in modulo 3.
- Once the children are confident with writing numbers in modulo 3, they can they investigate writing numbers in modulo 4 and modulo 5.

- The numbers 19 and 34 are 'congruent modulo 5'; ask the children to explain what this means:

(19 mod 5 = 19 ÷ 5 = 3 r 4, so 19 mod 5 = 4

34 mod 5 = 34 ÷ 5 = 6 r 4, so 34 mod 5 = 4).

Ask the children to suggest other pairs of congruent modulo 5 / modulo 4 / modulo 3 numbers.

### Let's Investigate

- Most children will probably be familiar with Pascal's Triangle. If not, you may need to spend some time discussing it with the children.
- The important part of this activity is not identifying the rule and extending Pascal's Triangle, rather it is expressing it in modulo 3 and identifying different patterns.

## Page 3

### Around the World

- The two most important aspects of this activity are getting the children to think about how and when the different types of numbers are used in different jobs, and also thinking about those jobs that use a combination of all the different types of numbers.
- Ask the children to think about the times when they are calculating with numbers that are not whole numbers (not integers), and whether they prefer to work with fractions, decimals, percentages or ratio and proportion. Why?

### Money Matters

- You may wish to suggest that the children differentiate their two lists further by indicating those effects that would be advantageous and those that would not.

### Around the World

- You will need to discuss the notion of a census with the children before they undertake this activity. You may also need to locate suitable websites to offer as suggestions to the children when they investigate the 2010 Chinese census.
- Children investigate other censuses including, if appropriate, the 2011 census in England and Wales.

## Page 4

### Around the World

- Flags that are suitable for children to use when describing the proportion of the different colours used include:
  - Malta and Monaco ($\frac{1}{2}$)
  - France, Germany, Italy and Ireland ($\frac{1}{3}$)
  - Austria ($\frac{2}{3}$ red, $\frac{1}{3}$ white)
  - Portugal (approx. 60% red and 40% green)
  - Thailand (approx. 30% red, 30% blue and 40% white)
  - United Arab Emirates (approx. 25% red, 25% green, 25% white and 25% black)

### The Puzzler

- Tell the children that the mathematical symbol needed is not in the illustration.

### The Language of Maths

- The children should write a different description for each of the examples of how they would work out an approximate number.
- What did you find out about different numeral systems?

## AfL

- Why do you think we use the base 10 numeral system rather than another numeral system?
- What did you notice about the values of numbers written in modulo 3 / modulo 4 / modulo 5?
- What patterns did you notice?
- What did you find as a result of your investigation?
- Tell me about your lists. What conclusions can you draw from them?
- When is it useful to use estimations and approximations? Why?

# Answers

### Page 1

**The Language of Maths**

| base 10 | 13 | 14 | 15 | 16 | 17 | 18 | 19 | 20 |
|---------|-----|-----|-----|-----|-----|-----|-----|-----|
| base 3 | 111 | 112 | 120 | 121 | 122 | 200 | 201 | 202 |

Other base numeral systems will vary.

**Technology Today**
Results of the investigation will vary. However the children should mention the fact that the binary numeral system is a number system with 2 as its base, and numbers are expressed as sequences of the digits 0 and 1.

### Page 2

**Technology Today**
Answers will vary.

**Let's Investigate**
In Pascal's Triangle, each number is produced by adding the two numbers above:

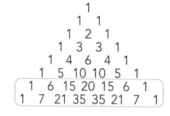

The next two rows of
Pascal's Triangle are:

```
            1
          1   1
        1   2   1
      1   3   3   1
    1   4   6   4   1
  1   5  10  10   5   1
1   6  15  20  15   6   1
1  7  21  35  35  21  7   1
```

Pascal's Triangle written with its values in modulo 3:
Answers will vary when commenting on the patterns that arise in a Pascal's Triangle written with its values in modulo 3.

```
                1
              1   1
            1   2   1
          1   0   0   1
        1   1   0   1   1
      1   2   1   1   2   1
    1   0   0   2   0   0   1
  1   1   0   2   2   0   1   1
1   2   1   2   1   2   1   2   1
1 0 0 0 0 0 0 0 0 1
```

### Page 3

**Around the World**
Lists will vary.

**Money Matters**
Lists will vary.

**Around the World**
Results of the investigation will vary.

### Page 4

**Around the World**
Results of the investigation will vary.

**The Puzzler**
Decimal point, i.e. 1·2

**The Language of Maths**
Answers will vary.

**Inquisitive ant**  irrational number
Any number that cannot be written as a fraction or a decimal with an infinite number of decimal places. Examples include $\pi$ and $\sqrt{2}$.

# Issue 2

## Negative numbers

### Prerequisites for learning

- Relate numbers to their position on a number line
- Recognise negative numbers in context, including temperature and how it is measured
- Recognise and continue number sequences formed by counting on or back in steps of constant size, including beyond zero when counting backwards
- Understand and use simple algebraic conventions
- Construct and interpret frequency tables, bar charts and line graphs

### Resources

pencil and paper
Resource sheet 2: My notes (optional)
Resource sheet 3: Pupil self assessment booklet (optional)
Resource sheet 5: 1 cm squared paper
ruler
bowl of ice
thermometer
empty frozen food packages, e.g. packet of peas, ice-cream carton, fish fingers box … (optional)
calculator
computer

## Teaching support

### Page 1

#### Let's Investigate

- At first, encourage the children to use a number line. However, after they have successfully demonstrated that they can add and subtract three (and four) positive and negative numbers, ask them to just write down the calculation.
- Discuss with the children what rules they can identify for adding and subtracting positive and negative numbers. This will assist them with the 🐜 Technology Today activity on page 2.

#### Focus on Science

- This activity requires the children to measure and record the temperature increase of a bowl of ice. It is advised therefore, that the children do this activity on a suitable day, i.e. a day without PE or an assembly.
- Children could repeat this activity at a different time of the year and compare the two different rates of temperature increase.

- Children can write their report using ICT.

### Page 2

#### Let's Investigate

- Ensure that children are familiar with letters used to represent numbers. Discuss with the children what rules they can identify for adding and subtracting a pair of positive and negative numbers. This will assist them with the 🐜 Technology Today activity.

#### At Home

- Ensure that children have access to frozen foods at home and / or are able to visit a supermarket during out-of-school hours. If this is not possible, then bring to school some empty frozen food packages as examples.
- Once the children have completed the activity at home, ensure that there is an opportunity in class for pairs or groups of children to discuss and compare the results. What conclusions can they make?

#### Technology Today

- Explain to the children that their poster will go on display in the classroom and that it should be designed to help other children when adding and subtracting positive and negative numbers.

### Page 3

**Around the World**

- Ensure that children understand the terms 'average minimum temperature' and 'record minimum temperature'.

- It may be necessary to assist some children in starting off their line graph, particularly with the numbering of the temperature axis. However, the  Around the World activity on page 4 should give most children a clue as to how this can be done.

**Looking for Patterns**

- When creating their own number sequences involving negative numbers, encourage the children to make them as challenging as possible.

- Children can rewrite their number sequences omitting some of the numbers, then swap their incomplete sequences with a partner. Pairs then discuss the different sequences.

### Page 4

**Around the World**

- Ensure the children understand the terms 'average daily temperature (max)' and 'average daily temperature (min)'.

- When writing their report, also ensure that children correctly identify the four seasons and make comparisons not only between seasons but also across the entire year.

- Children can write their report using ICT.

**Looking for Patterns**

- Suggest the children draw a number line to more easily identify those pairs of numbers with a difference of 0·2, i.e.

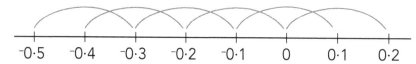

## AfL

- What is the difference between these two numbers?
- What is the rule for finding the difference between a positive and a negative number? What about the difference between two negative numbers?
- What about adding together a positive number and a negative number?
- How does a number line help when adding and subtracting positive and negative numbers?
- What does this graph tell us? Is this the best way to show this? How else could you have displayed the information?

## Answers

### Page 1

**Let's Investigate**
Calculations will vary.

**Focus on Science**
Results and reports will vary.

### Page 2

**Let's Investigate**
Answers will vary. Examples may include:
$a + b = 12$ (⁻5 + 17, 20 + ⁻8)
$a - b = 15$ (10 – ⁻5, 7 – ⁻8)
$a + b = ⁻8$ (⁻11 + 3, 10 + ⁻18)
$a - b = –16$ (⁻9 – 7, ⁻13 – 3)

**At Home**
Findings and conclusions will vary.

**Technology Today**
Posters will vary.

### Page 3

**Around the World**
The line graph should look something similar to the following:

Reports will vary.

**Looking for Patterns**
37, 25 , 13, 1, 11 , ⁻23, 35 , ⁻47 , ⁻59, 71 , ⁻83
Rule: subtract 12

41 , 33 , ⁻25, 17 , ⁻9, ⁻1, 7 , 15, 23
Rule: add 8

150, 80 , 10, 60 , 130 , ⁻200, ⁻270, 340
Rule: subtract 70

154 , ⁻117, ⁻80, 43 , ⁻6, 31 , 68, 105
Rule: add 37

Children's own number sequences will vary.

### Page 4

**Around the World**
Reports will vary.

**Looking for Patterns**
⁻0·5 – ⁻0·3; ⁻0·4 – ⁻0·2; ⁻0·3 – ⁻0·1; ⁻0·2 – 0; 0 – 0·2; ⁻0·1 – 0·1

Inquisitive ant
⁻5²
= ⁻5 × ⁻5
= 25

# Issue 3

## Addition

### Prerequisites for learning

- Identify prime numbers to at least 100
- Use tests of divisibility
- Calculate mentally with integers and decimals
- Use the formal written method to add whole numbers and decimals
- Use approximations to estimate and check results

### Resources

pencil and paper
Resource sheet 2: My notes (optional)
Resource sheet 3: Pupil self assessment booklet (optional)
ruler
dominoes
calculator (optional)

## Teaching support

### Page 1

**Looking for Patterns**

- Tell the children the value of one (or more) of the shapes in each of the grids, i.e.

**The Puzzler**

- Tell the children the value of one of the numbers (see Answers).

| | |
|---|---|
| ■ = 7 | ● = 6 |
| △ = 5 | □ = 5 |
| ⬟ = 4 | ▲ = 3 |
| ◆ = 3 | ⬠ = 8 |
| ○ = 2 | ◇ = 4 |
| | ▽ = 7 |

**The Puzzler**

- Ensure that the children are familiar with the term 'consecutive' and can identify consecutive odd numbers, e.g. 1, 3, 5, 7, ...
- Ask the children to show all their working as this will help them when writing about how they discovered what the numbers are.

**The Puzzler**

- Ensure that the children can identify prime numbers to at least 100. If not, provide them with a list:

| 2 | 3 | 5 | 7 | 11 |
|---|---|---|---|---|
| 13 | 17 | 19 | 23 | 29 |
| 31 | 37 | 41 | 43 | 47 |
| 53 | 59 | 61 | 67 | 71 |
| 73 | 79 | 83 | 89 | 97 |

### Page 2

**The Language of Maths**

- Before the children work independently on this activity, ensure that they understand how to work out a numerical tautonym.
- Children can spend as much or as little time on this activity as is appropriate. You may want some children to find only one or two four-, six- or eight-letter tautonyms, while other children might be expected to find more.

**Let's Investigate**

- Expect the children to use the given method to make several whole number palindromes before working with decimal numbers.
- Children should discover that the method is the same for decimal numbers as it is for whole numbers, but that the position of the decimal point plays an important role in creating perfect decimal palindromes such as 19·91 and 18·81, as opposed to imperfect decimal palindromes such as 111·1 and 66·6.

### Page 3

**Famous Mathematicians**

- Most children will probably be familiar with Pascal's Triangle. If not, you may need to spend some time discussing it with the children.
- The important part of this activity is not identifying the rule, rather it is in investigating other rules for producing triangles of numbers.

- If children have difficulty getting started with the investigation offer them some suggestions:
  - start with a different first number
  - find the difference between the two numbers above
  - find the product of the two numbers above
  - start with a sequence at the base of the triangle.

- Once two children have made their own triangle of numbers they can swap, identify the rule and write the next two lines of the pattern.

### Let's Investigate

- Ask the children to give reasons why coins in the UK are 1p, 2p, 5p, 10p, 20p, 50p, £1 and £2. Would another set of eight coins be just as affective? Why? Why not?

### The Arts Roundup

- The method, as opposed to the answer, is the most important aspect of this activity.
- Once the children have made a start on the activity, discuss with them their method of working.
- If children have difficulty getting started, suggest they organise their thoughts in a table. One possible method for working out the answer is:

| | | | |
|---|---|---|---|
| Gates open | 200 enter | 200 in grounds<br>＋ 200 more enter ground | 5:00 p.m. |
| 1st hour | 400 enter | 600 in grounds<br>(200 + 400)<br>＋ 200 more enter ground | 6:00 p.m. |
| 2nd hour | 800 enter | 1400 in grounds<br>(200 + 400 + 800)<br>＋ 200 more enter ground | 7:00 p.m. |
| 3rd hour | 1600 enter | 3000 in grounds<br>(200 + 400 + 800 + 1600)<br>＋ 200 more enter ground | 8:00 p.m. |
| 4th hour | 3200 enter | 6200 in grounds<br>(200 + 400 + 800 + 1600 + 3200) | 9:00 p.m. |

## Page 4

### Looking for Patterns

- Suggest the children record their findings in a table.

| Sum of 2<br>consecutive numbers | Sum of 3<br>consecutive numbers | Sum of 4<br>consecutive numbers | Sum of 5<br>consecutive numbers |
|---|---|---|---|
| 1 + 2 = 3 | 1 + 2 + 3 = 6 | 1 + 2 + 3 + 4 = 10 | 1 + 2 + 3 + 4 + 5 = 15 |
| 2 + 3 = 5 | 2 + 3 + 4 = 9 | 2 + 3 + 4 + 5 = 14 | 2 + 3 + 4 + 5 + 6 = 20 |
| 3 + 4 = 7 | 3 + 4 + 5 = 12 | 3 + 4 + 5 + 6 = 18 | 3 + 4 + 5 + 6 + 7 = 25 |
| 4 + 5 = 9 | 4 + 5 + 6 = 15 | 4 + 5 + 6 + 7 = 22 | 4 + 5 + 6 + 7 + 8 = 30 |

- A number is the sum of 2 consecutive numbers if the number is odd.

  A number is the sum of 3 consecutive numbers if the number is divisible by 3.

  A number is the sum of 4 consecutive numbers if the number is divisible by 4 after 10 has been subtracted from it.

  A number is the sum of 5 consecutive numbers if the number is divisible by 5 and is 15 or greater.

- The rule for finding whether a number is the sum of consecutive numbers is:

  *A* is the sum of *n* consecutive numbers if

  $$\frac{A - n\text{th triangular number}}{n} = \text{whole number}$$

  e.g.

  18 is the sum of 4 consecutive numbers if

  $$\frac{18 - 4\text{th triangular number (i.e. 10)}}{4} = \text{whole number}$$

  $$\frac{18 - 10}{4} = \frac{8}{4} = 2$$

  Therefore 18 is the sum of 4 consecutive numbers.

### Let's Investigate

- Encourage the children to find more than one solution.

### The Puzzler

- Most children will find this puzzle relatively easy. What is most important about this activity is how they went about it.

## AfL

- How did you work out the answer to this puzzle? What strategies did you use? How else could you have gone about it?
- Did you use trial and improvement to help you work out the answer to this puzzle? How did you know where to start? Then what did you do?
- How did you organise your thoughts? Did this help? What else could you have done? Why might this have been more effective?

# Answers

## Page 1

### Looking for Patterns

| 7 | 5 | 4 | 3 | 19 |
|---|---|---|---|----|
| 7 | 7 | 4 | 4 | 22 |
| 2 | 3 | 5 | 4 | 14 |
| 5 | 5 | 2 | 3 | 15 |
| 21 | 20 | 15 | 14 | |

| 6 | 5 | 3 | 8 | 22 |
|---|---|---|---|----|
| 3 | 4 | 6 | 5 | 18 |
| 6 | 7 | 3 | 8 | 24 |
| 5 | 8 | 4 | 7 | 24 |
| 20 | 24 | 16 | 28 | |

### The Puzzler

Other solutions are possible.

### The Puzzler

17, 19, 21, 23, 25, 27, 29, 31, 33

### The Puzzler

| 43 | 1 | 67 |
|----|----|----|
| 61 | 37 | 13 |
| 7 | 73 | 31 |

## Page 2

### The Language of Maths

Many words are possible.

Four-letter numerical tautonyms:
BUDS, BULK, CHEF, COME, DIAL, DONE, EXIT, FOIL, GRIP, HEAL, HUMP, LAID, LOVE, MEND, MOTH, NEAR, OKAY, PALE, PINK, RUST, SELL, SPOT, SPUN, TABS, TAIL, TAPE, THIS, TIDY, TOPS, UNTO, VAIN

Six-letter numerical tautonyms:
ASSENT, ASSUME, BOTTLE, BUTTER, CREATE, HUNTER, REPENT, SAVERS, SHADES, SMACKS, TIMERS, VACATE, WASTER

Eight-letter numerical tautonyms:
ANTIDOTE, BACKACHE, DISTILLS, FLOORING

### Let's Investigate

The same method applies for decimal numbers as for whole numbers. However, with decimal numbers the position of the decimal point does not always create a perfect palindrome, e.g.

8·6
8·6 + 6·8 = 15·4
15·4 + 45·1 = 60·5
60·5 + 50·6 = 111·1

13·5
13·5 + 53·1 = 66·6

A perfect palindrome can be made by altering the position of the decimal point, e.g.

8·6
8·6 + 6·8 = 15·4
15·4 + 4·51 = 19·91

13·5
13·5 + 5·31 = 18·81

## Page 3

### Famous Mathematicians

In Pascal's Triangle, each number is produced by adding the two numbers above:

### Let's Investigate

10 = 7 + 2 + 1
16 = 8 + 7 + 1
20 = 8 + 7 + 5
The numbers 4 and 19 cannot be made using the given set.
The set of numbers {1, 2, 3, 7, 8} can make all the numbers 1 to 21 and none above.

### The Arts Roundup

The gates opened at 5 p.m.

## Page 4

### Looking for Patterns

The numbers are consecutive.
The sums of two consecutive numbers are all odd numbers.
The sums of three consecutive numbers are all divisible by 3.
The sums of four consecutive numbers start at 10 and increase by 4 each time.
The sums of five consecutive numbers start at 15 and increase by 5 each time.

### Let's Investigate

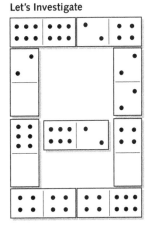

Other solutions are possible.

### The Puzzler

| AUGUST | | | | | | |
|---|---|---|---|---|---|---|
| M | T | W | T | F | S | S |
| | | | | | 1 | 2 |
| 3 | 4 | 5 | 6 | 7 | 8 | 9 |
| 10 | 11 | 12 | 13 | 14 | 15 | 16 |
| 17 | 18 | 19 | 20 | 21 | 22 | 23 |
| 24 | 25 | 26 | 27 | 28 | 29 | 30 |
| 31 | | | | | | |

| SEPTEMBER | | | | | | |
|---|---|---|---|---|---|---|
| M | T | W | T | F | S | S |
| | | 1 | 2 | 3 | 4 | 5 |
| 6 | 7 | 8 | 9 | 10 | 11 | 12 |
| 13 | 14 | 15 | 16 | 17 | 18 | 19 |
| 20 | 21 | 22 | 23 | 24 | 25 | 26 |
| 27 | 28 | 29 | 30 | | | |

Inquisitive ant

± plus or minus
The symbol is often used when describing a margin of error such as ±5 mm or ±2%.

## Subtraction

### Prerequisites for learning

- Identify prime numbers to at least 100
- Identify square roots of perfect squares to at least 12 × 12
- Find the square and square root of a number using a calculator
- Calculate mentally with integers and decimals
- Use the formal written method to subtract whole numbers and decimals
- Use approximations and inverse operations to estimate and check results

### Resources

pencil and paper
Resource sheet 2: My notes (optional)
Resource sheet 3: Pupil self assessment booklet (optional)
calculator (optional)

## Teaching support

### Page 1

#### Around the World

- Ensure that children understand the Yoruba number system, in particular the importance of the number 20 and how subtraction is used to express numbers.
- Rather than expressing all the numbers to 100 (or 200) using the Yoruba number system, ask the children to only write a selection of numbers less than 100 (or 200).

#### Let's Investigate

- By this stage most children should be able to identify prime numbers to at least 100. However, if they are unable to do so, tell the children to work in pairs. For this investigation do not give the children a list of prime numbers as it will make the activity too easy.

### Page 2

#### Famous Mathematicians

- Ask the children to further investigate the life and work of DR Kaprekar.

#### Looking for Patterns

- Tell the children to use prime numbers less than 100.
- Tell the children to use prime numbers greater than 100.

### Page 3

#### The Puzzler

- You may wish to use this activity as an opportunity to introduce or consolidate the terms 'minuend', 'subtrahend' and 'difference'.

$$\begin{array}{r} 587 \\ -\ 369 \\ \hline 218 \end{array}$$  minuend
subtrahend
difference

#### The Puzzler

- Ensure that children can find the square and square root of one-digit and two-digit numbers, including using a calculator.
- When working on the second puzzle, tell the children that the two-digit number is less than 50.

#### Let's Investigate

- This activity and the ⚘ Let's Investigate activity on page 4, offers a written method of subtraction.

## Page 4

### Let's Investigate

• This activity and the 🐝 Let's Investigate activity on page 3, offers a written method of subtraction.

### What's the Problem?

• The most important aspect of this activity is not in calculating the answers to the four calculations but in the children's explanations as to which method of subtraction they prefer to use for each calculation and why.

## AfL

• What is the answer to the puzzle? How did you work it out? What strategies did you use?

• Use your own words to explain to me this method of subtraction.

• Which of these methods of subtraction do you prefer? Why?

• How would you work out the answer to this calculation? Why would you use this method?

## Answers

### Page 1

**Around the World**
Calculations will vary

**Let's Investigate**
Pairs of consecutive primes less than 100 that have a difference of 2: 3 and 5, 5 and 7, 11 and 13, 17 and 19, 29 and 31, 41 and 43, 59 and 61, 71 and 73.
Pairs of consecutive primes less than 100 that have a difference of 4: 3 and 7, 7 and 11, 13 and 17, 19 and 23, 37 and 41, 43 and 47, 67 and 71, 79 and 83.

### Page 2

**Famous Mathematicians**
The largest number of subtraction calculations needed before the calculation starts repeating itself is five.
If you start with a four-digit number you will eventually end up with an answer of 6174 (known as Kaprekar's constant).

**Looking for Patterns**
Different calculations are possible. For example, for consecutive prime numbers:
$41 - 11 - 13 - 17 = 0$
$829 - 271 - 277 - 281 = 0$

For non-consecutive prime numbers:
$59 - 11 - 19 - 29 = 0$
$919 - 103 - 307 - 509 = 0$

### Page 3

**The Puzzler**
$$\begin{array}{r} 987654321 \\ -\ 123456789 \\ \hline 864197532 \end{array}$$

**The Puzzler**

| 4 | 36 |
|---|---|
| $4^2 = 16$ | $36^2 = 1296$ |
| $\sqrt{4} = 2$ | $\sqrt{36} = 6$ |
| $16 - 2 = 14$ | $1296 - 6 = 1290$ |

**Let's Investigate**
The method always works including for calculations involving decimals, e.g.

$$\begin{array}{r} 37 \cdot 8 \\ -\ 14 \cdot 3 \\ \hline \end{array}$$
$9 - 1 = 8$
$9 - 4 = 5$
$9 - 3 = 6$

$$\begin{array}{r} 37 \cdot 8 \\ +\ 85 \cdot 6 \\ \hline 123 \cdot 4 \end{array}$$

$123 \cdot 4$
$23 \cdot 4 + 0 \cdot 1 = 23 \cdot 5$

### Page 4

**Let's Investigate**
The method always works including for calculations involving decimals, e.g.

$$\begin{array}{r} 37 \cdot 8 \\ -\ 14 \cdot 3 \\ \hline \end{array}$$
$9 - 3 = 6$
$9 - 7 = 2$
$9 - 8 = 1$

$$\begin{array}{r} 62 \cdot 1 \\ +\ 14 \cdot 3 \\ \hline 76 \cdot 4 \end{array}$$
$9 - 7 = 2$
$9 - 6 = 3$
$9 - 4 = 5$

$23 \cdot 5$

**What's the Problem?**
Preferences and reasoning will vary.

**Inquisitive ant**

mathematical constant
A mathematical constant is a special number that occurs naturally in mathematics. Pi ($\pi$) is an example of a constant.

# Issue 5

## Multiplication

### Prerequisites for learning

- Understand squares, cubes and other powers
- Understand how the commutative, associative and distributive laws, and the relationships between operations, including inverse operations, can be used to calculate more efficiently
- Calculate mentally with integers and decimals
- Use the formal written methods of short multiplication and long multiplication
- Use approximations to estimate and check results

### Resources

pencil and paper
Resource sheet 2: My notes (optional)
Resource sheet 3: Pupil self assessment booklet (optional)
ruler
calculator

## Teaching support

### Page 1

#### The Puzzler

- The grid method of multiplication will assist children in seeing the relationship between $41 \times 51 = 2091$ and the other two calculations:

$41 \times 51$

| | 40 | 1 | |
|---|---|---|---|
| 50 | 2000 | 50 | 2050 |
| 1 | 40 | 1 | 41 |
| | | | 2091 |

$41 \times 52$

| | 40 | 1 | |
|---|---|---|---|
| 50 | 2000 | 50 | 2050 |
| 2 | 80 | 2 | 82 |
| | | | 2132 |

$42 \times 52$

| | 40 | 2 | |
|---|---|---|---|
| 50 | 2000 | 100 | 2100 |
| 2 | 80 | 4 | 84 |
| | | | 2184 |

$41 \times 52 = (41 \times 51) + (40 + 1)$
$= 2091 + 41$
$= 2132$

$42 \times 52 = (41 \times 52) + (50 + 2)$
$= 2132 + 52$
$= 2184$

- Discuss with the children the relationships between the numbers in each of the calculations, i.e.

$34 \times 202$

$34 = 2 \times 17$

Therefore:

$34 \times 202 = 2 \times (17 \times 202)$
$= 2 \times 3434$
$= 6868$

$34 = 404$

$34 = 2 \times 17$

$404 = 2 \times 202$

Therefore:

$34 \times 404 = 2 \times 17 \times 2 \times 202$
$= (2 \times 2) \times (17 \times 202)$
$= 4 \times 3434$
$= 13\,736$

#### The Puzzler

- 3! (referred to as 'factorial 3') is the product of all the positive numbers less than and equal to 3, i.e. $3 \times 2 \times 1 = 6$.

  Work through other examples such as 2! ($2 \times 1 = 2$).

  When solving the equation $(4 \times 2)!$ remind the children of the order of operations, i.e. $(4 \times 2)! = 8! = 40\,320$.

#### Money Matters

- Discuss with the children that if one £1 is just over 3 mm, then £10 is just over 3 cm (encourage answers that have been rounded down).

  Therefore:

  £170 = 17 × 3 cm
  = 51 cm

£174 = 51 cm + (4 × 3 mm)
     = 51 cm + 1·2 cm
     = 52·2 cm

### Focus on Science

- Calculations for the three problems are:
  - How far is the Earth from the Sun?

    8 min and 9 sec is 489 sec

    Distance from Earth to Sun = 489 sec × speed of light
               = 489 × 299 792 km
               = 146 598 288 km

  - How far is Mercury from the Sun?

    3 min and 13 sec is 193 sec

    Distance from Mercury to Sun = 193 sec × speed of light
               = 193 × 299 792 km
               = 57 859 856 km

  - How far is Venus from the Sun?

    6 min and 1 sec is 361 sec

    Distance from Venus to Sun = 361 sec × speed of light
               = 361 × 299 792 km
               = 108 224 912 km

## Page 2

### Around the World

- Draw children's attention to the following aspects of the method:
  - partitioning the tens and ones digits after multiplication, e.g. 7 × 8 = 56
  - the carry digits, e.g. 2 + 8 = 10
- Children write about the similarities and differences between this method and the grid method for multiplication.

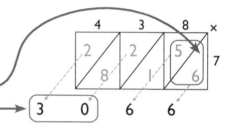

### Looking for Patterns

- Assist the children by giving them one or more of the missing digits, e.g

```
      ☆☆              8 ☆
  ×   ☆ 7         ×    ☆ ☆
      3 3 6          ☆ ☆ ☆ 7
    2 8 8 0          ☆ ☆ 5 ☆
    3 2 1 6          4 ☆ ☆ ☆
```

### Let's Investigate

- Remind the children to pay careful attention to the rules.
- Tell the children that there are seven possible calculations.

## Page 3

### Let's Investigate

- Ask the children to write an explanation as to how they worked out what the greatest product is.
- What if the digits were 5, 6, 7, 8 and 9? (876 × 95 = 83 220)

### Looking for Patterns

- If children have difficulty explaining what is happening, ask them to multiply 12 345 679 by 9 (answer: 111 111 111). Point out the relationship between these answers to the answers to the 11 times-tables. This should help them to identify the pattern.

## Page 4

### Looking for Patterns

- Draw children's attention to the two examples and discuss each line of the calculations, asking the children to comment on what they notice. If necessary, provide further examples, e.g. $5^3 \times 5^4 = $ ; $2^4 \div 2^2 = $

### Let's Investigate

- When investigating whether or not the method works for similar pairs of three-digit and four-digit numbers, remind the children that pairs of numbers must be near multiples, e.g. $237 \times 243$ $(240^2 - 3^2)$ and $1488 \times 1492$ $(1490^2 - 2^2)$.

## AfL

- What answer did you get for this puzzle? When you first looked at the puzzle how did you begin to work it out?
- What relationships / patterns did you notice? How did this help you?
- Talk me through your method of working out the puzzle.
- What do you think about this method?  Is it a method that you might use? When? Why not?

# Answers

## Page 1

### The Puzzler
41 × 51 = 2091
Explanations will vary. Possible explanations include:
41 × 52 = (41 × 51) + (41 × 1)
        = 2091 + 41
        = 2132
42 × 52 = (41 × 52) + (1 × 52)
        = 2132 + 52
        = 2184
*or*
42 × 52 = (41 × 51) + (41 × 1) + (1 × 52)
        = 2091 + 41 + 52
        = 2184

17 × 202 = 3434
Explanations will vary. Possible explanations include:
34 × 202 = 2 × (17 × 202)     34 × 404 = 2 × 17 × 2 × 202
         = 2 × 3434                    = 2 × 2 × (17 × 202)
         = 6868                        = 4 × 3434
                                       = 13 736

### The Puzzler
4! = 24
4! × 2 = 48
(4 × 2)! = 40 320

### Money Matters
52·2 cm

### Focus on Science
146 598 288 km
57 859 856 km
108 224 912 km

## Page 2

### Around the World
83 × 76 = 6308          537 × 49 = 26 313
886 × 356 = 315 416     73·9 × 34·6 = 2556·94

### Looking for Patterns

```
     48          89      or        83
×    67      ×   53          ×      59
   ------       ----              ----
    336         267               747
   2880        4450              4150
   ----        ----              ----
   3216        4717              4897
```

### Let's Investigate
5 × 5 = 25        3 × 75 = 225       5 × 75 = 375
5 × 7 = 35        5 × 55 = 275       7 × 75 = 525
3 × 25 = 75

## Page 3

### Let's Investigate
431 × 52 = 22 412

### Looking for Patterns
9 × 12 345 679 = 111 111 111.
Therefore, it is the digit chosen in step 2 that creates the pattern. For example, 7 × (9 × 12 345 679) = 777 777 777. When 111 111 111 is multiplied by a one-digit number, the answer consists only of that digit. This pattern is similar to 11 multiplied by a one-digit number.
Similarly, when 9 × 12 345 679 (i.e. 111 111 111) is multiplied by a number less than 19, the pattern is similar to 11 multiplied by that number.
For example: 12 × 11 = 132
            12 × 111 111 111 = 1 333 333 332

## Page 4

### Looking for Patterns
The index laws for multiplication and division of positive integer powers are:
$n^a \times n^b = n^{a+b}$
e.g. $4^2 \times 4^3 = 4^{2+3} = 4^5 = 1024$
$n^a \div n^b = n^{a-b}$
e.g. $4^5 \div 4^3 = 4^{5-3} = 4^2 = 16$

### Let's Investigate
This method works for similar pairs of three-digit and four-digit numbers.

**Inquisitive ant**

factorial
This is the product of all the positive numbers less than and equal to a specific number (n) and is written as 'n!'
For example, 3! means 3 × 2 × 1 = 6 (3! = 6).

# Issue 6

## Division

### Prerequisites for learning

- Understand tests of divisibility
- Recognise and use multiples, factors, divisors, common factors, highest common factors and lowest common multiples in simple cases
- Calculate mentally with integers and decimals, including with mixed operations
- Divide numbers up to 4 digits by a one-digit number using the formal written method of short division
- Divide numbers up to 4 digits by a two-digit number using the formal written method of long division
- Use approximations and inverse operations to estimate and check results

### Resources

pencil and paper

Resource sheet 2: My notes (optional)

Resource sheet 3: Pupil self assessment booklet (optional)

calculator (optional)

computer with Internet access

## Teaching support

### Page 1

#### Focus on Science

- Discuss with the children how rounding will help with calculating approximations.

  *For example,*

  Light travels at 299 792 km per second, which rounds to 300 000 km per second

  Mercury is approximately 58 million km from the Sun.

  *So:*

  58 000 000 km ÷ 300 000 km per sec ≈ 193 sec

  193 sec ÷ 60 sec ≈ 3 min

#### Let's Investigate

- Ask the children to investigate whether or not the statement is also true for decimal numbers. Children should provide examples to justify their conclusions.

#### The Puzzler

- Give the children the order of the digits, i.e.

  1 5 2 3 4

  (152 × 3 ÷ 4)

### Page 2

#### Around the World

- Ensure that children fully understand the concept of 'population density' and how; when referring to the population density of countries; is it expressed as the number of people per square kilometre (per km²).
- Work through one of the calculations with the children, for example:

  *Using a calculator*

  Australia: 24 062 755 ÷ 7 682 300 = 3·13 …

  Therefore approx 3 people per km².

  *Rounding*

  Australia: 24 000 000 ÷ 8 000 000 = 3

  Therefore approx 3 people per km².

#### The Puzzler

- Tell children one or more of the numbers in each puzzle (see Answers).

## Page 3

### The Puzzler

- Puzzle 1: Assist the children in realising that by rewriting the three-digit number to create a six-digit number you have actually multiplied the three-digit number by 1001 (i.e. 527 × 1001 = 527 527).
- Puzzle 2: Ensure that children are confident with the previous puzzle before they embark on the second puzzle.
- For the second puzzle you may wish to give the children one of the divisors (see Answers).

### Looking for Patterns

- Children should have no difficulties in writing divisibility tests for 3, 4, 6, 8 and 9. They may however, need some assistance with divisibility tests for 7, 11 and 12.

## Page 4

### The Puzzler

- Through discussion, help the children realise that the smallest number must be a multiple of 7 but not a multiple of 2, 3, 4, 5 or 6.

### Looking for Patterns

- For one or two of the calculations, tell the children one of the digits in the other factor that is not 34, e.g.

$$\boxed{\phantom{0}}\boxed{8} \times \boxed{\phantom{0}}\,\boxed{\phantom{0}} = 1972 \qquad \boxed{2}\,\boxed{\phantom{0}} \times \boxed{\phantom{0}}\,\boxed{\phantom{0}} = 816$$

### At Home

- If more appropriate, ask the children to calculate the population density of the school or the neighbourhood around the school. Discuss with the children how in such cases answers will more than likely need to be expressed as the number of people per square metre ($m^2$).
- Once the children have completed the activity at home, ensure that there is an opportunity in class for pairs or groups of children to discuss their results.

## AfL

- How did you work out the answer? Did you make an approximation? What did you do?
- How accurate is your answer / approximation?
- Did you use trial and improvement to help you work out the answer to this puzzle? Where did you begin? Why did you start there?
- What do your results mean?
- How did knowing about multiples / factors / divisors help you with this activity?

# Answers

## Page 1

### Focus on Science

| Planet | Approximate time for light to travel from the Sun |
|--------|---------------------------------------------------|
| Mercury | 3 min |
| Venus | 6 min |
| Earth | 8 min |
| Mars | 13 min |
| Jupiter | 43 min |
| Saturn | 1 hr 18 min |
| Uranus | 2 hr 41 min |
| Neptune | 4 hr 4 min |
| Pluto | 5 hr 28 min |

Explanation will vary.

### Let's Investigate

The statement is true.
When you reverse the digits of any two-digit number to make a new number and find the total of the two numbers, the answer is always divisible by 11, e.g.

| 87 + 78 | 43 + 34 |
|---------|---------|
| = 165 ÷ 11 | = 77 ÷ 11 |
| = 15 | = 7 |

This only applies to numbers with an even number of digits, i.e. pairs of two-digit, four-digit, six-digit … numbers.

### The Puzzler

152 × 3 ÷ 4 = 114

## Page 2

### Around the World

| Country | Population density |
|---------|--------------------|
| Australia | 3 people per km² |
| India | 392 people per km² |
| Jamaica | 248 people per km² |
| United Kingdom | 267 people per km² |
| United States | 33 people per km² |

The countries with the greatest population densities are:
• Macau – China (21 224 people per km²)
• Monaco (18 713 people per km²)
• Singapore (7697 people per km²)
The countries with the smallest population densities are:
• Greenland (0·03 people per km²)
• Mongolia (2 people per km²)
• Namibia (3 people per km²)

### The Puzzler

6, 9, 12, 30, 45, 78          3, 6, 9, 24, 78, 105

## Page 3

### The Puzzler

Puzzle 1: The final answer will always be the three-digit number you started with. Dividing by 7, 11 and 13 is the same as dividing by 1001 (i.e. 7 × 11 × 13 = 1001). By rewriting the three-digit number to create a six-digit number you have actually multiplied the three-digit number by 1001 (i.e. 527 × 1001 = 527 527). Then by dividing by 1001 the result is the three-digit number you started with.

Puzzle 2: 686 868 ÷ 68 = 10 101.
Therefore you need to find three numbers that multiply together to make 10 101.
So, for the remainder of the puzzle many answers are possible:

| Divide this number by: | 13 | 7 | 7 | 3 | 3 |
|------------------------|----|----|-----|----|-----|
| Divide this number by: | 21 | 37 | 13 | 37 | 13 |
| Divide this number by: | 37 | 39 | 111 | 91 | 259 |

### Looking for Patterns

**3:** the sum of the digits is divisible by 3
**4:** the last two digits are divisible by 4
**6:** the number is even and divisible by 3 or the number is divisible by 2 and 3
**8:** the last 3 digits are divisible by 8
**9:** the sum of the digits is divisible by 9
**7:** Take the last digit, double it, and then find the difference between this answer and the rest of the number. Continue to do this until you come to a number you know is or is not, divisible by 7.
*Example:*

| 56: 6 × 2 = 12 | 12 – 5 = 7 |
|----------------|------------|
| 539: 9 × 2 = 18 | 53 – 18 = 35 |

Since 35 is divisible by 7 then so also is 539.
**11:** Subtract the last digit from the rest of the number. Continue to do this until you come to a number you know is or is not, divisible by 11.
*Example:*
374: 37 – 4 = 33. Since 33 is divisible by 11, then so also is 374.
**12:** The number is divisible by 3 and 4.
*Example:*
336: 3 + 3 + 6 = 12, which is divisible by 3.
36 ÷ 4 = 9, which means it is divisible by 4.
So 336 is divisible by 12.

## Page 4

### The Puzzler

49

### Looking for Patterns

34 is the two-digit factor
58 × 34 = 1972
24 × 34 = 816
79 × 34 = 2686

### At Home

Results and explanations will vary.

**Inquisitive ant**  dividend
A number or quantity that is to be divided by another number or quantity.
For example, in the calculation 14 ÷ 7 = 2, 14 is the dividend (dividend ÷ divisor = quotient).

# Mixed operations

## Prerequisites for learning

- Identify prime numbers to at least 100
- Find the prime factors of two-digit numbers
- Understand squares, cubes and other powers
- Understand square root and use the square root key on a calculator
- Calculate mentally with integers and decimals
- Use the formal written methods to add, subtract and multiply whole numbers
- Find fractions using division
- Find percentages of numbers and quantities
- Use approximations and inverse operations to estimate and check results

## Resources

pencil and paper
Resource sheet 2: My notes (optional)
Resource sheet 3: Pupil self assessment booklet (optional)
calculator

# Teaching support

## Page 1

### Let's Investigate

- Discuss the two examples with the children. Emphasise how in each example the primes have been grouped together to make two identical numbers (squares), i.e.

$$2 \times 2 \times 11 \times 11 \qquad\qquad 3 \times 3 \times 3 \times 3 \times 3 \times 3$$
$$\downarrow \qquad\qquad\qquad\qquad \downarrow$$
$$(2 \times 11) \times (2 \times 11) \qquad (3 \times 3 \times 3) \times (3 \times 3 \times 3)$$
$$\downarrow \qquad\qquad\qquad\qquad \downarrow$$
$$22 \times 22 \qquad\qquad\qquad 27 \times 27$$

- Provide the children with a list of all prime numbers to 100, i.e. 2, 3, 5, 7, 11, 13, 17, 19, 23, 29, 31, 37, 41, 43, 47, 53, 59, 61, 67, 71, 73, 79, 83, 89 and 97.

- Children comment on the strengths and limitations of this method.

### Looking for Patterns

- The important aspect of this activity is for the children to write about how they worked out what each pair of numbers is.

## Page 2

### Famous Mathematicians

- Ensure that children are able to perform the different types of calculations needed to use Heron's method for finding the square root of a number.

- Children comment on the strengths and limitations of this method.

### Money Matters

- Children need to realise that they are working with approximations. They also need to appreciate that when working out the quantities needed to make 180 cupcakes, given the quantities that each of the items are sold in, they will need to buy more of each item than is required to ensure that they have sufficient quantities.

- Discuss with the children that profit is calculated by finding the difference between the amount earned and the amount spent (£135 − £12.50 = £122.50).

## Page 3

### Around the World

- Ensure children are able to identify the pattern of numbers that are being subtracted, i.e. the pattern of odd numbers.

### Let's Investigate

- The important aspect of this activity is for the children to write about which method for finding the square root of a number they prefer and why.
- Children comment on the strengths and limitations of their chosen method.

## Page 4

### The Language of Maths

- Children investigate other powers and index notation.

### Money Matters

- There is a range of different income tax allowances in the UK. This activity has been simplified to only take into account the personal allowance. It makes no mention of the difference in the personal allowance for people with an income in excess of £100 000. Neither does it refer to the Marriage Allowance, Married Couple's Allowance nor the Blind Person's Allowance. You may wish to discuss these and other allowances with the children if you feel it is appropriate.
- Discuss the example with the children and ensure that they realise that when calculating the income tax due, that if the taxable income is above £32 000, then tax will need to be calculated at different rates, i.e.

  Amount of tax due on £37 000 (i.e. £48 000 – £11 000)

  = (£32 000 × 20%) + (£5000 × 40%)

  (taxable income = basic rate + higher rate)

  (Note: £37 000 – £32 000 = £5000)

## AfL

- Which method for finding the square root of a number do you prefer? Why?
- What are the benefits of this method? What are its limitations?
- Which patterns did you identify? How did this help you?
- What approximations did you make? What does this mean about the level of accuracy of your answer?

# Answers

### Page 1

**Let's Investigate**

$\sqrt{576} = 24$    $\sqrt{676} = 26$    $\sqrt{841} = 29$
$\sqrt{961} = 31$    $\sqrt{1225} = 35$    $\sqrt{1444} = 38$

**Looking for Patterns**

27 and 62
276 and 523

### Page 2

**Famous Mathematicians**

$\sqrt{28} \approx 5.29$    $\sqrt{39} \approx 6.24$    $\sqrt{46} \approx 6.78$
$\sqrt{88} \approx 9.38$    $\sqrt{73} \approx 8.54$    $\sqrt{62} \approx 7.87$

**Money Matters**

To make 180 cupcakes you would need the following quantities of each ingredient:
825 g butter
825 g sugar
15 drops vanilla essence
15 large eggs
825 g self-raising flour
$7\frac{1}{2}$ teaspoons baking powder

To make 180 cupcakes you would need to buy the following quantities of each ingredient:

| | |
|---|---|
| 4 × 250 g butter | 4 × £1.10 = £4.40 |
| 1 × 1 kg sugar | 1 × 95p = 95p |
| 1 × 28 ml vanilla essence | 1 × £1.20 = £1.20 |
| 3 × 6 large eggs | 3 × £1.20 = £3.60 |
| 1 × 1 kg self-raising flour | 1 × £1.50 = £1.50 |
| 1 × 170 g baking powder | 1 × 85p = 85p |

Therefore the approximate cost to make 180 cupcakes is £12.50.
If all the cupcakes are sold at 75p each you would take £135.
This is a profit of £122.50.

### Page 3

**Around the World**

$\sqrt{289} = 17$    $\sqrt{576} = 24$    $\sqrt{361} = 19$
$\sqrt{529} = 23$    $\sqrt{961} = 31$    $\sqrt{784} = 28$

This method can only be used to find the square roots of perfect squares.

**Let's Investigate**

Results of the investigation will vary depending on the child's preference.

### Page 4

**The Language of Maths**

$3^5 = 243$    $5^3 = 125$    $2^7 = 128$    $8^5 = 32\ 768$    $7^4 = 2401$

**Money Matters**

£56 000: £11 600    £82 000: 22 000    £195 000: £68 900

**Inquisitive ant**

$\sqrt[3]{\phantom{x}}$
cube root

A cube root is a number that when multiplied by itself twice gives the stated number.
e.g. $\sqrt[3]{8} = 2$ (i.e. $2 \times 2 \times 2 = 8$)

# Issue 8

## Mixed operations and algebra

### Prerequisites for learning

- Represent information or unknown numbers in an equation
- Understand and use simple algebraic conventions
- Derive quickly squares of numbers to 10 × 10
- Use the order of operations, including brackets
- Calculate mentally with integers and decimals
- Use the formal written methods to add, subtract, multiply and divide
- Use approximations and inverse operations to estimate and check results

### Resources

pencil and paper
Resource sheet 2: My notes (optional)
Resource sheet 3: Pupil self assessment booklet (optional)
ruler
calculator (optional)

## Teaching support

### Page 1

#### Sports Update

- Assist the children in deriving a formula for working out the total number of games played for any number of teams. NOTE: Every team plays every other team twice (once at home and once away).

| Number of teams | Number of games |
|---|---|
| 2 | 2 |
| 3 | 6 |
| 4 | 12 |
| 5 | 20 |
| 6 | 30 |
| $n$ | $n(n-1)$ |

- Introduce the children to the pattern in the relationship between the number of players and the number of games, for example.

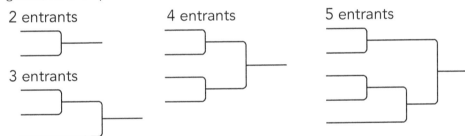

2 entrants    4 entrants    5 entrants

3 entrants

#### Sports Update

- Assist the children in deriving a formula for working out the total number of matches played.

| Number of entrants | Number of matches |
|---|---|
| 2 | 1 |
| 3 | 2 |
| 4 | 3 |
| 5 | 4 |
| 6 | 5 |
| $n$ | $n-1$ |

#### Let's Investigate

- Ensure children understand the diagram.
- Ask the children to present their results in a format different from that in the pupil issue.

### Page 2

#### Sports Update

- Ensure children understand the information presented in the tables and the requirements of the activity.
- Work with the children to begin writing one of the programmes.

## Page 3

### Let's Investigate

- Children need to be confident with using the correct order of operations, including brackets. If necessary, draw children's attention to the BODMAS diagram.
- Ensure that children are also able to understand and use simple expressions in symbols, and substitute positive numbers into simple linear expressions. If necessary, go through one or two of the expressions with the children.

### Let's Investigate

- Tell the children to find at least two different ways of making each of the numbers.

### What's the Problem?

- As well as having a secure understanding of the points mentioned in the above activity, children also need to understand and use simple algebraic conventions for multiplication ($a \times b = ab$) and division ($a \div b = \frac{a}{b}$).

## Page 4

### Looking for Patterns

- Ensure that the children fully understand how the first number trick can be expressed using algebra. This will assist the children when using algebra to explain the second number trick and when writing their own.

### What's the Problem?

- If children are having difficulties in one or more of the calculations, tell them the correct position of one of the other digits (see Answers).

### The Puzzler

- Ask the children to make their own puzzle, perhaps involving other shapes, e.g.

## AfL

- Explain to me what this expression means.
- How would you write that using symbols rather than numbers or words?
- Can you find an alternative calculation / expression / formula?
- What relationships / patterns did you notice?
- Apply your formula to this situation. Does it work?

# Answers

## Page 1

**Sports Update**
90
Formula = $n(n-1)$

**Sports Update**
11 matches
Formula = $n - 1$

**Let's Investigate**
Results of the investigation will vary.

## Page 2

**Sports Update**
Children's programmes will vary.

## Page 3

**Let's Investigate**

$41 = (4 \times 9) + 5$
$\quad = (5 \times 9) - 4$
$87 = (7 \times 9) + (2 \times 7) + (2 \times 5)$
$\quad = (2 \times 5 \times 9) - (6 \div 2)$
$120 = 6 \times 5 \times 4$
$\quad = 3 \times 5 \times 2 \times 4$

$59 = (6 \times 9) + 5$
$\quad = (7 \times 7) + (2 \times 5)$
$93 = (7 \times 9) + (4 \times 7) + 2$
$\quad = (2 \times 42) + (6 \div 2)$

Other calculations are possible.

**Let's Investigate**

$(5 + 7) - 10 = 2$
$5 + (7 - 10) = 2$
$(5 - 7) + 10 = 8$
$5 \times (7 - 10) = {}^-15$
$(5 \times 7) - 10 = 25$

$5 + 7 + 10 = 22$
$5 - (7 + 10) = {}^-12$
$(5 + 7) \times 10 = 120$
$(5 - 7) \times 10 = {}^-20$

## What's the Problem?

$(3 \times 5) - 8 + 24 = 31$
$34 + 5(8 - 5) = 49$
$(4 \times 8) - 84 + (8 \times 5) + 68 = 56$
$12(8 + 5) - 7(8 - 5) = 135$
$\frac{40}{8} - \frac{15}{5} = 2$
$6([4 \times 5] - [2 \times 8]) + (6 \times 8) - (6 \times 5) = 42$

## Page 4

**Looking for Patterns**
- Think of a number.     $n$
  - Add 5.     $n + 5$
- Multiply the result by 2.     $2n + 10$
  - Subtract 4.     $2n + 6$
  - Halve it.     $n + 3$
- Subtract your original number.     3

Answers will vary. Check that the children's algebraic expressions work.

## What's the Problem?

| | |
|---|---|
| $58 + 7 = 65$ | $74 - 6 = 68$ |
| $32 \times 9 = 288$ | $112 \div 7 = 16$ |
| $75 + 68 = 143$ | $107 - 59 = 48$ |
| $23 \times 14 = 322$ | $468 \div 26 = 18$ |

## The Puzzler

**Inquisitive ant**     slide rule
A mechanical device for carrying out calculations particularly those involving multiplication and division.

# Fractions

## Prerequisites for learning

- Understand and use the term 'highest common factor' (HCF)
- Find equivalent fractions
- Simplify fractions by cancelling common factors
- Order a set of fractions by converting them to fractions with a common denominator
- Express a smaller whole number as a fraction of a larger one
- Relate fractions to multiplication and division
- Tabulate systematically the information in a problem

## Resources

pencil and paper
Resource sheet 2: My notes (optional)
Resource sheet 3: Pupil self assessment booklet (optional)
fraction wall (optional)

## Teaching support

### Page 1

#### Famous Mathematicians

- Demonstrate how to use Euclid's Algorithm using question 1 as an example:

$$162 \overline{)189}$$
$$\underline{162}$$
$$27 \overline{)162}$$
$$\underline{162}$$
$$0$$

HCF is 27.

$$\frac{162 \div 27 = 6}{189 \div 27 = 7}$$

#### The Puzzler

- Ask the children to make their own puzzle similar to the one given.

#### The Puzzler

- Tell the children the position of one or two of the digits in the fraction, e.g.

### Page 2

#### Looking for Patterns

- Discuss with the children the relationship between the sequence number, i.e. $F_1$, $F_2$, $F_3$ ... and the numbers that appear as denominators in those sequences, i.e. $F_1$: 1; $F_2$: 1 and 2; $F_3$: 1, 2 and 3.
- Also draw children's attention to the layout of the fractions that highlights which fractions have been added to each subsequent sequence. This will help them identify the pattern and then continue it, i.e.

$$F_1 = \frac{0}{1}, \qquad\qquad\qquad\qquad\qquad\qquad\qquad\qquad\qquad\qquad \frac{1}{1}$$

$$F_2 = \frac{0}{1}, \qquad\qquad\qquad\qquad\qquad \frac{1}{2}, \qquad\qquad\qquad \frac{1}{1}$$

$$F_3 = \frac{0}{1}, \qquad\qquad\qquad \frac{1}{3}, \quad \frac{1}{2}, \quad \frac{2}{3}, \qquad\qquad \frac{1}{1}$$

$$F_4 = \frac{0}{1}, \qquad\qquad \frac{1}{4}, \frac{1}{3}, \quad \frac{1}{2}, \quad \frac{2}{3}, \frac{3}{4}, \qquad \frac{1}{1}$$

$$F_5 = \frac{0}{1}, \quad \frac{1}{5}, \frac{1}{4}, \frac{1}{3}, \frac{2}{5}, \frac{1}{2}, \frac{3}{5}, \frac{2}{3}, \frac{3}{4}, \frac{4}{5}, \quad \frac{1}{1}$$

$$F_6 = \frac{0}{1}, \frac{1}{6}, \frac{1}{5}, \frac{1}{4}, \frac{1}{3}, \frac{2}{5}, \frac{1}{2}, \frac{3}{5}, \frac{2}{3}, \frac{3}{4}, \frac{4}{5}, \frac{5}{6}, \frac{1}{1}$$

- Ensure that children understand how to check their Farey sequences using the given formula.
- Ask the children to extend the sequence to $F_{10}$.

## Page 3

### What's the Problem?

- Ask prompting questions such as:
  - What if Cloe got £6 pocket money? What would a third of that be?
  - Can you think of an amount for Taylah so her half is the same as Cloe's third?
  - Can you think of an amount for Taylah so her half is less than Cloe's third?

### Let's Investigate

- Provide the children with a fraction wall to assist them when comparing and ordering the fractions, i.e.

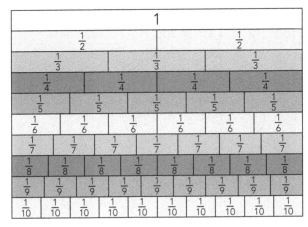

### The Arts Roundup

- Children need to first convert $\frac{1}{8}$ and $\frac{2}{3}$ into equivalent fractions, i.e. $\frac{3}{24}$ and $\frac{16}{24}$. That leaves $\frac{5}{24}$ remaining. Therefore $\frac{5}{24}$ equals the fraction of musicians, $\frac{3}{24}$ the technicians and $\frac{16}{24}$ the singers – which means the total number of people in The Reggio Opera Company is 24.

## Page 4

### Looking for Patterns

- A possible method for working out the answer is by tabulating systematically the information, for example:

| Teacher announcement | Number of children in the hall | Number of children who left the hall | Number of children remaining in the hall |
|---|---|---|---|
| 1 | 190 | 96 | 94 |
| 2 | 94 | 48 | 46 |
| 3 | 46 | 24 | 22 |
| 4 | 22 | 12 | 10 |
| 5 | 10 | 6 | 4 |
| 6 | 4 | 3 | 1 |

### What's the Problem?

- Answers will obviously vary. However possible calculations may be:
  - fraction of life so far spent asleep:

$$\frac{8 \text{ hours}}{24 \text{ hours}} = \frac{1}{3}$$

  - fraction of life so far spent eating:

$$\frac{2 \text{ hours}}{24 \text{ hours}} = \frac{1}{12}$$

– fraction of life so far spent in school:

(11 years old × 365 days) + 3 leap year days = 4018 days

4018 days × 24 hours a day = 96 432 hours

7 years in school × 36 weeks a year × 5 days a week × 6 hours = 7560 hours

$$\frac{7560 \text{ hours}}{96 \text{ } 432 \text{ hours}} = \frac{45}{574} \approx \frac{1}{13}$$

## AfL

- What patterns do you notice?
- What is the next fraction in the sequence? How do you know?
- Is there another way to work that out?
- How did you work that out? What clues did you use? How did they help?

# Answers

## Page 1

### Famous Mathematicians

$\frac{162}{189} = \frac{6}{7}$ (HCF = 27)  $\frac{68}{153} = \frac{4}{9}$ (HCF = 17)  $\frac{65}{91} = \frac{5}{7}$ (HCF = 13)

$\frac{38}{95} = \frac{2}{5}$ (HCF = 19)  $\frac{72}{135} = \frac{8}{15}$ (HCF = 9)  $\frac{424}{477} = \frac{8}{9}$ (HCF = 53)

### The Puzzler

### The Puzzler

$\frac{5832}{17\,496} = \frac{1}{3}$

## Page 2

### Looking for Patterns

$F_4 = \frac{0}{1}, \frac{1}{4}, \frac{1}{3}, \frac{1}{2}, \frac{2}{3}, \frac{3}{4}, \frac{1}{1}$

$\frac{1}{4}$ and $\frac{3}{4}$ are in $F_4$ but not in $F_3$.

$F_5 = \frac{0}{1}, \frac{1}{5}, \frac{1}{4}, \frac{1}{3}, \frac{2}{5}, \frac{1}{2}, \frac{3}{5}, \frac{2}{3}, \frac{3}{4}, \frac{4}{5}, \frac{1}{1}$

$F_6 = \frac{0}{1}, \frac{1}{6}, \frac{1}{5}, \frac{1}{4}, \frac{1}{3}, \frac{2}{5}, \frac{1}{2}, \frac{3}{5}, \frac{2}{3}, \frac{3}{4}, \frac{4}{5}, \frac{5}{6}, \frac{1}{1}$

## Page 3

### What's the Problem?

Half of Taylah's money can be less than a third of Cloe's. If, for example, Taylah has £1 and Cloe has £3, then half of Taylah's pocket money is 50p and a third of Cloe's is £1.
Amounts will vary.

### Let's Investigate

Results of the investigation will vary.

### The Arts Roundup

3 technicians.
16 singers.
24 people are in The Reggio Opera Company.

## Page 4

### Looking for Patterns

There were 190 children in the hall to start with.

### What's the Problem?

Answers will vary. However most approximations should be similar to the following:

asleep: $\frac{1}{3}$    in school: $\frac{1}{13}$    eating: $\frac{1}{12}$

**Inquisitive ant**

non-unitary fraction
A non-unitary fraction is a fraction with a numerator of 2 or more, e.g. $\frac{2}{3}, \frac{3}{4}, \frac{4}{5} \ldots$
Fractions with a numerator of 1, e.g. $\frac{1}{2}, \frac{1}{3}, \frac{1}{4} \ldots$ are called unitary (or unit) fractions.

# Issue 10

## Fractions

### Prerequisites for learning

- Tabulate systematically the information in a problem or puzzle
- Recognise and use lowest common multiples
- Identify equivalent fractions
- Interpret mixed numbers
- Simplify fractions by cancelling common factors
- Order a set of fractions by converting them to fractions with a common denominator
- Use mental methods of calculation with fractions

### Resources

pencil and paper
Resource sheet 2: My notes (optional)
Resource sheet 3: Pupil self assessment booklet (optional)
calculator (optional)

## Teaching support

### Page 1

#### Let's Investigate

- You may wish to draw children's attention to the 🐝 Let's Investigate activity on page 4 which sets out a method for multiplying a mixed number by a mixed number. This may help children in writing a method for multiplying a fraction by a fraction.

  Alternatively, discuss the following method with the children:

  1. If possible, simplify the numerators and denominators by cancelling.
  2. Multiply the numerators together to get the numerator.
  3. Multiply the denominators together to get the denominator.
  4. Reduce the fraction to its simplest form or change an improper fraction to a mixed number.

#### Money Matters

- Suggest the children record their working in a table that records what the girls did (Action) and how much money each girl had after each action.

  A possible method for working out the answer is:

|  | Lucy | Melinda |
|---|---|---|
| Action 1 | £10.50 | £1.50 |
|  | − £ 3.00 | + £3.00 |
| Action 2 | £ 7.50 | £4.50 |
|  | + £ 1.50 | − £1.50 |
| Action 3 | £ 9.00 | £3.00 |
|  | − £ 3.00 | + £3.00 |
|  | £ 6.00 | £6.00 |

### Page 2

#### Around the World

- An illustration of the problem may help children see the solution.

## Money Matters

- Suggest the children record their working in a table that records how much money Greg spent at each shop and how much money he had left after spending each amount.

A possible method for working out the answer is:

|  | Amount spent | Amount remaining |
|---|---|---|
| Florist | £14 $\left(\frac{1}{2}\right)$ | £14 $\left(\frac{1}{2}\right)$ |
| Dry cleaning | £20 $\left(\frac{1}{3} + £4\right)$ | £28 $\left(\frac{2}{3} - £4\right)$ |
| Supermarket | £60 $\left(\frac{1}{2} + £6\right)$ | £48 $\left(\frac{1}{2} - £6\right)$ |

Total started = £60 + £20 + £14 + £14 = £108

## The Puzzler

- For this puzzle children need to be confident with adding and subtracting fractions.

Tell the children that:

– for the first puzzle all the mixed numbers are either halves or quarters (including $\frac{3}{4}$)

– for the second puzzle all the mixed numbers are either halves or fifths (including $\frac{2}{5}$, $\frac{3}{5}$ or $\frac{4}{5}$)

## Let's Investigate

- Draw children's attention to the  Let's Investigate activity on page 1 which shows how a fraction calculation can be presented as a diagram.

- Suggest the children use shapes such as circles or rectangles to draw their diagrams.

- Ask children to draw two different diagrams to represent each of the fraction statements – perhaps one of the diagrams using shapes and the other diagram a completely different type of picture.

- If children have difficulty in knowing how to approach the puzzle, tell them that Greg spent £60 in the supermarket.

# Page 3

## Let's Investigate

- Ensure that children understand the method for adding fractions with different denominators. Therefore it is important that they fully comprehend the examples provided.

Children also need to be able to identify equivalent fractions, simplify fractions, recognise and use lowest common multiples (LCM), and interpret mixed numbers.

The degree of difficulty in this activity depends upon the fractions that children choose to add together. Adding unitary fractions in most cases will be easier than adding non-unitary fractions. Adding pairs of mixed numbers will probably be the most challenging.

## In the Past

- Referring to the example of $\frac{3}{4}$, discuss with the children how $\frac{3}{4}$ can also be written as $\frac{1}{4} + \frac{1}{4} + \frac{1}{4}$, but that $\frac{1}{2} + \frac{1}{4}$ is more 'elegant' than $\frac{1}{4} + \frac{1}{4} + \frac{1}{4}$ because it has two terms rather than three, and because it starts with the largest fraction with a numerator of 1 $\left(\frac{1}{2}\right)$ that can be taken out of $\frac{3}{4}$.

Remind the children that they should aim to write each fraction as a sum with the least number of unitary fractions.

# Page 4

## Let's Investigate

- Ensure that children understand the method for subtracting fractions with different denominators. Therefore it is important that they fully comprehend the examples provided.

Children also need to be able to identify equivalent fractions, simplify fractions, recognise and use lowest common multiples (LCM), and interpret mixed numbers.

The degree of difficulty in this activity depends upon the fractions that children choose to subtract. Subtracting unitary fraction in most cases will be easier than subtracting non-unitary fractions. Finding the difference between pairs of mixed numbers will probably be the most challenging.

**Let's Investigate**

- This Let's Investigate activity deals with multiplying mixed numbers, and is an extension of the Let's Investigate activity on page 1 where children were asked to find a method for multiplying fractions.

**AfL**

- Explain to me how to add / subtract / multiply a pair of fractions. What about a pair of mixed numbers?
- How did you work out the answer to this problem / puzzle? Where did you start? How did you record your working? Did you draw a table / diagram? Did this help? How?

# Answers

## Page 1

### Let's Investigate
$$\frac{3}{5} \times \frac{5}{6} = \frac{1}{2} \qquad \frac{1}{4} \times \frac{7}{8} = \frac{7}{32} \qquad \frac{2}{3} \times \frac{5}{9} = \frac{10}{27} \qquad \frac{5}{8} \times \frac{6}{7} = \frac{15}{28}$$
$$\frac{5}{6} \times \frac{1}{4} \times \frac{3}{8} = \frac{5}{64}$$

### Money Matters
Lucy £10.50
Melinda £1.50

## Page 2

### Around the World
12·5 miles

### Money Matters
£108

### The Puzzler
$$\boxed{3\tfrac{1}{2}} + \boxed{4\tfrac{1}{4}} - \boxed{3\tfrac{1}{4}} + \boxed{1\tfrac{1}{4}} - \boxed{2\tfrac{3}{4}} = \boxed{3}$$
$$\boxed{2\tfrac{3}{5}} + \boxed{4\tfrac{2}{5}} + \boxed{3\tfrac{1}{2}} - \boxed{1\tfrac{4}{5}} - \boxed{2\tfrac{1}{5}} = \boxed{6\tfrac{1}{2}}$$

Other answers are possible.

### Let's Investigate
Diagrams will vary.

## Page 3

### Let's Investigate
Results of the investigation will vary.

### In the Past
Results of the investigation will vary.

## Page 4

### Let's Investigate
Results of the investigation will vary.

### Let's Investigate
Results of the investigation will vary.

**Inquisitive ant**

LCM
lowest or least common multiple
For example, the LCM of 3 and 4 is 12.

# Issue 11

## Decimals

### Prerequisites for learning

- Calculate mentally with integers and decimals
- Use efficient written methods to add and subtract decimals with up to two places
- Use understanding of place value to multiply and divide decimals by 10, 100 or 1000
- Use a calculator to solve problems, including those involving decimals
- Select and use standard metric units of measure and convert between units using decimals to two places
- Use the order of operations, including brackets

### Resources

pencil and paper
Resource sheet 2: My notes (optional)
Resource sheet 3: Pupil self assessment booklet (optional)
Resource sheet 5: 1 cm squared paper (optional)
ruler
section from a newspaper showing exchange rates
calculator
cheques from a range of different banks
material for making a poster
computer with Internet access

## Teaching support

### Page 1

#### Money Matters

- Either provide the children with the section from a newspaper that shows exchange rates (financial and / or travel section) or access exchange rates from the Internet.
- Ensure that children understand the difference between imports and exports.
- The most important aspect of this activity is the last section – drawing conclusions about the effects of exchange rates on the prices of imported and exported goods.

- Ask the children to draw a conversion graph showing the relationship between the pound and another major currency such as the Euro or US dollar.

#### Let's Investigate

- Using two, three or four digits it is possible to make the following combinations of decimals with one, two or three places:
    - decimals with one place: O·t, TO·t, HTO·t
    - decimals with two places: O·th, TO·th
    - decimals with three places: O·tht$^h$

#### Let's Investigate

- Ensure that children understand the difference between a terminating decimal and a recurring decimal.
- Children also need to be confident with using a calculator and understand the error display 'e'.

### Page 2

#### Money Matters

- The main purpose of this activity is for the children to investigate for themselves how cheques work, what are their advantages and disadvantages, and how they are designed to ensure security.
- Ensure that there is a range of cheques from different banks available for the children to refer to when designing their school's cheque.

#### At Home

- After children have completed the activity at home, ensure that there is an opportunity in class for pairs or groups of children to compare and discuss their lists, and to draw conclusions about the usage of decimals with different decimal places.

#### The Language of Maths

- Encourage the children to be as detailed as possible when defining the word 'decimal'.

## Page 3

### Let's Investigate

- Ensure that children are confident in using the order of operations, including brackets.

### Looking for Patterns

- Remind the children that they are designing a poster with the purpose of explaining to others how to effectively and efficiently convert between different metric units for length, mass and capacity. Therefore, the poster needs to be easy to read and follow, and illustrated with examples.

### The Language of Maths

- Children should be able to infer the meaning of the prefixes 'centi', 'milli' and 'deci' from their association with words such as centimetre, millimetre and decimal. Likewise, they should be able deduce the meaning of the words 'decimetre', 'centigram', 'centilitre' and 'decilitre'.

## Page 4

### The Puzzler

- The amount of money in each envelope can be found by subtracting the total of the other two pairs of envelopes from £10. For example, Envelope E = £10 – (£5.20 + £3.40) = £1.40.

### The Puzzler

- Tell the children that the common total is 3·4.

## AfL

- What did you find out? How did you find this out? What does it mean?
- How do you know that you have found all the different possibilities?
- How did you organise your work?
- Explain to me how you worked that out. What strategies did you use? How did they help you?

# Answers

## Page 1

### Money Matters
Results of the investigation will vary.

### Let's Investigate
Results of the investigation will vary.

### Let's Investigate
$$\frac{1}{2}, \frac{1}{4}, \frac{1}{5}, \frac{1}{8}, \frac{1}{10}, \frac{1}{16}, \frac{1}{20}, \frac{1}{25}, \frac{1}{32}, \frac{1}{40}, \frac{1}{50}, \frac{1}{64}, \frac{1}{80}$$

## Page 2

### Money Matters
Results of the investigation will vary.

### At Home
Results of the investigation will vary.

### The Language of Maths
'Decimal' means using the number ten as a base. Numbers are expressed in a counting system that uses units of ten.

## Page 3

### Let's Investigate
Results of the investigation will vary.

### Looking for Patterns
Results will vary.

### The Language of Maths
*centi* – one hundredth   *milli* – one thousandth   *deci* – one tenth

decimetre – metric unit of length that is equal to one tenth of a metre

centigram – metric unit of mass that is equal to one hundredth of a gram

decilitre – metric unit of capacity that is equal to one tenth of a litre

centilitre – metric unit of capacity that is equal to one hundredth of a litre

## Page 4

### The Puzzler
A = £2.70
B = £2.50
C = £1.80
D = £1.60
E = £1.40

### The Puzzler

| 1·6 | 0·3 | 0·2 | 1·3 |
|-----|-----|-----|-----|
| 0·5 | 1   | 1·1 | 0·8 |
| 0·9 | 0·6 | 0·7 | 1·2 |
| 0·4 | 1·5 | 1·4 | 0·1 |

Each row, column and diagonal totals 3·4.
Other solutions are possible.

**Inquisitive ant**  $10^{-3}$
$= 0.001$ (milli)

# Issue 12

## Percentages

### Prerequisites for learning

- Recognise the per cent symbol (%) and understand that per cent relates to 'number of parts per hundred'
- Express tenths and hundredths as percentages
- Express one quantity as a percentage of another
- Recognise approximate proportions of a whole and use percentages to describe and compare them

### Resources

pencil and paper
Resource sheet 2: My notes (optional)
Resource sheet 3: Pupil self assessment booklet (optional)
ruler
pair of compasses
protractor
newspapers, magazines and catalogues
data-handling software
calculator (optional)
computer with Internet access

## Teaching support

### Page 1

#### Let's Investigate

- Discuss with the children all the different regular activities they do in a weekday. Encourage the children to organise all the activities into six to ten different categories. This will make it easier for the children to draw their pie chart.
- It is advised that children create their pie chart using ICT.
- Children draw their pie chart using a pair of compasses, a protractor and a ruler.

#### The Puzzler

- Ensure children are familiar with magic squares.
  Ask the children to create a 4 × 4 magic percent square.

#### Focus on Science

- Children will need to use the Internet for this activity.

### Page 2

#### The Language of Maths

- Briefly introduce the children to the terms 'deposit', 'down-payment' and 'balance'. Ensure that they are secure in their understanding of these terms before setting them to work on the activity.

#### Let's Investigate

- At this stage, children should be able to recognise approximate proportions of a whole and use percentages to describe and compare them. Encourage the children to make comparisons between three, four or more groups.

#### Money Matters

- Most children should be able to calculate successfully the VAT on goods and services and the new price once VAT has been added.
- It will be easier to find prices in magazines and catalogues that are VAT inclusive. Services, as opposed to goods, are often quoted without VAT. To find prices of goods and services that do not include VAT refer to appropriate websites.
- If the price of an item already includes VAT, some children may need assistance in calculating the cost of the item before VAT (see Answers).

## Page 3

### Money Matters

- Below are the VAT rates for some European countries:

  18% – Malta             19% – Germany

  20% – Austria and France     21% – Belgium and Spain

  22% – Italy              23% – Ireland, Poland and Portugal

  24% – Finland and Greece

  25% – Denmark and Sweden

  Note: Rates current as of 1 June 2016

### The Language of Maths

- This activity requires children to be able to recognise approximate proportions of a whole and use percentages to describe and compare them.

- Explain to the children that each sector of the pie chart is a multiple of 5%.

### Money Matters

- You may wish to provide children with appropriate clippings from newspapers rather than have them look for them themselves.

## Page 4

### Money Matters

- Draw children's attention to the illustrations displaying different percentages and talk about what they all have in common (they are multiples of 10% or 25%).

### Technology Today

- To be able to answer this problem, children need to be able to express successfully one quantity as a percentage of another.

- Work through one or more examples with the children. If appropriate, provide the children with a calculator.

  e.g. 58 out of 80.

  $$\frac{58}{80} \times \frac{100}{1} = \frac{580}{8} = 72 \cdot 5\%$$

## AfL

- What did you find out? What does it mean? How did you go about this?
- How did you go about working out the percentage? How would you do this on a calculator?
- What calculation did you do? What does the answer tell you?
- Approximately what percentage of the pie chart is this sector? Why do you think it is that percent?

# Answers

## Page 1

### Let's Investigate
Results of the investigation will vary.

### The Puzzler

| | | |
|---|---|---|
| 60% | 10% | 80% |
| 70% | 50% | 30% |
| 20% | 90% | 40% |

The magic percent is 150%.
Other solutions are possible.

### Focus on Science
A humidity meter measures the amount of moisture in the air. RH% refers to the percentage of relative humidity in the air. Relative humidity is the amount of water vapour in the air expressed as a percentage of the maximum amount of water vapour that can exist in the air at that temperature.

## Page 2

### The Language of Maths
Results of the investigation will vary.

### Let's Investigate
Results of the investigation will vary.

### Money Matters
VAT stands for Value-Added Tax. It is a tax added to the value of a product at its production or distribution and is paid by the consumer when they purchase the product. Every quarter, the producer (or distributor) pays to the government the VAT they receive from consumers. The rate of VAT in the UK as of 1 January 2011 is 20%.

To calculate the price of an item including VAT:
(price of item before VAT x percentage rate of VAT) + price of item e.g. price of item before VAT costs £24
VAT rate is 20%
(£24 × 0·2) + £24 = £28.80

To find the price of an item before VAT: $\dfrac{\text{price of item including VAT} \times 100}{100 + \text{percentage rate of VAT}}$

e.g. price of item including VAT costs £28.80
VAT rate is 20%
$$\frac{£28\cdot80 \times 100}{100 + 20} = \frac{2880}{120} = £24$$

## Page 3

### Money Matters
Results of the investigation will vary.

### The Language of Maths
Answers will vary. However, they should be similar to the following:

| | | |
|---|---|---|
| Sector 1: 25% | Sector 2: 10% | Sector 3: 5% |
| Sector 4: 5% | Sector 5: 5% | Sector 6: 5% |
| Sector 7: 15% | Sector 8: 10% | Sector 9: 20% |

### Money Matters
Results of the investigation will vary.

## Page 4

### Money Matters
Results of the investigation will vary. However, most sales have discounts of multiples of 10% (or 25%). This is because such percentage discounts are easy to calculate, which means consumers can quickly work out how much money they are saving.

### Technology Today
Hector did best on Friday. He did worst on Wednesday. Gomez did best on Tuesday and Friday. He did worst on Saturday.

**Inquisitive ant**  ‰

'Per mil' means parts per thousand. It is a tenth of a percent.

# Issue 13

## Percentages

### Prerequisites for learning

- Recognise the per cent symbol (%) and understand that per cent relates to 'number of parts per hundred'
- Find percentages of numbers and quantities
- Express one quantity as a percentage of another
- Calculate percentage increases or decreases
- Recognise approximate proportions of a whole and use percentages to describe and compare them
- Make and justify estimates and approximations to calculations

### Resources

pencil and paper

Resource sheet 2: My notes (optional)

Resource sheet 3: Pupil self assessment booklet (optional)

calculator (optional)

map of the local area and a contrasting area

## Teaching support

### Page 1

**Money Matters**

- Ensure that the children are familiar with the following terms: 'increment', 'original price', 'percentage increase', 'discount' and 'percentage decrease'.
- Children also need to understand and use the formulas to calculate a percentage increase or decrease. Work through the first problem with the children, i.e.

original price = £60

decrease in price (discount) = £60 – £42 = £18

$= \frac{18}{60} \times 100\%$

$= \frac{3}{10} \times 100\%$

$= 30\%$

- It is recommended that children work in pairs for the second part of this activity.

### Page 2

**Money Matters**

- Ensure that the children understand the concept of commission and can use the formulas to calculate a commission in pounds and a commission as a percentage. It is important that they fully comprehend the examples provided.

### Page 3

**Around the World**

- Discuss with the children how they are only expected to provide approximate percentages of land that is allocated to each of the different categories.
- It is important that children are able to explain how they arrived at their approximations.

**Focus on Science**

- As the calculations in this activity require the children to find percentages of multiples of 100 (i.e. 2000, 1500 and 800) they should be encouraged to use mental and written methods to work out the answers, and not use a calculator.
- Do children identify and use the relationship between 9%, 18% and 36%?

### Focus on Science

- As with the previous  Focus on Science activity, the children should be encouraged to use mental and written methods to work out the percentages and not use a calculator.
- Can the children work out one of the percentages, i.e. for canines, and then use the relationship for the number of pairs of each different kind of teeth to work out the remaining percentages? For example,
    - Percentage of adult teeth that are molars is three times the percentage of adult teeth that are canine.
    - Percentage of adult teeth that are incisors or bicuspids is twice the percentage of adult teeth that are canine.

## Page 4

### Focus on Science

- Remind the children how they are only expected to provide approximate percentages. Discuss with them how rounding can help with their approximation, and also what degree of rounding is appropriate given the context of the problem.

### What's the Problem?

- Children should be encouraged to use mental and written methods to work out the answers and not use a calculator.

### The Arts Roundup

- Assist the children with working out the problem, i.e.

    the number of female musicians that also perform with smaller ensembles: $\frac{40}{100} \times \frac{30}{1} = \frac{1200}{100} = 12$.

    So, the total number of musicians that also perform with smaller ensembles: $12 + 16 = 28$.

    So, the percentage of the 70 orchestra members that also perform with smaller ensembles: $\frac{28}{70} \times \frac{100}{1} = \frac{2800}{70} = 40\%$.

### The Puzzler

- Provide the children with an example (see Answers).
- Ask the children to complete other statements such as:

    ☐ is ◯ % of 32

    ☐ is 14% of ◯

    Alternatively, children can make up statements of their own.

## AfL

- How did you work out that percentage?
- How did you work out that percentage increase / decrease?
- What is this expressed as a percentage?
- What did you use to help you work out that answer? Was there a percentage that you already knew that you used to help you? How did this help? Why did you do that?
- How did rounding help you with your calculation? What does that mean in terms of the accuracy of your answer?

# Answers

## Page 1

**Money Matters**

30%    15%
50%    20%

## Page 2

**Money Matters**

| Agent | Value of goods sold | Commission as a percentage | Commission in pounds |
|-------|---------------------|----------------------------|----------------------|
| D Rogers | £34 000 | 6% | £2040 |
| M Quincy | £194 000 | 5% | £9700 |
| A Leech | £29 500 | 8% | £2360 |
| W Ali | £67 800 | 4% | £2712 |
| C T Adams | £45 350 | 3% | £1360.50 |

Best agent: M Quincy (sold the most value of goods yet has only the third-highest percentage commission).
Worst agent: A Leech (sold the least value of goods yet has the highest percentage commission).

## Page 3

**Around the World**
Results of the investigation will vary.

## Focus on Science

| | Head and neck | Both arms and hands | Torso | Both legs and feet |
|-------|---------------|---------------------|-------|--------------------|
| Adult | 180 cm² | 360 cm² | 740 cm² | 720 cm² |
| Teenager | 135 cm² | 270 cm² | 555 cm² | 540 cm² |
| Child | 72 cm² | 144 cm² | 296 cm² | 288 cm² |

## Focus on Science
molars: 37·5%
incisors: 25%
bicuspids: 25%
canines: 12·5%

## Page 4

**Focus on Science**
38·67%
72·34%
Answers may vary depending on the degree of rounding that children did.

**What's the Problem?**
The approximate total surface area of the Earth is 494 300 000 km².
Approximately 346 000 000 km² of the Earth's surface is covered by water.

**The Arts Roundup**
40%

**The Puzzler**
Statements will vary. Examples may include:
5 is 10% of 50
12 is 15% of 80
18 is 30% of 60
55 is 44% of 125

**Inquisitive ant**  percentage points
Percentage points refers to the difference between two percentages. For example, a percentage rise from 20% to 30% can be described as a rise of 10 percentage points.

# Issue 14

## Ratio and proportion

### Prerequisites for learning

- Use the vocabulary of ratio and proportion to describe the relationship between two quantities
- Use sequences to scale numbers up or down
- Solve problems involving ratio and proportion
- Understand and use ratio notation
- Calculate mentally with integers and decimals
- Use the formal written method to multiply and divide whole numbers and decimals
- Use approximations and inverse operations to estimate and check results

### Resources

pencil and paper
Resource sheet 2: My notes (optional)
Resource sheet 3: Pupil self assessment booklet (optional)
calculator
child's reading book
two 1, 2, 3, 1, 2, 3 dice
computer with Internet access

## Teaching support

### Page 1

#### Around the World

- Ensure children are familiar with ratio notation, e.g. 8 : 5, before attempting this activity.
- Allow the children to use a calculator for this activity.
- As this activity requires the children to use sequences to scale numbers up or down, you may wish to introduce them to the following method as a way of working out the answers.
- Take, for example, the Great Pyramid of Khufu, with a base width of 230 m. The height of the pyramid can be calculated using the following diagram:

| base | height | |
|------|--------|--|
| 8 | 5 | 28·75 |
| 230 m | 143·75 m | |

(230 m ÷ 8 = 28·75 m
28·75 m × 5 = 143·75 m)

### Page 2

#### Money Matters

- Ensure children are familiar with ratio notation, e.g. 5 : 8, before attempting this activity.
- Allow the children to use a calculator for this activity.
- Discuss with the children the use of the inverse ratio to change back dollars into pounds, i.e. 8 : 5.

#### What's the Problem?

- Allow the children to record their ratios and proportions in their own way.
- Once several children have completed the activity, hold a discussion and allow individual children to present their method of recording. What are the similarities and differences?

### Page 3

#### Let's Investigate

- Mercury is the closest planet to the Sun. What is the approximate ratio of the time that each of the other planets takes to the time that Mercury takes?

**The Language of Maths**

- What is the second most frequently used letter in your book?

## Page 4

### Let's Investigate

- What is the approximate ratio of the totals 2 to 3 to 4 to 5 to 6?

### Money Matters

- The ratios give (1 × 50p) + (3 × 20p) + (2 × 10p) + (2 × 5p) = £1.40. £5.60 is four times this amount, so there are four times these numbers of coins.

- What is the ratio of 50p to 20p to 10p to 5p coins? (1 : 3 : 2 : 2)

### Looking for Patterns

- Ensure children are familiar with ratio notation, e.g. 6 : 5, before attempting this activity.
- The minimum number of yellow counters there can be is 5. If this is the right number, there must be 8 blue counters (ratio 8 : 5), therefore 10 green counters (ratio 5 : 4), therefore 12 red counters (ratio 6 : 5). This makes 35 counters in total, so not enough.
- Doubling the number of each coloured counter keeps the ratios the same and gives a total of 70 counters, which fits the clues.

## AfL

- What does the word 'ratio' mean? What about 'proportion'?
- How did you use ratio to work out the answer to this problem?
- How did you work out that proportion? Is it an approximation or the actual proportion?
- How do you write a ratio / proportion? How else can you express a ratio / proportion?
- What ratio / proportion is this?
- Tell me some of your statements / problems that involve ratio and proportion.

# Answers

## Page 1

### Around the World
The Great Pyramid of Khufu: 143·75 m
The Pyramid of Khafre: 133·75 m
The Pyramid of Menkare: 65·625 m

## Page 2

### Money Matters
Peter received $160.
Aslan received $80.
Silvia received $224.
Tommi received $280.
Rada received $512.

Silvia returned with £45.
Tommi returned with £72.50.
Rada returned with £101.25.

### What's the Problem?
The ratio of starfish to shells is 5 : 7.
$\frac{7}{12}$ of the bucket is shells.
$\frac{5}{12}$ of the contents are starfish.
The ratio of fish to starfish to shells is 3 : 5 : 7.
$\frac{1}{3}$ of the contents of the bucket are starfish now.

## Page 3

### Let's Investigate
Mercury : Earth 1 : 4
Venus : Earth 2 : 3
Mars : Earth 2 : 1
Jupiter : Earth 12 : 1
Saturn : Earth 30 : 1
Uranus : Earth 84 : 1
Neptune : Earth 165 : 1

### The Language of Maths
3 : 1
Providing there is enough text, the ratio should be the same on any page.

## Page 4

### Let's Investigate
The most frequent total is 4. The least frequent totals are 2 and 6.
Ratio of the most frequent total to the least frequent total is 3 : 1.

### Money Matters
4 × 50p, 12 × 20p, 8 × 10p, 8 × 5p

### Looking for Patterns
There are 24 red, 20 green, 16 blue and 10 yellow counters in the bag.

**Inquisitive ant**  : Mathematical symbol for writing a ratio.

## Ratio and proportion

### Prerequisites for learning

- Use the vocabulary of ratio and proportion to describe the relationship between two quantities
- Use sequences to scale numbers up or down
- Solve problems involving ratio and proportion
- Understand and use ratio notation
- Use and record standard metric units to estimate and measure length to a suitable degree of accuracy
- Calculate mentally with integers and decimals
- Use the formal written method to multiply and divide whole numbers and decimals
- Use approximations and inverse operations to estimate and check results

### Resources

pencil and paper
Resource sheet 2: My notes (optional)
Resource sheet 3: Pupil self assessment booklet (optional)
Resource sheet 4: Scale drawing
recipe books (optional)
local telephone directory
pack of playing cards (optional)
access to different sized children's classroom chairs
measuring equipment
set of dominoes
2 sheets of A4 paper
coloured pencils
computer with Internet access

## Teaching support

### Page 1

**The Arts Roundup**

- Ask the children to enlarge their small picture to a given ratio, e.g. 1 : 5.

**At Home**

- You may wish the children to undertake this activity in school rather than at home. If so, provide them with a recipe book.

- If the children do undertake this activity at home, once they have completed the task ensure that there is an opportunity in class for pairs or groups of children to discuss their results.

**Let's Investigate**

- Remind the children that this activity involves finding an approximate proportion, not the actual proportion.

**Looking for Patterns**

- Length of 4 of Johannes' strides:
  30 cm × 4 strides = 120 cm
  Length of 1 of Martine's strides:
  120 cm ÷ 5 strides = 24 cm
  Total length of 18 of Martine's strides:
  24 cm × 18 = 432 cm.

### Page 2

**Sports Update**

- One method of working out the answer to this activity is by scaling up the measurements and recording the results in a table, e.g.

| Lance | 6 miles | 12 miles | 18 miles | 24 miles | 30 miles | 36 miles | 39 miles |
|-------|---------|----------|----------|----------|----------|----------|----------|
| Fabio | 4·5 miles | 9 miles | 13·5 miles | 18 miles | 22·5 miles | 27 miles | 29·25 miles |

### The Language of Maths

- Ensure children understand ratio notation, i.e. 2 : 3.
- This activity requires the children to make two different diagrams for each given ratio and proportion. The purpose of making two different diagrams is so that children can identify relationships. For example, the relationship between 1 : 5 and 2 : 10; and the relationship between $\frac{2}{3}$ and $\frac{4}{6}$. This also allows for discussion with the children as to how ratios and proportions should be expressed in their simplest form.

### What's the Problem?

- Ensure children understand ratio notation, i.e. 2 : 5.
- Once children have written their word problems they can swap them to check that the problems match the given ratios, proportions and amounts.

## Page 3

### Let's Investigate

- For this activity children will need to have access to a range of different sized children's classroom chairs.

### Let's Investigate

- Give the child a set of dominoes, but remove those with a blank side, and ask them to make tally charts of the odd and even products and odd and even sums.

### The Language of Maths

- There are 58 letters in the name of the village.

  13 letters are vowels.

  11 are the letter 'l'.

  6 are the letter 'o'.

  7 are the letter 'g'.

## Page 4

### In the Past

- Other measurements of the human body that show the golden ratio are:
  - top of head to foot : navel to foot
  - navel to foot : top of head to navel
  - top of shoulders to navel : top of head to top of shoulders
  - navel to bottom of knee : bottom of knee to foot

### Let's Investigate

- The ratio between the width and the length of A4 and all the A sizes of paper is 1 : √2.
- This means that each time a sheet is cut in half, the two resultant sheets keep the same ratio of width to length as the original.

### Let's Investigate

- Ensure that children realise that column A = 1, B = 2, C = 3 etc.

## AfL

- What do scale drawings have to do with ratio?
- What does the word 'ratio' mean? What about 'proportion'?
- How did you work out that proportion? Is it an approximation or the actual proportion?
- How do you write a proportion? How else can you express a proportion?
- What proportion / ratio is this?
- How did you use ratio to work out the answer to this problem?
- Tell me some of your statements / problems that involve ratio and proportion.

# Answers

## Page 1

**The Arts Roundup**
1 : 3

**At Home**
Results of the investigation will vary.

**Let's Investigate**
Results of the investigation will vary.

**Looking for Patterns**
432 cm

## Page 2

**Sports Update**
29·25 miles

**The Language of Maths**
Proportion of red – 1 : 6, blue – 5 : 6
Proportion of green – 4 : 11, yellow – 7 : 11
Proportion of red – 1 : 3, black – 1 : 6, blue – 1 : 2

Descriptions will vary for the other questions.

**What's the Problem?**
Word problems will vary.

## Page 3

**Let's Investigate**
Results of the investigation will vary.

**Let's Investigate**
The ratio of even products to odd products is 5 : 2.
The proportion of odd products is $\frac{2}{7}$.
The proportion of even products is $\frac{5}{7}$.

The ratio of even totals to odd totals is 4 : 3.
The proportion of odd totals is $\frac{3}{7}$.
The proportion of even totals is $\frac{4}{7}$.

**The Language of Maths**
The ratio of vowels to consonants is 13 : 45.
The ratio of the letter 'l' to the letter 'o' is 11 : 6.
The proportion of the letters that are vowels is $\frac{13}{58}$.
The proportion of the letters that are the letter 'g' is $\frac{7}{58}$.
Other descriptions will vary.

## Page 4

**In the Past**
Results of the investigation will vary.

**Let's Investigate**
Both the lengths and widths double from one sheet to the next.
The ratio of length to width of sheets of A4 to A10 paper is approximately 1 : 1·4.

**Let's Investigate**
Results of the investigation will vary.

**Inquisitive ant**
scale factor
Refers to the ratio between the size of a representation of something and its actual size.

# Issue 16

## Ratio and proportion

### Prerequisites for learning

- Use the vocabulary of ratio and proportion to describe the relationship between two quantities
- Use sequences to scale numbers up or down
- Solve problems involving ratio and proportion
- Understand and use ratio notation
- Calculate mentally with integers and decimals
- Use the formal written method to multiply and divide whole numbers and decimals
- Use approximations to estimate and check results

### Resources

pencil and paper
Resource sheet 2: My notes (optional)
Resource sheet 3: Pupil self assessment booklet (optional)
recipe books
material for making a poster
computer with Internet access

## Teaching support

### Page 1

#### The Puzzler

- Using direct proportion, assist the children in seeing the relationship between the two ratios, e.g.

  7 parts orange juice mixed with 3 parts water

  $$= \frac{7 \times 4}{3 \times 4} = \frac{28}{12}$$

  8 parts orange juice mixed with 4 parts water

  $$= \frac{8 \times 3}{4 \times 3} = \frac{24}{12}$$

#### At Home

- Children should not only write male and female ratio and proportion statements about their extended family but also about other topics. For example, the ratio and proportion of family members that are:

  – under the age of 40 and over the age of 40

  – married or not married

  – live in the same city / town as they do or live elsewhere.

  Discuss with the children other suitable topics.

- After children have completed the activity at home, ensure that there is an opportunity in class for pairs or groups of children to compare and discuss the different ratio and proportion statements they wrote about their families.

#### The Language of Maths

- Children should be familiar with the term 'direct proportion'. However you may need to spend some time discussing and providing examples of 'inverse proportion'.

- Work through the first problem with the children, i.e.

  As there are fewer men, the work will take longer.

  The ratio of men has decreased 6 : 8 or 3 : 4.

  So, the number of hours is increased in the ratio 4 : 3.

  The inverse of 3 : 4 is 4 : 3. The amount of time is in inverse proportion to the number of men.

  Number of hours $= 12 \times \frac{4}{3}$

  $$= \frac{48}{3} = 16 \text{ hours}$$

## Page 2

### What's the Problem?

• Work through the first problem with the children.

### What's the Problem?

• Ensure that children are familiar with ratio notation, e.g. 2 : 3, and how this can be extended to include three-part ratios such as 5 : 1 : 2.

### Sports Update

• Some children may need assistance in working out the answer to the problem and in particular organising their work. One example may be:

8 people in the stadium = 7 Nawra Rovers supporters

9 Nawra Rovers supporters = 1 Nawra Rovers season ticket holder

819 Nawra Rovers supporters = 91 Nawra Rovers season ticket holders

819 Nawra Rovers supporters $\times \frac{8}{7} \left(1\frac{1}{7}\right)$ people in the stadium = 936 people in the stadium

## Page 3

### Let's Investigate

• This is an open-ended investigation where, depending on the amount of time and effort children are prepared to invest in the activity, they can be as detailed and as accurate as they wish.

• The important aspects of this activity are the justifications that children give for the decisions that they made during the investigation.

### Let's Investigate

• Either provide the children with a recipe book or direct them to a suitable website.

• When children are rewriting the quantities needed of each ingredient, suggest that one is for fewer people than given in the recipe, i.e. scaling down the recipe; and the other is for more people, i.e. scaling up the recipe.

## Page 4

### What's the Problem?

• For this problem, children need to find out, on average, how many children each day have school dinners as opposed to packed lunches. A precise number is not essential for this activity.

### The Language of Maths

• Explain to the children that their poster will go on display in the classroom and that it should be designed so that other children can easily understand both the difference and relationship between ratio and proportion.

**AfL**

• What does the word 'ratio' mean? How do you write a ratio?
• What is the difference between 'direct proportion' and 'inverse proportion'?
• How do you write a proportion? How else can you express a proportion? Which do you prefer? Why?
• What does scaling have to do with ratio and proportion? Can you give me an example?
• Give me some other examples of when and how we use ratio and proportion.

# Answers

## Page 1

**The Puzzler**
7 parts orange juice mixed with 3 parts water is stronger.

**At Home**
Answers and statements will vary.

**The Language of Maths**
16 hours
6 days
37 minutes 30 seconds

## Page 2

**What's the Problem?**
15 men
7·5 days
Explanations will vary.

**What's the Problem?**
Books = 1235
CDs = 247
DVDs = 494

**Sports Update**
There are 936 people in the stadium.

## Page 3

**Let's Investigate**
Results of the investigation will vary.

**Let's Investigate**
Results of the investigation will vary.

## Page 4

**What's the Problem?**
Results will vary.

**The Language of Maths**
Posters will vary. However, they should convey the idea that ratio compares part to part (using terms such as *to every*), and proportion compares part to whole (using terms such as *in every*). The relationship between ratio and proportion can be explained through examples such as: *'two to every three' (a ratio)* is equivalent to *'two in every five' (a proportion)*.

**Inquisitive ant**

a : b = b : a
Using ratio notation, a : b shows the relationship between two numbers or quantities. It can also be expressed in the form b : a. For example, in a class of 30 children, 14 boys and 16 girls, the ratio of boys to girls is 14 : 16 (or 7 : 8) and is equal to the ratio of girls to boys, i.e. 16 : 14 (or 8 : 7).

# Algebra

## Prerequisites for learning

- Use simple expressions and formulas in words and symbols
- Generate and describe linear number sequences
- Enumerate possibilities of combinations of two variables
- Calculate mentally with integers and decimals
- Use the formal written methods to add, subtract, multiply and divide
- Use approximations and inverse operations to estimate and check results

## Resources

pencil and paper
Resource sheet 2: My notes (optional)
Resource sheet 3: Pupil self assessment booklet (optional)
calculator (optional)
computer with Internet access

# Teaching support

## Page 1

### Famous Mathematicians

- Most children should know square numbers up to and including $10^2$, but not all may be familiar with triangular numbers and oblong numbers.
- The important aspect of this activity is not being able to write the 5th to 10th square, triangular and oblong numbers, but rather working out a rule or formula for finding any square, triangular or oblong number.
- If children are not confident with writing a mathematical rule or formula, discuss with them possible ways of writing this, including the use of symbols such as $a$ or $n$.
- If appropriate, discuss with the children the algebraic convention for omitting the multiplication sign when writing an algebraic expression, i.e. $n(n + 1)$ rather than $n \times (n + 1)$.

## Page 2

### Famous Mathematicians

- Ensure children have completed the  Famous Mathematicians activity on page 1 before attempting this activity.
- Work with the children, drawing a dot array for the first statement, e.g.

 +  =

### Famous Mathematicians

- Most children should be able to successfully complete the table. However, some difficulty may arise when writing a rule or formula.
- If children are not confident with writing a mathematical rule or formula, discuss with them possible ways of writing this, including the use of symbols such as $a$ or $n$.
- If appropriate, discuss with the children the algebraic convention for omitting the multiplication sign when writing an algebraic expression, i.e. $\dfrac{n(n + 1)}{2}$ rather than $\dfrac{n \times (n + 1)}{2}$.
-  Children investigate further the life and work of Carl Gauss.

## Page 3

### Famous Mathematicians

- Ensure children fully understand the table and the problem before setting them off to work independently on the activity.
- Once the children have completed the activity, discuss with them their methods of working. Were they able to identify the pattern and apply the rule to working out how many pairs of rabbits there would be at the end of the year?

### Looking for Patterns

- Ensure children have completed the  Famous Mathematicians activity above before starting on this activity.
- Children investigate further the life and work of Fibonacci.

## Page 4

### Looking for Patterns

- Encourage the children to work out how many sides there are in a row of 4 and 5 greenhouses, if necessary, drawing a diagram.
- When devising a formula, encourage the children to look for the relationship between the number of greenhouses in a row and the total number of sides.

### Looking for Patterns

- When writing a formula for the rule, discuss with the children the algebraic convention of referring to a number in the sequence as the $n$th term. Also explain the convention of omitting the multiplication sign when writing an algebraic expression, i.e. how: $n \times (n + 1) \times (n + 2)$ can be expressed as: $n(n + 1)(n + 2)$.

### Looking for Patterns

- Briefly discuss each of the sequences with the children. What patterns do they notice?

### Sports Update

- Discuss with the children why the final score of 4 – 3 could also be a possible half-time score.
- Some children may need assistance in identifying the formula. When writing a formula for the rule, discuss with the children the algebraic convention of assigning a letter to represent a term, and also for omitting the multiplication sign when writing an algebraic expression, i.e. how: $(a + 1) \times (b + 1)$ can be expressed as: $(a + 1)(b + 1)$.

## AfL

- What is happening in this sequence?
- What pattern do you notice? What is the rule?
- How would you express this rule in words? What about using symbols?
- How else can you express this rule?
- How does this diagram show this relationship?
- What are all the different possibilities? How can you be sure that you have accounted for them all?

# Answers

## Page 1

**Famous Mathematicians**

|  | Square number | Triangular number | Oblong number |
|---|---|---|---|
| 5th | 25 | 15 | 30 |
| 6th | 36 | 21 | 42 |
| 7th | 49 | 28 | 56 |
| 8th | 64 | 36 | 72 |
| 9th | 81 | 45 | 90 |
| 10th | 100 | 55 | 110 |
| 50th | 2500 | 1275 | 2550 |
| Rule for any number | $n^2$ | $\dfrac{n(n+1)}{2}$ | $n(n+1)$ |

## Page 2

**Famous Mathematicians**
Diagrams will vary.

**Famous Mathematicians**
Formula is:
$$\frac{n(n+1)}{2}$$

| Counting numbers | Number in set ($n$) | Total |
|---|---|---|
| 1 | 1 | 1 |
| 1 + 2 | 2 | 3 |
| 1 + 2 + 3 | 3 | 6 |
| 1 + 2 + 3 + 4 | 4 | 10 |
| 1 + 2 + 3 + 4 + 5 | 5 | 15 |
| 1 + 2 + 3 + 4 + 5 + 6 | 6 | 21 |
| 1 + 2 + 3 + 4 + 5 + 6 + 7 | 7 | 28 |
| 1 + 2 + 3 + 4 + 5 + 6 + 7 + 8 | 8 | 36 |
| 1 + 2 + 3 + 4 + 5 + 6 + 7 + 8 + 9 | 9 | 45 |
| 1 + 2 + 3 + 4 + 5 + 6 + 7 + 8 + 9 + 10 | 10 | 55 |

The numbers are all triangular numbers.
The total of the first 100 numbers is 5050.

## Page 3

**Famous Mathematicians**
There would be 144 pairs of rabbits at the end of the year.

**Looking for Patterns**
The Fibonacci sequence is the sum of the previous two numbers in the sequence.

The first 20 Fibonacci numbers are: (0), 1, 1, 2, 3, 5, 8, 13, 21, 34, 55, 89, 144, 233, 377, 610, 987, 1597, 2584, 4181, 6765

## Page 4

**Looking for Patterns**
There would be 41 sides in a row of 10 green houses.
Answers will vary for the formula, e.g. if $n$ = number of green houses in the row and $s$ = total number of sides then $s = 4n + 1$.

**Looking for Patterns**
336, 504
Answers will vary for an explanation in words, e.g. each number in the sequence is obtained by multiplying its position number in the sequence by the next two position numbers, i.e. $6 = 1 \times 2 \times 3$; $24 = 2 \times 3 \times 4$; ...
Answers will vary for the formula, e.g. if $n$ = the position in the sequence then $nth\ term = n \times (n + 1) \times (n + 2)$ or $n(n + 1)(n + 2)$.
So, the 6th term = $6 \times 7 \times 8 = 336$.

**Looking for Patterns**
Sequence D will be the first to reach 1000 or more.
A = 32nd term is 1024 (Rule: increase the difference by 2 each time – sequence of square numbers)
B = 46th term is 1081 (Rule: increase the difference by 1 each time – sequence of triangular numbers)
C = 18th term is 1597 (Rule: add the previous two terms – Fibonacci sequence)
D = 11th term is 1024 (Rule: double the previous term)

**Sports Update**
There are 20 possible half-time scores:

| | | | | |
|---|---|---|---|---|
| 0 – 0 | 1 – 0 | 2 – 0 | 3 – 0 | 4 – 0 |
| 0 – 1 | 1 – 1 | 2 – 1 | 3 – 1 | 4 – 1 |
| 0 – 2 | 1 – 2 | 2 – 2 | 3 – 2 | 4 – 2 |
| 0 – 3 | 1 – 3 | 2 – 3 | 3 – 3 | 4 – 3 |

If $a$ = one team's final score and $b$ = the other team's final score then the formula for calculating the number of possibilities is:
$(a + 1) \times (b + 1)$ or $(a + 1)(b + 1)$
So for a final score of 4 – 3
$(4 + 1)(3 + 1) = 5 \times 4 = 20$

**Inquisitive ant**

formula
A special type of equation that shows a mathematical relationship or rule expressed in symbols.

## Algebra – The Financial Issue

### Prerequisites for learning

- Find fractions using division
- Find percentages of numbers and quantities
- Use simple expressions and formulas in words and symbols
- Calculate mentally with integers and decimals
- Use the formal written methods to add, subtract, multiply and divide
- Use approximations and inverse operations to estimate and check results

### Resources

pencil and paper
Resource sheet 2: My notes (optional)
Resource sheet 3: Pupil self assessment booklet (optional)
calculator (optional)

## Teaching support

### Pages 1–2

**Money Matters**

- Ensure that the children are familiar with the following terms and their abbreviations: 'principal' (P), 'fixed rate of interest' (R), 'fixed length of time' (T), 'per annum' (p.a.), 'fixed term deposit' and 'simple interest' (I).

- Children also need to understand and use the formulas to calculate simple interest and the total amount due. Therefore it is important that they fully comprehend the example provided.

- It is recommended that children work in pairs for the second part of this activity where they investigate savings rates in newspapers and offer advice as to the most favourable option available.

### Pages 2–3

**Money Matters**

- As well as an understanding of the terms used in the 🏦 Money Matters activity on page 1, children also need to understand the terms 'loan' and 'repayment'. Point out to the children that the expression 'how much money is being borrowed (P)' refers to the 'principal' as previously discussed.

- Children also need to understand and use the formulas to calculate simple interest, the total amount due and monthly repayments. Therefore it is important that they fully comprehend the example provided.

- It is recommended that children work in pairs for the second part of this activity where they investigate loan rates in newspapers and offer advice as to the most favourable option available.

### Pages 3–4

**Money Matters**

- The concepts involved in this activity are more complex than in the previous two 🏦 Money Matters activities. Therefore it is important that children fully understand the following terms: 'shares', 'investors / shareholders', 'nominal value', 'face value', 'market price', 'par', 'premium', 'discount' and 'dividend'.

  It is advised that time is spent with the children going through and discussing in detail the two examples provided.

## AfL

- What have you learnt in this issue?
- Explain to me how savings / loans / shares work.
- Talk me through this formula.
- What does this mean?
- Do you think that this would be a good option? Why? Why not? What are the alternatives? How are these better / worse?

# Answers

## Pages 1–2

**Money Matters**

Mr J Brown
Simple interest = £120
Total amount = £2120
Mr T Kanu
Simple interest = £2160
Total amount = £14 160
Options will vary.

Mrs A Williams
Simple interest = £800
Total amount = £4800
Mrs B Andersen
Simple interest = £9912.50
Total amount = £40 412.50

## Pages 2–3

**Money Matters**

Mr Charles
a. £3720
b. £96 720
c. £4030

Net Works
a. £1 687 500
b. £3 187 500
c. £10 625
Options will vary.

Mr & Mrs Lee
a. £129 600
b. £489 600
c. £3400

Crystal Pools
a. £630 000
b. £1 530 000
c. £6375

## Pages 3–4

**Money Matters**

| £20 000 | £132 | £20 |
|---------|------|-----|
| £1650 | £450 000 | |

**Inquisitive ant**

economics
The study of how goods and services are produced and distributed.

# Issue 19

## Length

### Prerequisites for learning

- Recognise the square roots of perfect squares
- Understand and use simple algebraic conventions
- Represent information or unknown numbers in an equation
- Understand the word 'scale' in the contexts of maps and in drawing enlargements and reductions
- Understand and identify properties of a circle, including radius, diameter and circumference
- Solve simple problems involving ratio
- Understand compound units for speed, such as miles per hour and kilometres per hour
- Calculate mentally with integers and decimals
- Use the formal written methods to add, subtract, multiply and divide
- Use approximations and inverse operations to estimate and check results
- Measure and calculate using imperial units and know their approximate metric values
- Collect, select, process, present and interpret data

### Resources

pencil and paper
Resource sheet 2: My notes (optional)
Resource sheet 3: Pupil self assessment booklet (optional)
Resource sheet 5: 1 cm squared paper
ruler
selection of maps showing different scales
calculator
pair of compasses
eight pieces of paper
tape measure
trundle wheel
computer with Internet access

## Teaching support

### Page 1

#### Around the World

- Show the children how to measure the distance between two places on the map and then use the scale to calculate the actual distance.
- You may wish to discuss with the children the difference between the actual distance between two places on a map and the distance 'as the crow flies'.

#### Construct

- This activity involves measuring, converting and drawing. Encourage the children to be as accurate as possible throughout each stage of the activity.

### Page 2

#### Focus on Science

- The second column in the table below shows the diameter (in kilometres) of each of the planets. You may wish to provide this information for the children rather than have them find it out for themselves. The final column offers a possible scale drawing size for each of the planets.
- Some of the planets will either be too large or too small to draw if they are all based on the same scale, e.g. Sun (too large), Pluto, Mercury and Mars (too small). For such planets suggest children just write the diameter.

| Planet | Diameter in km | Diameter in km (rounded) | To scale |
|---|---|---|---|
| Sun | 1 391 000 | 1 400 000 | 140 cm |
| Mercury | 4879 | 5000 | 5 mm |
| Venus | 12 104 | 12 000 | 12 mm |
| Earth | 12 756 | 13 000 | 13 mm |
| Mars | 6794 | 7000 | 7 mm |
| Jupiter | 142 984 | 140 000 | 14 cm |
| Saturn | 120 536 | 120 000 | 12 cm |
| Uranus | 51 118 | 51 000 | 51 mm |
| Neptune | 49 528 | 50 000 | 5 cm |
| Pluto | 2390 | 2000 | 2 mm |

### Around the World

• Work through an example with the children, e.g.

| Metric units | Imperial units |
|---|---|
| For a height of 1·5 metres | For a height of 5 feet |
| $d = \sqrt{12 \cdot 7h}$ | $d = \sqrt{1 \cdot 50h}$ |
| $d = \sqrt{12 \cdot 7 \times 1 \cdot 5}$ | $d = \sqrt{1 \cdot 50 \times 5}$ |
| $d = 4 \cdot 36$ km | $d = 2 \cdot 74$ miles |

## Page 3

### Let's Investigate

• Ensure that children understand all the terms involved with staircases.

### Sports Update

• The degree of complexity of this activity depends on how detailed the children make their scale drawing.

### Let's Investigate

• Assist children to work out the percentage error, i.e.

$$\frac{\text{Actual error (cm)}}{10 \text{ cm}} \times \frac{100}{1}$$

• Repeat the activity, only this time asking the children to cut a piece of string as close to 30 cm long as possible.

## Page 4

### Around the World

• The answer to this activity will depend on the mode of transportation children use. They need to find out kilometres per hour or miles per hour for their chosen mode of transport and calculate accordingly, i.e.
  – plane: average cruising speed = 800 km/h or 500 MPH
  – running: 10 km/h or 6 MPH
  – walking: 5 km/h or 3 MPH
  – boat: average cruising speed = 35 knots or 65 km/h or 40 MPH.

### The Language of Maths

• You may wish to discuss with the children how in the book, the reference to 20 000 leagues (or 111 120 kilometers or 69 047 miles) does not mean depth. It actually refers to the distance travelled underwater. 20 000 leagues / 111 120 kilometers / 69 047 miles is almost three times the circumference of the Earth.

• Children investigate maths in books / stories.

### Money Matters

• A 10p coin is 1·85 mm thick.
  Methods will vary. One method is:
  1 km = 1 000 000 mm
  1 000 000 ÷ 1·85 = 540 541 coins = £54 054.10

### At Home

• You may wish for the children to undertake this activity in school rather than at home.

• If the children do undertake this activity at home, once they have completed the task, ensure that there is an opportunity in class for pairs or groups of children to discuss their results.

### AfL

• Tell me the scale of your map / diagram. What does this mean?
• What did you find out?
• What were the results of your investigation? What conclusions can you draw?
• What do your estimates / approximations mean? How accurate are they? What does this mean?

# Answers

## Page 1

**Around the World**
Answers will vary.

**Construct**
Plans will vary.

## Page 2

**Focus on Science**
Diagrams will vary.

**Around the World**
Answers will vary depending on the unit of measure used and the children's heights.

## Page 3

**Let's Investigate**
Results will vary depending on the staircases children investigate.

**Sports Update**
Diagrams will vary depending on the chosen sport.

**Let's Investigate**
Results of the investigation will vary.

## Page 4

**Around the World**
Answers will vary depending on the mode of transport used.

**The Language of Maths**
A league is a unit of length.
1 league = 5·55600 kilometres or 3·45233834 miles
Alternative titles for *20,000 Leagues Under the Sea* could be *111 120 Kilometres Under the Sea* or *69 047 Miles Under the Sea.*

**Money Matters**
£54 054.10

**At Home**
Results of the investigation will vary.

**Inquisitive ant**  nanometre
One billionth of a metre.

# Issue 20

## Mass

### Prerequisites for learning

- Understand logic puzzles
- Calculate mentally with integers and decimals
- Use the formal written methods to add, subtract, multiply and divide
- Use approximations and inverse operations to estimate and check results
- Measure and calculate using imperial units and know their approximate metric values
- Understand compound units, such as kilogram per cubic metre
- Collect, select, process, present and interpret data

### Resources

pencil and paper
Resource sheet 2: My notes (optional)
Resource sheet 3: Pupil self assessment booklet (optional)
Resource sheet 5: 1 cm squared paper
ruler
material for making a poster
calculator
selection of food packaging (optional)
computer with Internet access

## Teaching support

### Page 1

#### Around the World

- Most children will find this activity relatively easy. Ensure children know that 1 tonne is equivalent to 1000 kg.

#### Around the World

- Children can produce their results in a graph or chart using ICT.
- Children investigate other commodities such as gold, iron-ore, zinc, rubber and copper.

### Page 2

#### Looking for Patterns

- These logic problems can be solved in various ways. However, all methods are based on identifying patterns and relationships. One way of solving such problems is to assign values to the shapes. For example, in the first problem:

  - By looking at the second set of scales, we can see that:

    $3 \times \bigcirc = 1 \times \triangle$

    $\therefore \bigcirc = 1$ and $\triangle = 3$

  - By looking at the first set of scales, we can work out using what we have discovered above that:

    $2 \times \bigcirc = 1 \times \square$

    $\therefore \bigcirc = 1$ and $\square = 2$

  - So, $\triangle \square \square = 3 + 2 + 2 \bigcirc$

    $\therefore 7 \times \bigcirc$ balance the third scale.

- Possible values for the other puzzles are:

**Puzzle 2:**

$\bigcirc = 3$

$\square = 5$

$\triangle = 7$

$\therefore 5 \times \bigcirc$ balance the third scale.

**Puzzle 3:**

$\bigcirc = 3$

$\square = 1$

$\triangle = 5$

$\therefore 3 \times \bigcirc$ balance the third scale.

#### The Language of Maths

- Explain to the children that their poster should include a combination of words and illustrations to explain the difference between mass and weight.

### Focus on Science

• Children comment of the buoyancy of each of the objects. What conclusions can they draw from their investigation?

## Page 3

### Focus on Science

• You may prefer to leave out the first part of the activity where children find out their own weight on each of the planets. If so, tell the children to go straight onto finding the Earth weight of other objects and then to calculate their approximate weight on each of the other planets.

### Let's Investigate

• Ensure children understand the difference between mass and volume, and are able to calculate (and / or approximate) volume (see Issue 21).

• The important aspect of this activity is the inferences that children make as a result of their investigation.

## Page 4

### At Home

• Remind the children that they are only expected to make approximations in this activity. Discuss with the children how they might arrive at these approximations and averages.

• You may wish for the children to undertake this activity in school rather than at home. If so, have available a selection of food packaging.

• If the children do undertake this activity at home, once they have completed the task, ensure that there is an opportunity in class for pairs or groups of children to discuss their results.

### What's the Problem?

• Explain to the children the relationship between stones and pounds, and their metric equivalent, i.e.

1 pound (lb) = 0·454 kg        14 pounds = 1 stone (st)

• One method of working out the answer is:

If 1lb = 0·454 kg, then 63 kg ÷ 0·454 ≈ 139 lb

If 14 lb = 1 st, then 139 lb ÷ 14 = 9 st 13 lb

### What's the Problem?

• Explain to the children the relationship between stones and pounds, and their metric equivalent, i.e.

1 pound (lb) = 0·454 kg        14 pounds = 1 stone (st)

• One method of working out the answer is:

If 14 lb = 1 st, then (12 st × 14) + 8 lb = 176 lb

If 1 lb = 0·454 kg, then 176 lb × 0·454 ≈ 80 kg

## AfL

• What did you find out? How did you record your results? Why did you decide to present them in this way?

• What conclusions can you draw from your investigation?

• How did you work out these puzzles? What strategies did you use?

• What calculations did you do?

# Answers

## Page 1

### Around the World
1260 kg

Trader B / 80 kg

Trader G

Trader H

Traders C and F

Trader D / 800 kg

Trader F / 1320 kg

Trader D (800 kg), Trader C (840 kg), Trader G (900 kg), Trader A (1200 kg), Trader H (1250 kg), Trader E (1260 kg), Trader B (1280 kg) and Trader F (1320 kg)

### Around the World
Presentation and reports will vary however, the top three producers of each commodity are shown in the table below:

| Commodity | Top three producers (tonnes) (*million tonnes) |
|-----------|------------------------------------------------|
| wheat | EU (157*) / China (126*) / India (95*) |
| sugar | Brazil (768*) / India (341*) / China (128*) |
| rice | China (204*) / India (153*) / Indonesia (69*) |
| tea | China (2*) / India (1*) / Kenya (432 000) |
| coffee | Brazil (3*) / Vietnam (2*) / Colombia (696 000) |

NOTE: Figures may vary depending on source.

## Page 2

### Looking for Patterns
Puzzle 1: 7 × ○ balance the third scale.

Puzzle 2: 5 × ○ balance the third scale.

Puzzle 3: 3 × ○ balance the third scale.

### The Language of Maths
Posters will vary. However definitions should be similar to the following:
- The mass of an object is how much matter it contains.
- The weight of an object is the force caused by gravity pulling down on the mass of an object.

### Focus on Science
The mass of the materials are:
- balsa wood: 170 kg/m³
- pine wood: 560 kg/m³
- gold: 19 320 kg/m³
- silver: 10 490 kg/m³
- lead: 11 340 kg/m³
- aluminium: 2600 kg/m³

Notes: – kg/m³ refers to the number of kilograms per cubic metre.
  – Answers may vary depending on the type of material used.

## Page 3

### Focus on Science
Results of the investigation will vary.

### Let's Investigate
Results of the investigation will vary.

## Page 4

### At Home
Results of the investigation will vary.

### What's the Problem?
9 st 13 lb

### What's the Problem?
80 kg

**Inquisitive ant**

inference

An inference is a conclusion drawn from evidence or reasoning.

# Issue 21

## Volume and capacity

### Prerequisites for learning

- Understand the concept of volume
- Understand and use simple algebraic conventions
- Use simple expressions and formulas in symbols
- Understand pi (π) as the ratio of the circumference of a circle to its diameter and is equal to 3·14
- Calculate mentally with integers and decimals
- Use the formal written methods to add, subtract, multiply and divide
- Use approximations and inverse operations to estimate and check results

### Resources

pencil and paper

Resource sheet 2: My notes (optional)

Resource sheet 3: Pupil self assessment booklet (optional)

collection of cylinders, e.g. tin can, tube of sweets, drinking glass, toilet roll … (optional)

material for making a poster

100 ml can

sand or rice

measuring cylinder with scale in cubic centimetres

water

collection of small solid objects, e.g. small stone, coin, ball of modelling clay …

calculator (optional)

computer with Internet access

## Teaching support

### Page 1

**Around the World**

- Ensure children understand and can use the formula for calculating the volume of a cuboid.

**Around the World**

- Rates for both national and international freightage can easily be found on the Internet.
- The important aspect of this activity is how the volume of a parcel, as opposed to distance, affects pricing.
- Suggest the children record their results in a table.

### Page 2

**Let's Investigate**

- This activity introduces children to the formulas for calculating the volume of a cylinder and a triangular prism. Ensure that they understand and can use these formulas before working independently on this activity and the ⌂ At Home activity on page 3. You may also need to remind / introduce children to pi (π).

Volume of a cylinder

$V = \pi r^2 l$

$\quad = 3·14 \times 10^2 \times 32$

$\quad = 3·14 \times 100 \times 32$

$\quad \approx 10\ 048\ cm^3$

Volume of a triangular prism

$V = \frac{1}{2} bhl$

$\quad = \frac{1}{2} \times 4 \times 5 \times 7$

$\quad = \frac{140}{2}$

$\quad = 70\ cm^3$

### Page 3

**At Home**

- You may wish for the children to undertake this activity in school rather than at home. If so, have available a collection of cylinders, e.g. tin can, tube of sweets, drinking glass, toilet roll …
- If the children do undertake this activity at home, once they have completed the task, ensure that there is an opportunity in class for pairs or groups of children to discuss their results.

### Sports Update

- Ensure children understand and can use the formula for calculating the volume of a sphere.

  Tennis ball with a radius of 3 cm

  $\frac{4}{3} \pi r^3$

  $\frac{4}{3} \times 3 \cdot 14 \times 3^3$

  $= \frac{4}{3} \times 3 \cdot 14 \times 27$

  $= \frac{339}{3}$

  $\approx 113 \text{ cm}^3$

### Focus on Science

- Remind the children that the formula for calculating the volume of the cylinder is $V = \pi r^2 h$. Ask them to find out what the formula is for calculating the volume of a cone ($V = \frac{1}{3}\pi r^2 h$).
- Given that both the cylinder and cone have the same radius and height then three conesful should fill the can.

### The Language of Maths

- Explain to the children that their poster should include a combination of words and illustrations to explain the difference between volume and capacity.

## Page 4

### Famous Mathematicians

- Be sure to provide children with measuring cylinders with scales in cubic centimetres.

### Let's Investigate

- This investigation assumes that most classrooms will be cuboid in shape and therefore children will be able to use the formula $V = lwh$. However, classrooms do come in shapes other than cuboids. In such cases children will need to make approximations. When doing so, children should write about the assumptions they have made when arriving at their approximations.

## AfL

- How do you calculate volume? What about for a different solid?
- Explain this formula to me in your own words.
- What were the results of your experiment? What conclusions can you make?
- What did your investigation discover? Why do you think this is?

# Answers

## Page 1

### Around the World
10 264 800 mm³
1026 m³
201·67 cm³
91·125 m³
50 120 692 mm³
One possible answer is 50 cm × 115·5 cm, but there are endless possibilities.

### Around the World
Results of the investigation will vary.

## Page 2

### Let's Investigate
A = 70 cm³
B = 10 048 cm³
C = 441 cm³
D = 942 cm³

## Page 3

### At Home
Results of the investigation will vary.

### Sports Update
Tennis ball = 113 cm³
Volley ball = 9198 cm³
Cricket ball = 523 cm³
Basket ball = 7235 cm³

### Focus on Science
Three conesful should fill the can.
The volume of the cone is $\frac{1}{3}$ that of the cylinder.

### The Language of Maths
Posters will vary. However the definition should be similar to the following:
Volume and capacity measure the same thing: three-dimensional space, but they are slightly different in usage. Capacity refers to how much a container can hold (with contents measured commonly in litres or its derived units); while volume is the space actually occupied by an object or the bulk of some substance.

## Page 4

### Famous Mathematicians
Results of the investigation will vary.

### Let's Investigate
Results of the investigation will vary.

## Inquisitive ant

SI

SI is the International System of Units (abbreviated SI from the French Le Système International d'Unités). It is the world's most widely used system of measurement.

It is based on the metric system and the number ten and involves seven 'base' units: metre, kilogram, second, ampere, kelvin, candela, mole. Litre is also an SI unit but is not considered a 'base' unit.

## Time

### Prerequisites for learning

- Understand and use simple algebraic conventions
- Use simple expressions and formulas in symbols
- Understand compound units for speed, such as kilometres per hour
- Calculate mentally with integers and decimals
- Use the formal written methods to add, subtract, multiply and divide
- Use approximations and inverse operations to estimate and check results

### Resources

pencil and paper
Resource sheet 2: My notes (optional)
Resource sheet 3: Pupil self assessment booklet (optional)
time/clock interactive teaching tool (optional)
digital clock (optional)
mirror (optional)
tape measure
stopwatch
calculator (optional)

## Teaching support

### Page 1

#### The Puzzler

- If children have an analogue wristwatch, they may find this activity very easy.
- You may wish to show the children the answer using a time/clock interactive teaching tool.

- Children investigate what number the minute hand is pointing to when the hour hand is pointing to 9, 19, 39, 49 or 59. What about if the hour hand is pointing to 1, 11, 21, 31, 41, 51?

#### Looking for Patterns

- A method for working out each answer is:

*Low-pitched bell*

Every hour the low-pitched bell strikes four times – on the hour, at 15 minutes past, 30 minutes past and 45 minutes past. Given that there are two 12-hour periods in 24 hours the calculation is
$[(1 \times 4) + (2 \times 4) + (3 \times 4) \dots (12 \times 4)] \times 2$ which totals 624 strikes.

*High-pitched bell*

Every hour the high-pitched bell strikes once at quarter past the hour, twice at half past the hour and thrice at quarter to the hour. Given that there are 24 hours a day the calculation is $24 \times (1 + 2 + 3)$ which totals 144 strikes.

#### Let's Investigate

- A digital clock and a mirror may help children to see which digits, and subsequently which times, are affected by reflection.

### Page 2

#### Sports Update

- One method for working out how long it would take the male and female 100-metre record holders to run the marathon at the same speed as they ran 100 metres is:

42·195 km × 1000 = 42 195 m

42 195 m ÷ 100 m = 421·95

∴ Usain Bolt would take 421·95 × 9:58 sec to run this distance

= 4042:28 sec

= 67 min 22 sec

= 1 h 7 min 22 sec

- Give the children time to discuss the results of the racing activity back in the classroom.
- Ask the children to work out how long it would take them to run a marathon if they ran the whole distance at this speed.

### Page 3

**Focus on Science**

- Work through the first two problems with the children, i.e.

  total distance travelled = 525 km

  total time taken = 7 hours

  $$\text{average speed} = \frac{\text{total distance travelled}}{\text{total time taken}}$$

  $$= \frac{525 \text{ km}}{7 \text{ hours}}$$

  $$= 75 \text{ km/h}$$

  total distance travelled = 7·5 km

  total time taken = $\frac{1}{2}$ hour

  $$\text{average speed} = \frac{\text{total distance travelled}}{\text{total time taken}}$$

  $$= \frac{7\text{·}5 \text{ km}}{30 \text{ min}} = \frac{15 \text{ km}}{1 \text{ h}}$$

  average speed = 15 km/h

  time taken = $3\frac{1}{2}$ hours

  total distance travelled = average speed × total time taken

  = 15 km/h × $3\frac{1}{2}$ hours

  total distance travelled in $3\frac{1}{2}$ h = 52·5 km

  total distance travelled = 60 km

  $$\text{total time taken} = \frac{\text{total distance travelled}}{\text{average speed}}$$

  $$= \frac{60 \text{ km}}{15 \text{ km/h}}$$

  total time taken = 4 hours

**The Puzzler**

- Suggest children work in pairs doing the calculations for both birthdays together.

### Page 4

**Let's Investigate**

- Remind the children of the order of operations.
- Work through an example with the children.

  For example, 29 January 2002.

  $$f = k + \left[\frac{(13 \times m - 1)}{5}\right] + D + \left[\frac{D}{4}\right] + \left[\frac{C}{4}\right] - 2 \times C$$

  $$= 29 + \left[\frac{(13 \times 11 - 1)}{5}\right] + 1 + \left[\frac{1}{4}\right] + \left[\frac{20}{4}\right] - 2 \times 20$$

  $$= 29 + \left[(28\text{·}4)\right] + 1 + \left[0\text{·}25\right] + \left[5\right] - 40$$

  $$= 29 + 28 + 1 + 5 - 40$$

  $$= 23$$

  To find the day of the week divide $f$ by 7: $\frac{f}{7}$

  $$= \frac{23}{7}$$

  $$= 3 \text{ r } 2 \ (2 = \text{Tuesday})$$

  So, 29 January 2002 was a Tuesday.

## AfL

- How did you work out the answer to the puzzle? What conclusions can you draw from it? Is there a rule? If so, what is it?
- Explain the formula to me.
- Talk me through your calculation. How did you work that out?

# Answers

## Page 1

**The Puzzler**
48 minutes past

**Looking for Patterns**
Low-pitched bell: 624 strikes
High-pitched bell: 144 strikes

**Let's Investigate**
12-hour digital clock

01:10    02:50    05:20
10:01    11:11    12:51

24-hour clock – the six times above and the following:

00:00    15:21    20:05
21:15    22:55

## Page 2

**Sports Update**
Usain Bolt: 1 h 7 min 22 sec
Florence Griffith Joyner: 1 h 13 min 46 sec
Answers will vary for the paired activity.

## Page 3

**Focus on Science**
Barry's average speed is 75 km/h.
The man could cycle 52·5 km in $3\frac{1}{2}$ hours.
It would take it him 4 hours to 60 km.

| Total distance travelled | Total time taken | Average speed |
|---|---|---|
| 160 km | 4 h | 40 km/h |
| 60 km | 30 min | 120 km/h |
| 315 km | 3 h 30 min | 90 km/h |
| 93 km | $7\frac{3}{4}$ h | 12 km/h |
| 21 km | 4 h 12 min | 5 km/h |

**The Puzzler**
Answers will vary.

## Page 4

**Let's Investigate**
Answers will vary.

**Inquisitive ant**  horology
The study or science of measuring time.

## Area

### Prerequisites for learning

- Use simple expressions and formulas in symbols
- Understand and use simple algebraic conventions
- Use fractions to describe and compare proportions
- Calculate the area of rectilinear shapes
- Understand and identify properties of a circle, including diameter and radius
- Understand pi ($\pi$) as the ratio of the circumference of a circle to its diameter which is equal to 3·14
- Calculate mentally with integers and decimals
- Use the formal written methods to add, subtract, multiply and divide
- Use approximations and inverse operations to estimate and check results

### Resources

pencil and paper
Resource sheet 2: My notes (optional)
Resource sheet 3: Pupil self assessment booklet (optional)
Resource sheet 8: Squared dot paper
ruler
scissors (optional)
11 × 11 geoboard
elastic bands
calculator (optional)
access to a range of measuring equipment
access to a daily supply of newspapers at home

## Teaching support

### Page 1

#### Looking for Patterns

- Suggest that the children draw and cut out several squares and semi-circles and label them $a$ and $b$ accordingly. They can then use these to construct the shapes on the page. This will provide a useful visual cue.

- Drawing lines to separate the compound shapes may assist in identifying the individual shapes, e.g.

- Discuss with the children some algebraic conventions. For example, that $a + b + b$ can be expressed as $a + 2b$, or that $a \div 2$ can be written as $\frac{1}{2}a$.

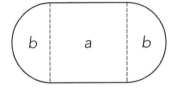

### Page 2

#### In the Past

- Most children should require little or no assistance in answering questions 1 or 2.

- Some children may require help in redesigning Tutankhamun's tomb. If this is the case, allow the children to work in pairs to discuss and reason appropriate alternatives.

### Page 3

#### Let's Investigate

- Ensure that the children fully understand Pick's Formula before setting them off to work independently.

- Using a geoboard is an easier alternative to using squared paper.

#### What's the Problem?

- There are different methods to solve this problem. One possible method is to imagine the four right-angled triangles put together as two squares, each with sides 8 cm. Therefore, the area of each square is 64 cm² and 2 × 64 cm² = 128 cm².

#### Let's Investigate

- Discuss the difference between regular and irregular polygons. The largest octagon that can be made on the geoboard is an irregular octagon.

## Page 4

### Sports Update

- The shape of a football is not a sphere. It is actually a truncated icosahedron. It is made from 32 polygons: 12 regular pentagons and 20 regular hexagons.

- Most children will probably solve this problem using an informal method. However if appropriate, introduce the children to the formula for finding the area of a sphere: $A = 4\pi r^2$ as a method of calculating the approximate surface area of a football (approximate given that a football is actually a truncated icosahedron and not a sphere). In order to be able to apply this formula the children will need to be familiar with the meaning of both pi ($\pi$) and radius ($r$).

### The Puzzler

- Encourage the children to use what they know, i.e. that C is one square unit, to work out what they don't know, e.g. that A and E are both half the size of C.

### At Home

- Ensure that the children have access to a daily supply of newspapers. If this is not possible, try and provide them with a daily (preferably free) paper.

- Once children have completed the home activity, provide them with an opportunity to share what they did with others. What conclusions can they make?

## AfL

- How would you express this in words? What about using letters and symbols?

- How did you work that out? Is there another way you could have arrived at that answer? What is the most effective and efficient method? Why is this the best method?

- Is there another answer / possibility? Are there any more?

- What have you discovered? How might this help you in the future?

# Answers

## Page 1

### Looking for Patterns

$a + b + b$ or $a + 2b$

$a + a$ or $2a$

$a \div 2$ or $\frac{1}{2} a$

$a + \frac{1}{2} a$ or $1\frac{1}{2} a$

$a + b + b$ or $a + 2b$

Answers will vary for different shapes whose areas are $2a + b$.

## Page 2

### In the Past
Passage = 931·26 m²
Antechamber = 2790·3 m²
Annex = 1118 m²
Burial Chamber = 2649·6 m²
Treasury = 1819·25 m²
Total area = 9308·41 m²
Answers will vary for the redesigned tomb.

## Page 3

### Let's Investigate
Results of the investigation will vary.

### What's the Problem?
128 cm²

### Let's Investigate

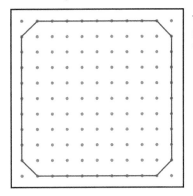

$\frac{2}{100}$ or $\frac{1}{50}$ of the geoboard is outside of the octagon.

## Page 4

### Sports Update
Answers will vary for informal methods.
If using the formula $A = 4\pi r^2$,
then: $A = 4 \times 3·14 \times 121 = 1520$ cm²

### The Puzzler
Tangram pieces A and E = 0·5 square unit
Tangram pieces B and D = 2 square units
Tangram pieces F and G = 1 square unit
Total = 8 square units

### At Home
Results and comparisons will vary.

---

**Inquisitive ant**

hectare
A metric unit of area equal to 100 acres or 10 000 square metres (2·471 acres).

# Perimeter

## Prerequisites for learning

- Calculate the area and perimeter of rectilinear shapes
- Understand and use simple algebraic conventions
- Represent information or unknown numbers in an equation
- Calculate mentally with integers and decimals
- Use the formal written methods to add, subtract, multiply and divide
- Use approximations and inverse operations to estimate and check results

## Resources

pencil and paper

Resource sheet 2: My notes (optional)

Resource sheet 3: Pupil self assessment booklet (optional)

Resource sheet 5: 1 cm squared paper

Resource sheet 8: Squared dot paper

ruler

world atlas

trundle wheel

geoboard

elastic bands

matchsticks

computer with Internet access

# Teaching support

### Page 1

**Construct**

- Most children should find this activity relatively easy. When they have worked out which tile can be removed without changing the overall perimeter, ask them to explain their thinking.

**What's the Problem?**

- Assist the children in seeing the squares as follows:

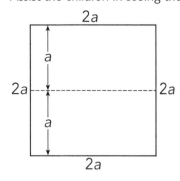

As the square was folded in half, the length of the rectangle is half the width.

So, perimeter of the rectangle

$= (2a \times 2) + (a \times 2) = 36$ cm

$\therefore 4a + 2a = 36$ cm

$\therefore 6a = 36$ cm

$\therefore a = 6$ cm

So, perimeter of the square

$= 2a \times 4$

$= 12$ cm $\times 4$

$= 48$ cm

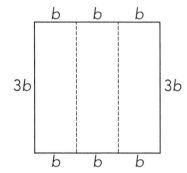

The perimeter of one rectangle

$= (3b \times 2) + (b \times 2) = 40$ cm

$\therefore 6b + 2b = 40$ cm

$\therefore 8b = 40$ cm

$\therefore b = 5$ cm

So, perimeter of the square

$= 3b \times 4$

$= 15$ cm $\times 4$

$= 60$ cm

### Around the World

- This activity is best suited for pairs or small groups of children.
- A trundle wheel is an excellent resource for measuring the dimensions of the land on which the school is built. Ensure that children are familiar with, and are able to use, a trundle wheel before they start on this activity.
- The  Let's Investigate activity on page 4 depends on children having successfully completed this activity.

### The Language of Maths

- Remind the children that shapes are congruent if they are exactly the same size and shape.

## Page 2

### Around the World

- Children can find out about borders either on the Internet or using a world atlas. Prior to the activity, you may wish to discuss these options with the children and decide which one is most appropriate.
- For either option, you will probably need to discuss with the children how their borders / perimeters will be approximates.

### Construct

- Explain to the children that there are five different lengths of fencing possible.

### Let's Investigate

- Suggest children move straight onto using squared dot paper.

## Page 3

### What's the Problem?

- One method of working is:

  $12 \cdot 6 \div 6 = 2 \cdot 1$

  $2 \cdot 1 \times 1 = 2 \cdot 1$

  $2 \cdot 1 \times 2 = 4 \cdot 2$

  $(2 \cdot 1 + 4 \cdot 2) \times 2 = 12 \cdot 6$

### Let's Investigate

- Children investigate other polygons whose perimeters are greater than their areas.

### The Language of Maths

- Children will easily be able to offer formulas for the square and rectangle.
- To write the formulas for the two other quadrilaterals and the circle, children need to understand and use both Pythagoras' theorem and the formula for calculating the circumference of a circle. Both these concepts are covered in Issue 26.

## Page 4

### Looking for Patterns

- Children should have no difficulty in drawing the next two shapes in each sequence. Nor should they have trouble in stating the number of extra squares and the number of matches used to make them.
- Some children may need help in writing the formulas and may benefit from drawing a table of the number of squares and the number of matches used, e.g. for the first sequence:

| No. of squares ($n$) | 1 | 2 | 3 | 4 | 5 |
| --- | --- | --- | --- | --- | --- |
| No. of matches used | 4 | 7 | 10 | 13 | 16 |
| No. of matches in perimeter | 4 | 6 | 8 | 10 | 12 |

- When working out the formula for number of matches used: each increase in n increases the number of matches by 3. Therefore for n extra squares, the number of extra matches is $3n$. The total number of matches needed for one square is 4 (= $3n + 1$). Therefore $3n + 1$ is the formula.

- When working out the formula for the number of matches in the perimeter: each increase in $n$ increases the number of matches by 2. Therefore for $n$ extra squares, the number of extra matches is $2n$. The total number of matches needed for one square is 4 (= $2n + 2$). Therefore $2n + 2$ is the formula.

- Discuss with the children why the formulas for the first three sequences are the same.

**Let's Investigate**

- Children should use the measurements they made in the 🌍 Around the World activity on page 1.

## AfL

- What relationships do you notice? What is the rule / pattern? How can you express this as a formula?

- Is this statement completely true? Why?

- What is the answer to this problem / puzzle? How did you work it out?

- What are the results of your investigation?

# Answers

## Page 1

### Construct
Tile G

### What's the Problem?
48 cm
60 cm

### Around the World
Plans will vary.

### The Language of Maths
Shapes that are congruent do have the same perimeter, however shapes that have the same perimeter are not necessarily congruent.

## Page 2

### Around the World
Results of the investigation will vary. However Canada has the largest combined land and sea border and the Vatican City has the smallest border. Cuba and the Bahamas have similar sized borders, as do the Philippines and China.

### Construct

| Sides of rectangle (m) | Total length of fencing (m) |
|---|---|
| 1 | 80 | 162 |
| 2 | 40 | 84 |
| 4 | 20 | 48 |
| 8 | 10 | 36 |
| 16 | 5 | 42 |

### Let's Investigate
A 4 × 4 square has a perimeter and area that are numerically equal. This is also true for a 3 × 6 rectangle.
There are many possible pairs of shapes where the two perimeters are the same and the two areas are the same, e.g.

## Page 3

### What's the Problem?
Length: 4·2 m
Width: 2·1 m

### Let's Investigate
Answers will vary. However, rectangles whose perimeters are greater than their areas include 2 × 3, 2 × 4, 2 × 5, 2 × 6 … rectangles.

### The Language of Maths
Formulas or rules will vary, However possible formulas are:
- for a square: $4a$
- for a rectangle: $2(a + b)$
- for the irregular quadrilateral: $a + b + c + \sqrt{b^2 + (c - a)^2}$
- for the parallelogram: $2a + 2\sqrt{b^2 + c^2}$
- for the irregular hexagon: $2(a + b)$
- for the circle: $\pi a$

## Page 4

### Looking for Patterns
NOTE: For each formula below $n$ = number of squares

1 square using 3 matches are added each time.
The formula for the number of squares and the number of matches used: $3n + 1$
The formula for the number of squares and the number of matches around the perimeter: $2n + 2$.

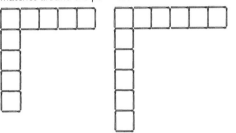

2 squares using 6 matches are added each time.
The formula for the number of squares and the number of matches used: $3n + 1$.
The formula for the number of squares and the number of matches around the perimeter: $2n + 2$.

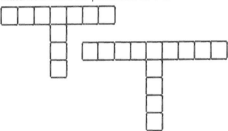

3 squares using 9 matches are added each time.
The formula for the number of squares and the number of matches used: $3n + 1$
The formula for the number of squares and the number of matches around the perimeter: $2n + 2$.

2 squares using 5 matches are added each time.
The formula for the number of squares and the number of matches used: $\frac{5n}{2} + 2$
The formula for the number of squares and the number of matches around the perimeter: $n + 4$

### Let's Investigate
Plans will vary.

**Inquisitive ant**

circumference
The distance around a closed curve. It is a special perimeter.

# Issue 25

## Measurement

### Prerequisites for learning

- Understand and use simple algebraic conventions
- Represent information or unknown numbers in an equation
- Know and use imperial measures still in everyday use and their metric equivalents
- Calculate mentally with integers and decimals
- Use the formal written methods to add, subtract, multiply and divide
- Use approximations and inverse operations to estimate and check results

### Resources

pencil and paper

Resource sheet 2: My notes (optional)

Resource sheet 3: Pupil self assessment booklet (optional)

Resource sheet 5: 1 cm squared paper

ruler

globe or world atlas

string

calculator (optional)

road atlas

computer with Internet access

## Teaching support

### Page 1

#### Famous Mathematicians

- By referring to the first four rows in the table, children should be able to easily identify the relationship between the measurements for Person 1 and Person 2, and therefore the rule and formula (i.e. $W1 \times D1 = W2 \times D2$).

- Children investigate further the life and discoveries of Archimedes.

### Page 2

#### Famous Mathematicians

- By referring to the table, children should be able to identify the relationship between the time it takes an object to fall to the ground and the distance it travels during the fall.

  However, you may need to discuss with the children how to represent this as a formula, i.e. $4{\cdot}8 \times t^2$ or $4{\cdot}8t^2$. Depending on how the formula is expressed, you may also need to remind the children of the order of operations (i.e. find $t^2$ first then multiply the result by $4{\cdot}8$), and the algebraic convention of omitting the multiplication sign.

- Children investigate further the life and discoveries of Galileo.

#### Focus on Science

- This activity, Inquisitive Ant and the  Let's Investigate activity on page 3 are all aimed at introducing children to unusual and very specific units of measures.

- You may wish to discuss with the children that the decibel scale is a logarithmic scale, i.e. 20 decibels is 10 times louder than 10 decibels; 30 decibels is 100 times louder than 10 decibels; 40 decibels is 1000 times louder than 10 decibels, ...

#### Around the World

- In order for children to make their approximations, the globe will need to have some form of scale. If such a globe is not available, then suggest to the children that they use a world atlas.

- Children work out the distances in nautical miles.

  1 km = 0·54 nautical miles

  1 nautical mile = 1·852 km

## Page 3

### Let's Investigate

- This activity, Inquisitive Ant and the  Focus on Science activity on page 2 are all aimed at introducing children to unusual and very specific units of measures.
- The most important aspect of this activity is finding, where appropriate, the equivalent metric measurement.

### Famous Mathematicians

- In Issue 21, Inquisitive Ant required the children to investigate SI – the International System of Units. This system is based on the metric system and is an ideal starting point for the first part of this activity.
- Children should know the imperial unit equivalents for some of the metric units. They should be encouraged to investigate those equivalents they do not yet know.

### Around the World

- Children can continue this activity at home by asking their parents or grandparents about what they consider to be the advantages and disadvantages of both the metric and imperial systems.

## Page 4

### Let's Investigate

- Most UK road atlases include a chart that shows the distances in miles by road between various cities. Provide children with such a chart and ask them to draw their own chart for just five different cities with the measurements given in kilometres.

### Let's Investigate

- Children may be able to use the measurements they made in the  Around the World activity on page 1 of Issue 24 to help them calculate the total area of the plot of land that the school is on.
- As there are various tasks involved in this activity, you may want the children to work on this in groups, with individuals or pairs working on different aspects. Children then share their results with the group before writing their report.

**AfL**

- What patterns did you notice? What is the relationship? Is there a rule?
- What formula did you discover? Describe this to me in words. What about using symbols?
- Show me an example that applies this formula.
- What did you find out about this investigation?
- What was your reasoning for making these decisions? Why are they valid reasons?

# Answers

## Page 1

### Famous Mathematicians
Archimedes' formula is W1 × D1 = W2 × D2.

| Person 1 | | Person 2 | |
|---|---|---|---|
| Weight (W1) | Distance from fulcrum (D1) | Weight (W2) | Distance from fulcrum (D2) |
| 24 kg | 2 m | 32 kg | 1·5 m |
| 40 kg | 1 m | 20 kg | 2 m |
| 20 kg | 1·5 m | 24 kg | 1·25 m |
| 80 kg | 0·5 m | 20 kg | 2 m |
| 45 kg | 2 m | 60 kg | 1·5 m |
| 70 kg | 1 m | 35 kg | 2 m |
| 36 kg | 1·25 m | 30 kg | 1·5 m |
| 52·5 kg | 2 m | 84 kg | 1·25 m |

## Page 2

### Famous Mathematicians
Galileo's formula is $4·8t^2$ ($4·8 \times t^2$).
It would take approximately 13 seconds for an object to fall to the ground from the top of Burj Khalifa.

### Focus on Science
Answers will vary.
However, a decibel scale may look something like:

```
0    20    40    60    80    100    120    140
```

### Around the World
Estimated sailing distances will vary.
The actual sailing distance from:
• London to New York is 6189 km (3342 nautical miles)
• London to Sydney via the Suez Canal is 21 351 km (11 529 nautical miles).

## Page 3

### Let's Investigate
Fathom: depth of water.   1 fathom = 8 feet or 1·8 m
Hand: height of a horse.   1 hand = 4 inches or 10·2 cm
Knot: speed of a boat.   1 knot = 1·15 mph =1·852 km/h
Furlong: measure of distance.   1 furlong = one-eighth of a mile, 220 yards or 201·2 m
Quintal: measure of mass.   1 quintal = 100 base units of either pounds or kilograms
Results of the investigation will vary.

### Famous Mathematicians
Answers will vary. However some of the common equivalents may include the following:

| Length | 1 millimetre = 0·03937 inches |
|---|---|
| | 1 centimetre = 0·3937 inches |
| | 1 metre = 3·281 feet |
| | 1 metre = 1·0936 yards |
| | 1 kilometre = 0·6214 miles |
| Mass | 1 gram = 0·0352 ounces |
| | 1 kilogram = 2·2046 pounds |
| Volume and capacity | 1 millilitre = 0·035 ounces |
| | 1 litre = 1·76 pints |
| | 1 litre = 0·22 gallons |

### Around the World
Reports will vary, however, things that would need to change include road signs, weight information on packaging, weather reporting …

## Page 4

### Let's Investigate
Both formulas give the same answer.
Reasons as to which formula children prefer will vary.

### Let's Investigate
Results of the investigation will vary.

**Inquisitive ant**

Richter scale
A scale from 1 to 10 used to measure the severity of earthquakes according to the amount of energy released. The larger the number, the stronger the earthquake.

# Issue 26

## 2-D shapes

### Prerequisites for learning

- Recognise squares of numbers and the square roots of perfect squares
- Understand and identify properties of a circle, including centre, radius, diameter and circumference
- Understand pi ($\pi$) as the ratio of the circumference of a circle to its diameter, equal to 3·14
- Use a pair of compasses to draw circles
- Represent information or unknown numbers in an equation
- Understand and use simple algebraic conventions
- Calculate mentally with integers and decimals
- Use the formal written methods to add, subtract, multiply and divide
- Use approximations and inverse operations to estimate and check results

### Resources

pencil and paper

Resource sheet 2: My notes (optional)

Resource sheet 3: Pupil self assessment booklet (optional)

Resource sheet 6: 2 cm squared paper

ruler

set-square

matchsticks

calculator

at least six circular objects, all different sizes, e.g. plates of different sizes, wastepaper basket, analogue clock, geometric circular shape

tape measure

## Teaching support

| Number of points ($p$) | Number of chords ($c$) |
|---|---|
| 2 | 1 |
| 3 | 3 |
| 4 | 6 |
| 5 | 10 |
| 6 | 15 |
| 7 | 21 |
| 8 | 28 |

### Page 1

#### Let's Investigate

- Ensure children understand what a 'chord' is.

- Suggest the children tabulate the information to help them identify the pattern and then write the formula, e.g.

- Some children may need assistance with writing the formula. This can either be written in words or using symbols.

  Encourage children to write the formula using symbols.

### Page 2

#### Let's Investigate

- This is a practical activity where children discover pi ($\pi$) for themselves, and realise that the circumference of a circle is approximately 3·14 or $3\frac{1}{7}$ $\left(\frac{22}{7}\right)$ times the diameter.
- Ensure that the children understand the terms 'circumference', 'diameter' and 'radius'.

#### Let's Investigate

- Ensure children understand that the word 'congruent' means that the pieces are identical in size and shape and that they can be exactly superimposed. Note: This is the Inquisitive Ant activity for this issue.

#### The Puzzler

- Diagonal BD is the same as diagonal AC. The diagonal AC is the radius of the circle. Therefore, the diameter of the circle is 12 cm.

### Page 3

#### What's the Problem?

- Discuss with the children the formulas for calculating the circumference of a circle given the diameter or radius, and the diameter of a circle when given the circumference. Ensure that they understand that $\pi d$ means $\pi \times d$ and that $2\pi r$ means $2 \times \pi \times r$.

- If necessary, work through the questions with the children, i.e.
  - Calculate the circumference of a circle with a diameter of 18 cm.

    $c = \pi d$

    $= 3\cdot14 \times 18$

    $= 56\cdot52$ cm
  - Calculate the circumference of a circle with a radius of 6 cm.

    $c = 2\pi r$

    $= 2 \times 3\cdot14 \times 6$

    $= 37\cdot68$ cm
  - To the nearest centimetre, calculate the diameter and radius of a circle with a circumference of 173 cm.

    diameter = circumference $\div \pi$

    $= 173$ cm $\div \frac{22}{7} = 173$ cm $\times \frac{7}{22}$

    $= \dfrac{173 \times 7}{22}$

    $= \frac{1211}{22}$

    $=$ approximately 55 cm

    radius = diameter $\div 2$

    $= 55 \div 2$

    $=$ approximately 27·5 cm

## The Puzzler

- Children make some matchsticks puzzles of their own.

## Page 4

### Famous Mathematicians

- Ensure children fully understand Pythagoras' theorem, i.e.

  $c^2 = a^2 + b^2$

  $\therefore c = \sqrt{a^2 + b^2}$

  Because $c^2 = a^2 + b^2$

  then $a^2 = c^2 - b^2$      or      $b^2 = c^2 - a^2$

  $\therefore a = \sqrt{c^2 - b^2}$      $\therefore b = \sqrt{c^2 - a^2}$
- If necessary, provide an example substituting two of the letters for numbers, e.g.

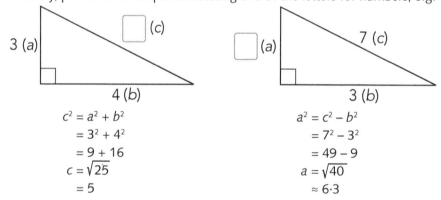

$c^2 = a^2 + b^2$          $a^2 = c^2 - b^2$

$= 3^2 + 4^2$          $= 7^2 - 3^2$

$= 9 + 16$           $= 49 - 9$

$c = \sqrt{25}$          $a = \sqrt{40}$

$= 5$               $\approx 6\cdot3$

### Sports Update

- Remind the children that the lengths given are approximates, but that they should aim to draw and label their diagrams as accurately as possible.
- Work with the children as they draw their first triangle, e.g.

  $b^2 = c^2 - a^2$

  $= 5\cdot1^2 - 2\cdot1^2$

  $= 26\cdot01 - 4\cdot41$

  $b = \sqrt{21\cdot6}$

  $\approx 4\cdot65$

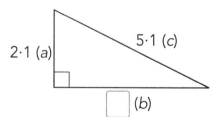

## AfL

- Explain the formula to me in your own words.
- How might we write this using symbols rather than words?
- What did you find out as a result of your investigation? What does this mean? Can you make a generalisation?
- How did you work out the answer to that puzzle? What patterns / relationships did you notice?

# Answers

## Page 1

### Let's Investigate

5 points = 10 chords
6 points = 15 chords
7 points = 21 chords
8 points = 28 chords

The sequence of chords for circles with 2, 3, 4, 5, 6, 7 and 8 points is the sequence of triangular numbers.

*Formula*

$$\text{no. of chords} = \frac{\text{no. of points (no. of points – 1)}}{2}$$

$$c = \frac{p\,(p-1)}{2}$$

24 points = 276 chords

## Page 2

### Let's Investigate

The average should be approximately equal to the value of pi ($\pi$), i.e. 3·14.

### Let's Investigate

Squares will vary. Some possibilities may include:

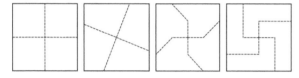

### The Puzzler

The diameter of the circle is 12 cm.
Explanations will vary.

## Page 3

### What's the Problem?

The circumference of a circle with a diameter of 18 cm is 56·52 cm.
The circumference of a circle with a radius of 6 cm is 37·68 cm.
The diameter of a circle with a circumference of 173 cm is approximately 55 cm.
The radius of a circle with a circumference of 173 cm is approximately 27·5 cm.
Results of the investigation will vary.

## The Puzzler

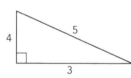

## Page 4

### Famous Mathematicians

13 miles

$$c = \sqrt{a^2 + b^2}$$
$$= \sqrt{5^2 + 12^2}$$
$$= \sqrt{25 + 144}$$
$$= \sqrt{169}$$
$$= 13$$

4 m

$$a = \sqrt{c^2 - b^2}$$
$$= \sqrt{5^2 - 3^2}$$
$$= \sqrt{25 - 9}$$
$$= \sqrt{16}$$
$$= 4$$

### Sports Update

Triangles should show the following measurements:

| | Arm length (cm) | Body length (cm) | Ground level line length |
|---|---|---|---|
| Lisa | 42 cm ÷ 20 = 2·1 cm | 102 cm ÷ 20 = 5·1 cm | 21·6 cm |
| Dan | 64 cm ÷ 20 = 3·2 cm | 150 cm ÷ 20 = 7·5 cm | 41·6 cm |
| Michelle | 36 cm ÷ 20 = 1·8 cm | 84 cm ÷ 20 = 4·2 cm | 14·4 cm |
| Joseph | 48 cm ÷ 20 = 2·4 cm | 112 cm ÷ 20 = 5·6 cm | 25·6 cm |
| Ian | 58 cm ÷ 20 = 2·9 cm | 136 cm ÷ 20 = 6·8 cm | 37·83 cm |

**Inquisitive ant**

congruent

Shapes are congruent if they are exactly the same size and shape and can be exactly superimposed.

# Issue 27

## 3-D shapes

### Prerequisites for learning

- Identify, visualise and describe properties of 3-D shapes
- Identify and draw nets of 3-D shapes
- Represent and interpret sequences, patterns and relationships involving shapes; suggest and test hypotheses; construct and use simple expressions and formulas in words then symbols

### Resources

pencil and paper
Resource sheet 2: My notes (optional)
Resource sheet 3: Pupil self assessment booklet (optional)
ruler
collection of different polyhedrons (optional)
12 straws
eight joiners
commercially produced skeletal construction kits, e.g. Frameworks Set (optional)
six paper squares, ideally each a different colour
interlocking cubes (optional)
stiff cardboard, scissors and colouring materials (optional)
1–6 dice (optional)

## Teaching support

### Page 1

#### Famous Mathematicians

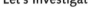

- Provide the children with a collection of different polyhedrons including cube, cuboid, triangular-based pyramid, square-based pyramid, triangular prism, octahedron, dodecahedron and icosahedron. This will enable them to count the number of faces, vertices and edges and therefore more easily identify Euler's formula.

#### Construct

- This very practical activity enables children to create different cubes and cuboids.
- Suggest that children use more than 12 straws and eight joiners. This will enable them to make other polyhedrons.
- If available, provide the children with commercially produced skeletal construction kits.

### Page 2

#### Let's Investigate

- Provide the children with eight interlocking cubes all of the same colour.
- If children cannot use the results of the $2 \times 2 \times 2$ cube investigation to answer the same questions for the two other cubes, then provide them with 27 and 64 interlocking cubes all of the same colour so that they can create their own $3 \times 3 \times 3$ and $4 \times 4 \times 4$ cubes.

#### Construct

- Children use stiff cardboard, a ruler, scissors and colouring materials to construct their own calendar.

### Page 3

#### Construct

- If appropriate, allow the children to work in pairs or groups to make their own origami cube.
- Children can investigate other origami shapes.

## Page 4

**The Puzzler**

• Provide the children with a 1–6 dice.

**Let's Investigate**

• Discuss with the children different orientations of the same arrangements. For example, how these four 2 × 2 × 2 cubes are considered to be the same:

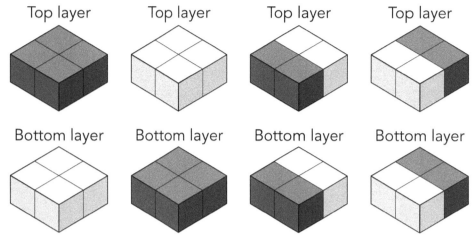

• Provide the children with four interlocking cubes of one colour and four of another colour.

**AfL**

• What is the rule / formula?

• What did you discover as a result of your investigation? What generalisations can you make?

• What mental image did you have? How did this help you? How do you know that you are correct?

# Answers

## Page 1

### Famous Mathematicians

$F + V = E + 2$ or $F + V - 2 = E$

| Polyhedron | Faces (F) | Vertices (V) | Edges (E) |
|---|---|---|---|
| cube (hexahedron) | 6 | 8 | 12 |
| cuboid | 6 | 8 | 12 |
| triangular-based pyramid (tetrahedron) | 4 | 4 | 6 |
| square-based pyramid | 5 | 5 | 8 |
| triangular prism | 5 | 6 | 9 |
| octahedron | 8 | 6 | 12 |
| dodecahedron | 12 | 20 | 30 |
| icosahedron | 20 | 12 | 30 |

A football has 60 vertices.

### Construct
Results of the investigation will vary.

## Page 2

### Let's Investigate
8 small cubes make up the large 2 × 2 × 2 cube
3 yellow faces: 8
2 yellow faces: 0
1 yellow face: 0
0 yellow faces: 0
The total of the answers to the second questions (8) is equal to the answer to the first question (8).
27 small cubes make up the large 3 × 3 × 3 cube
3 yellow faces: 8
2 yellow faces: 12
1 yellow face: 6
0 yellow faces: 1
64 small cubes make up the large 4 × 4 × 4 cube
3 yellow faces: 8
2 yellow faces: 24
1 yellow face: 24
0 yellow faces: 8
Regardless of the size of the large square, the number of small squares with 3 yellow faces is always 8.

### Construct
Many answers are possible. However the digits 0, 1 and 2 must appear on both cubes. The remaining faces must have the digits 3–8 on them (the digit 6 is used upside down as the digit 9). One possible solution is:

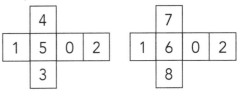

## Page 3

### Construct
No answer required.

## Page 4

### The Puzzler

Other answers are possible.

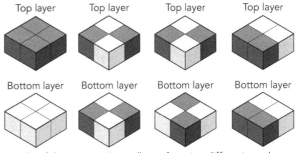

### Let's Investigate
There are four completely different arrangements possible.

Top layer   Top layer   Top layer   Top layer

Bottom layer   Bottom layer   Bottom layer   Bottom layer

Results of the investigation will vary for using different numbers of each colour.

**Inquisitive ant**

icosidodecahedron
A polyhedron with 20 triangular faces and 12 pentagonal faces. It has 30 identical vertices, with two triangles and two pentagons meeting at each. It has 60 edges, each separating a triangle from a pentagon.

### Prerequisites for learning

- Know that angles are measured in degrees and that one whole turn is 360°; compare and order angles
- Estimate, draw and measure acute and obtuse angles using an angle measurer or protractor to a suitable degree of accuracy
- Use a pair of compasses to draw circles
- Understand and identify properties of a circle, including centre, radius and arc
- Collect, select, process, present and interpret data

### Resources

pencil and paper

Resource sheet 2: My notes (optional)

Resource sheet 3: Pupil self assessment booklet (optional)

Resource sheet 5: 1 cm squared paper

Resource sheet 6: 2 cm squared paper

Resource sheet 8: Squared dot paper

Resource sheet 9: Triangular dot paper

Resource sheet 10: Isometric paper

Resource sheet 11: Diamond paper

magnetic / orienteering compass

ruler

pair of compasses

protractor

floor robot

chessboard (optional)

coin, 1–6 dice, 1–8 digit cards

a random number generating function on a computer, e.g. number spinner or similar

torch

tape measure

computer with Internet access

## Teaching support

### Page 1

#### Sports Update

  • Children investigate the importance of angles in other sports, e.g. football, golf (golf clubs), tennis …

#### Let's Investigate

- This activity is about knowing the size of interior angles in different polygons.
- Discuss with the children that if n represents the number of sides of a polygon, the formula for calculating the sum of interior angles is $180 \times (n - 2)$.

  So, the sums of angles in regular polygons are:

  – 3-sided shape (triangle): 180° ∴ Interior angle is 60°.

  – 4-sided shape (square): 360° ∴ Interior angle is 90°.

  – 5-sided shape (pentagon): 540° ∴ Interior angle is 108°.

  – 6-sided shape (hexagon): 720° ∴ Interior angle is 120°.

  – 7-sided shape (heptagon): 900° ∴ Interior angle is 128·5°.

  – 8-sided shape (octagon): 1080° ∴ Interior angle is 135°.

  – 9-sided shape (nonagon): 1260° ∴ Interior angle is 140°.

  – 10-sided shape (decagon): 1440° ∴ Interior angle is 144°.

  – 12-sided shape (dodecagon): 1800° ∴ Interior angle is 150°.

  Children need this information when writing their instructions.

 • Use a diagram to show the children the angle of turn in the example, i.e.

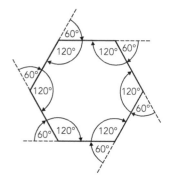

## Page 2

### Technology Today

• Pairs of children can compare the sets of instructions they wrote for the Let's Investigate activity on page 1, choose one set of instructions for each shape and use a floor robot.

### Construct

• To draw the shape of a 50p coin, children need to repeat step 6 a further five times.

• Knowing which two points form an arc depends on continuing the pattern in step 4 and step 5. If children cannot identify the pattern, suggest they tabulate the information.

| Point | Arc drawn between points: |
|-------|---------------------------|
| A | D and E |
| B | E and F |
| C | F and G |
| D | G and A |
| E | A and B |
| F | B and C |
| G | C and D |

### Around the World

• Ensure that children understand how bearings work.

• When giving bearings of places outside, it is recommended that children work in pairs.

• Children investigate the sport of orienteering.

## Page 3

### The Puzzler

• Explain to the children that there are different solutions possible for each board.

• Some children may find it helpful to refer to an actual chessboard and knight piece.

• Using the 3 × 4 board as an example, work with the children to record one of the possible solutions onto squared paper, i.e.

• Some children may find the 6 × 6 and 8 × 8 boards too challenging. If this is the case, suggest they only find solutions for the smaller boards.

You may wish to discuss with the children that a possible solution to the 8 × 8 chessboard can be made by using two 3 × 4 boards and two 4 × 5 boards, i.e.

### Let's Investigate

• Ensure children use a range of different dot paper.

## Page 4

### Let's Investigate

• Ensure children use a range of different dot paper and if available, a random number generating function on a computer, e.g. number spinner or similar.

### Focus on Science

• Suggest that one method of measuring the angle is to measure the distance of the light source from the object and the height of the light source above the object. From this children can draw a scale triangle and measure the angle of the light source.

### At Home

• After children have completed the activity at home, ensure that there is an opportunity in class for pairs or groups of children to discuss their results.

## AfL

• How did you work out / calculate what the size of the angle was?

• Describe your route to me.

• What instructions did you write?

• Where did you stand in the playground? Tell me an object that you chose. Give me the compass bearings for this.

• How did you work out the solution to the puzzle? Did you find another route?

• Tell me what you did in your experiment. What are the results? What does this tell us?

# Answers

## Page 1

### Sports Update

2 × 1 table: Pocket E
3 × 2 table: Pocket F
4 × 1 table: Pocket B
7 × 3 table: Pocket D

### Let's Investigate

Instructions will vary. However, they should be similar to the following:

- equilateral triangle: 3 angles each of 60°
- rectangle: 4 angles each of 90°
- regular pentagon: 5 angles each of 108°
- regular octagon: 8 angles each of 135°

## Page 2

### Technology Today

Instructions will vary depending on the ICT robotic equipment available.

### Construct

No answer required.

### Around the World

The arrow of a magnetic compass is a magnet. Therefore it always rotates to point to magnetic north.
Results of the investigation will vary.

## Page 3

### The Puzzler

Solutions will vary. One solution for each chessboard is:

3 × 4    4 × 5    5 × 5

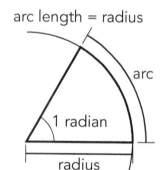

6 × 6    Normal 8 × 8

### Let's Investigate

Trails will vary.

## Page 4

### Let's Investigate

Paths will vary.

### Focus on Science

Reports, graphs and conclusions will vary.

### At Home

Lists of angles will vary.

**Inquisitive ant**

**radian**
A unit of angle, equal to an angle at the centre of a circle whose arc length is equal to the length of the radius.

arc length = radius

arc

1 radian

radius

# Issue 29

## Reflections

### Prerequisites for learning

- Understand and identify properties of a circle, including: centre, radius, diameter and circumference
- Use a pair of compasses
- Recognise reflective symmetry
- Complete patterns with up to two lines of symmetry
- Draw the position of a shape after a reflection

### Resources

pencil and paper

Resource sheet 2: My notes (optional)

Resource sheet 3: Pupil self assessment booklet (optional)

Resource sheet 6: 2 cm squared paper

ruler

postcards, travel brochures, books and magazines showing examples of reflective symmetry

camera (optional)

pair of compasses

coloured pencils

wallpaper samples showing examples of reflective symmetry (optional)

computer with Internet access

## Teaching support

### Page 1

#### Construct

- Allow the children to use the school camera to take photos of examples of reflective symmetry in and around the school.

  Encourage the children to look for examples of reflective symmetry in architecture from different cultures.

#### Around the World

- There are two aspects to this investigation. Firstly, investigating Ndebele art and culture, and secondly designing a Ndebele mural.
- After children have designed their mural, ask them to write a statement describing what makes it an example of Ndebele art and commenting on its symmetry.

### Page 2

#### Around the World

- Similar to the Around the World activity on page 1, there are two aspects to this investigation. Firstly, investigating Akan art and culture, and secondly drawing a design for an Akan stool.
- After children have designed their stool, ask them to write a statement describing what makes it an example of an Akan stool and commenting on its symmetry.

#### The Arts Roundup

- Patterns based on equilateral triangles and hexagons are easy to draw using a compass because the radius of a circle divides its circumference into six equal parts.
- The steps of the pattern should look as follows:

### Page 3

#### Looking for Patterns

- If appropriate, children can create their designs using ICT.

- When children have finished their design they swap their design, but not their description, with another child. Each child then writes a description of their partner's design. When they have finished, they compare the descriptions of the same design.

#### Sports Update

- Children investigate symmetry in the designs of different sports fields, for example, football, rugby, basketball and tennis.

### Page 4

#### In the Past

- There are two aspects to this investigation. Firstly, investigating mosaics from different civilisations and cultures, and secondly designing a mosaic pattern with reflective symmetry.

- Similar to the Looking for Patterns activity on page 3, children can create their patterns using squared paper or ICT.

- Ask the children to write a brief statement describing the symmetry in each design.

#### The Puzzler

- Suggest the children use squared paper to write their name in mirror lines placed at different angles.

- Children should not be limited to only horizontal, vertical and the diagonal angle shown. For example,

**LUCINDA**

#### At Home

- You may wish for the children to undertake this activity in school rather than at home. If so, provide wallpaper samples showing examples of reflective symmetry or ask them to find examples on the Internet.

- If the children do complete the activity at home, ensure that there is an opportunity in class for pairs or groups of children to discuss their results.

- Ask the children to write a brief statement describing the symmetry in each wallpaper design.

## AfL

- Describe to me the symmetry in this building / mural / stool / wallpaper.
- Tell me how your design / pattern / mural / stool shows reflective symmetry.
- What type of symmetry is this?

# Answers

## Page 1

**Construct**
Results of the investigation will vary.

**Around the World**
Results of the investigation will vary.

## Page 2

**Around the World**
Results of the investigation will vary.

**The Arts Roundup**
Children's patterns will vary.

## Page 3

**Looking for Patterns**
Children's patterns will vary.

**Sports Update**
Statement will vary. However, all the moves show examples of vertical and horizontal symmetry.

## Page 4

**In the Past**
Children's patterns will vary.

**The Puzzler**
Children's reflections will vary.

**At Home**
Results of the investigation will vary.

**Inquisitive ant**  plane of symmetry
Just as 2-D shapes have lines of symmetry, so 3-D shapes have planes of symmetry.

# Issue 30

## Translations

### Prerequisites for learning

- Understand tessellations
- Use coordinates in all four quadrants to draw, locate and complete shapes that meet given properties

### Resources

pencil and paper
Resource sheet 2: My notes (optional)
Resource sheet 3: Pupil self assessment booklet (optional)
Resource sheet 6: 2 cm squared paper
Resource sheet 8: Squared dot paper
Resource sheet 9: Triangular dot paper
ruler
cardboard
scissors
sticky tape
coloured pencils
geoboard (optional)
elastic bands (optional)
computer with Internet access

## Teaching support

### Page 1

#### Looking for Patterns

  • Instruct the children to create their tessellating patterns using ICT.

#### The Arts Roundup

 • Children make templates of greater complexity.

### Page 2

#### The Arts Roundup

 • Make a display of the work of MC Escher, including a brief description of how mathematics features in each of the works of art.

#### Construct

 • Children make templates of greater complexity.

### Page 3

#### In the Past

 • There are two aspects to this investigation. Firstly, investigating mosaic border patterns from different civilisations and cultures, and secondly designing a mosaic border pattern made from a translated shape.

 • Children can create their border pattern using mathematical paper or ICT.

#### Let's Investigate

 • Remind the children that a translation is the movement of a shape from one position to another without any rotation, reflection or change in size, and moving only vertically or horizontally.

• Children investigate which triangles triangle 2 can land on exactly after one or two translations.

## Page 4

### Let's Investigate

• The numerous variations in this activity mean that it is an extremely open-ended investigation that children can revisit several times. Encourage them to investigate:

– drawing other quadrilaterals and polygons

– using different grids

– using other types of transformations.

### The Puzzler

• Provide the children with a geoboard and elastic bands.

**AfL**

• Explain your pattern to me. How does it show translations?

• How has this shape been translated?

• What happened when you translated your shape? What was similar / different about the shapes when they were translated onto different paper?

• Can you tell me some things that show a translating pattern? How do they show it?

• What did you find out about the work of MC Escher / mosaic border patterns? How do they show translations?

• What can you tell me about tessellations? What makes this shape tessellate? Why doesn't this shape tessellate?

# Answers

### Page 1

**Looking for Patterns**
Tessellating patterns will vary.

**The Arts Roundup**
Templates and tessellations will vary.

### Page 2

**The Arts Roundup**
Results of the investigation will vary.

**Construct**
Templates and tessellations will vary.

### Page 3

**In the Past**
Children's border patterns will vary.

**Let's Investigate**
One translation:
    Shape A: 3
    Shape B: 0
    Shape C: 4 and 10
    Shape D: 2
    Shape E: 9
Two translations:
    Shape A: 1
    Shape B: 4
    Shape C: 12
    Shape D: 1, 3, 6 and 7
    Shape E: 4, 5, 8 and 10

### Page 4

**Let's Investigate**
Results of the investigation will vary.

**The Puzzler**
3 × 3 geoboard: 1
4 × 4 geoboard: 5
5 × 5 geoboard: 11
Results of the investigation will vary if the size of the right-angled triangle is different, e.g. 1-unit by 1-unit.

**Inquisitive ant**  transformation
Reflections, rotations and translations are all forms of transformation.

## Prerequisites for learning

- Begin to understand rotational symmetry
- Visualise and draw on grids of different types where a shape will be after rotation through 90° or 180° about its centre or one of its vertices
- Complete a simple symmetric figure
- Understand and identify properties of a circle, including centre
- Use a pair of compasses

## Resources

pencil and paper

Resource sheet 2: My notes (optional)

Resource sheet 3: Pupil self assessment booklet (optional)

Resource sheet 5: Squared paper

Resource sheet 8: Squared dot paper

Resource sheet 9: Triangular dot paper

Resource sheet 10: Isometric paper

ruler

camera (optional)

coloured pencils

pair of compasses

scissors

computer with Internet access

## Teaching support

### Page 1

**Around the World**

- Children make a poster / display of symmetrical Rangoli patterns found on the Internet. They write a brief description of each pattern describing its rotational symmetry.

**Looking for Patterns**

- Extend the activity by asking the children to draw a larger triangle and to use nine different colours, i.e.

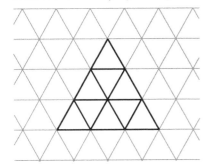

### Page 2

**Looking for Patterns**

- Referring to the example, discuss with the children how the shape has not only been rotated through a half turn, but also translated.

- Instruct the children to create their half-turn rotation tessellating patterns using ICT.

**Let's Investigate**

- Rather than drawing the hubcaps, allow the children to use the school camera to take photos of the hubcaps.

- Ask the children to find other examples of rotational symmetry in and around the school, e.g. toys and equipment from the Foundation stage.

### Page 3

**The Arts Roundup**

- Children investigate Islamic art, looking in particular for examples of rotational and reflective symmetry.

### Page 4

**Construct**

- The numerous variations in this activity means that it is an extremely open-ended investigation that children can revisit several times. Encourage them to investigate:

  - different templates (shapes)
  - overlapping shapes that result from the rotations, i.e.
  - lines drawn at different angles, i.e.

**Let's Investigate**

- There are 12 different pentominoes.

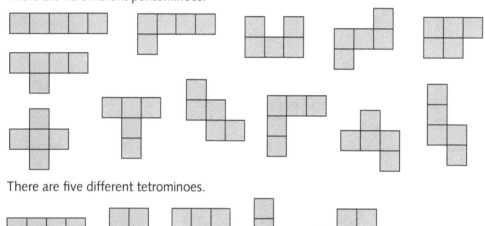

There are five different tetrominoes.

**AfL**

- Explain your pattern to me. How does it show rotational symmetry?
- How has this shape been rotated?
- Can you tell me some things that show rotational symmetry? How do they show it?
- What did you find out about Rangoli / Islamic patterns? How are they symmetrical?
- What can you tell me about tessellations? What makes this shape tessellate? Why doesn't this shape tessellate?

# Answers

## Page 1

**Around the World**
Results of the investigation will vary.

**Looking for Patterns**
Patterns will vary.

## Page 2

**Looking for Patterns**

Tessellating patterns made from other shapes will vary.

**Let's Investigate**
Results of the investigation will vary.

## Page 3

**The Arts Roundup**
Patterns will vary.

## Page 4

**Construct**
Templates and patterns will vary.

**Let's Investigate**
A pentomino is a 2-D shape made from five congruent squares, connected along their edges.
Results of the investigation will vary.

**Inquisitive ant**

order of symmetry
The order of symmetry of a shape is the number of times a shape can be fitted back onto its own outline during a complete turn. For example the order of symmetry of a square is 4, and a rectangle is 2.

## Prerequisites for learning

- Use coordinates in the first quadrant to draw, locate and complete shapes that meet given properties
- Identify, visualise and describe properties of triangles, quadrilaterals and other regular polygons; use knowledge of properties to draw 2-D shapes
- Use the eight compass points to describe direction
- Use simple expressions and formulas in symbols
- Understand squares and cubes of numbers
- Find the difference between a positive and a negative integer, or two negative integers

## Resources

pencil and paper
Resource sheet 2: My notes (optional)
Resource sheet 3: Pupil self assessment booklet (optional)
Resource sheet 5: 1 cm squared paper
Resource sheet 6: 2 cm squared paper
Resource sheet 8: Squared dot paper
ruler
material for making a poster
map of the local area (optional)
computer with Internet access

## Teaching support

### Page 1

**Famous Mathematicians**

- Ensure that children understand the formula, and special case formula, for "The Witch of Agnesi".
- As children need to find the squares of negative numbers when using the formula (e.g. $^-10^2$), you may need to discuss with them the multiplication of two negative integers. An effective way of demonstrating this is by linking known multiplication tables to negative number multiplication tables. For example:

$2 \times 2 = 4$ $\qquad$ $2 \times {}^-2 = {}^-4$
$1 \times 2 = 2$ $\qquad$ $1 \times {}^-2 = {}^-2$
$0 \times 2 = 0$ $\qquad$ $0 \times {}^-2 = 0$
$^-1 \times 2 = {}^-2$ $\qquad$ $^-1 \times {}^-2 = 2$
$^-2 \times 2 = {}^-4$ $\qquad$ $^-2 \times {}^-2 = 4$ (or $^-2^2 = 4$)
$^-3 \times 2 = {}^-6$ $\qquad$ $^-3 \times {}^-2 = 6$

### Page 2

**Construct**

- Along with their own mazes, children find other examples of mazes on the Internet to make a display.

**Around the World**

- You may wish the children to work in pairs or as a group on this activity.

### Page 3

**The Puzzler**

- Children write a similar puzzle of their own using the eight compass points to describe direction.

**Let's Investigate**

- Remind the children of the definition and properties of each of the following quadrilaterals:

  - *parallelogram:* 2 pairs of opposite parallel sides / opposite sides and angles are equal

  - *rhombus:* a special parallelogram / 4 equal sides / opposite sides equal and parallel / opposite angles equal / 2 lines of symmetry

– *rectangle:* a special parallelogram / 4 right angles / opposite sides equal and parallel / 2 lines of symmetry

– *square:* a special parallelogram and a special rhombus / 4 equal sides / 4 right angles / opposite sides equal and parallel / 4 lines of symmetry

– *kite:* 2 pairs of adjacent sides equal / 1 pair of opposite angles equal / 1 line of symmetry

– *trapezium:* 1 pair of parallel sides

- Children may need to use more than one coordinates grid.
- Children find the perimeter and area of each of their quadrilaterals.

**Around the World**

- You may wish to provide the children with a map of the local area.

## Page 4

### Construct

- Ensure that children understand the formula for drawing a parabola using coordinates.
- As children need to calculate with negative numbers when using the formula, for example, $y = (^-1 - 1)^2 + 1$, you may need to remind them of how to find the difference between a positive and a negative integer and how to multiply together two negative integers (see  Famous Mathematicians activity on page 200).
- Go through two examples with the children, one using a positive $x$-axis value, the other a negative $x$-axis value to work out the coordinates:

$$y = (x - 1)^2 + 1 \qquad\qquad y = (x - 1)^2 + 1$$
$$= (5 - 1)^2 + 1 \qquad\qquad = (^-2 - 1)^2 + 1$$
$$= 4^2 + 1 \qquad\qquad = ^-3^2 + 1$$
$$= 16 + 1 \qquad\qquad = 9 + 1$$
$$= 17 \qquad\qquad = 10$$
$$(5, 17) \qquad\qquad (^-2, 10)$$

### AfL

- Tell me some of your coordinates.
- What patterns do you notice in this list of coordinates?
- If you were to continue this curve what would be the next set of coordinates?
- How did you make your list of instructions as clear as possible? How did you ensure that your map conveyed all the necessary information while not being too detailed?

# Answers

## Page 1

**Famous Mathematicians**

(⁻10, 1)  (⁻9, 1·2)  (⁻8, 1·4)  (⁻7, 1·7)  (⁻6, 2)  (⁻5, 2·5)  (⁻4, 3)
(⁻3, 3·7)  (⁻2, 4·3)  (⁻1, 4·8)  (0, 5)  (1, 4·8)  (2, 4·3)  (3, 3·7)
(4, 3) (5, 2·5) (6, 2) (7, 1·7) (8, 1·4) (9, 1·2) (10, 1)

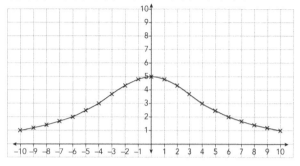

## Page 2

**Construct**
Mazes and conclusions will vary.

**Around the World**
Posters will vary.

## Page 3

**The Puzzler**
10 km

**Let's Investigate**
Coordinates of quadrilaterals will vary.

**Around the World**
Instructions will vary.

## Page 4

**Construct**

**Inquisitive ant**

GPS

Global Positioning System is a navigational and surveying facility which is based on receiving signals from different satellites.

### Prerequisites for learning

- Understand and identify properties of a circle, including circumference, chord and segment
- Use a pair of compasses to draw circles
- Understand and use simple algebraic conventions
- Represent information or unknown numbers in an equation

### Resources

pencil and paper
Resource sheet 2: My notes (optional)
Resource sheet 3: Pupil self assessment booklet (optional)
Resource sheets: 5–11 mathematical papers
ruler
chessboard (optional)
pair of compasses
coloured pencils
computer with Internet access

## Teaching support

### Page 1

#### The Language of Maths

- Some children may see this as a pattern made up of 12-sided shapes (dodecagons). However it is easier to describe the pattern by seeing it as a series of interconnecting regular hexagons, each one surrounded by rotated triangles and squares that form the hexagons' vertices and sides.
- Remind the children of the word 'regular' as it relates to 2-D shapes. The use of this term is important to describe the pattern successfully.

#### What's the Problem?

- Explain to the children that rotations are not considered different, i.e. the following are all the same solution.

- If children have difficulty identifying similarities suggest that they turn their sheet of squared paper around.
- Tell the children the fewest number of queens necessary to defend the chessboard:
  - 4 × 4 chessboard: 2 queens
  - 5 × 5 chessboard: 3 queens
  - 6 × 6 chessboard: 3 queens
  - 8 × 8 chessboard: 5 queens.
- Some children may find it helpful to refer to an actual chessboard and queen piece (they will need to use additional chess pieces as substitute queens).

### Page 2

#### Around the World

- State and country flags that are suitable for children to use when investigating different types of symmetry include:
  - vertical symmetry: Canada and India
  - horizontal symmetry: Norway and France
  - vertical and horizontal symmetry: United Kingdom and Jamaica

– rotational symmetry: European Union and Hong Kong

– no symmetry: Australia and USA.

### The Puzzler

- Explain to the children that the solution to this puzzle means that no two queens can share the same row, column, or diagonal.

- Tell the children that not allowing for repetitions of rotation and symmetry, there are 12 unique solutions. How many of them can they find?

- Some children may find it helpful to refer to an actual chessboard and queen piece (they will need to use additional chess pieces as substitute queens).

### Let's Investigate

- Suggest the children draw a table to assist them in identifying the rule, i.e.

| Number of chords (C) | Number of segments (S) | |
|:---:|:---:|:---|
| 2 | 4 | } +3 |
| 3 | 7 | } +4 |
| 4 | 11 | |
| 5 | 16 | } +5 |
| 6 | 22 | } +6 |

- You may need to provide some children with assistance when devising a formula for the maximum number of segments you can make for a particular number of chords:

$$S = \frac{C(C + 1)}{2} + 1$$

- Some children may also need reminding of the order of operations, and that $C(C + 1)$ is the same as $C \times (C + 1)$.

## Page 3

### Famous Mathematicians

- Ensure that children understand the difference between an odd and an even vertex.

- Children investigate the Konigsberg Bridge Problem.

## Page 4

### The Arts Roundup

- Children choose the mathematical paper that is best suited to their design.

### Technology Today

- If appropriate, children could reproduce on the computer the design they created in 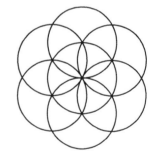 The Arts Roundup above.

### Construct

- Children follow steps 1 to 5. Then, without changing the compass settings, they draw six new circles using the six points around the circumference of the original circle for the centres. Children then colour their design to show examples of symmetry, rotation and translation.

### AfL

- Describe this design / pattern to me. What words are important in describing the design / pattern?

- How did you work out the solution to this problem / puzzle? Did you find more than one solution?

- What is the rule? Can you use this rule to write a formula?

- What was one of Euler's discoveries?

# Answers

## Page 1

**The Language of Maths**
Instructions will vary.

**What's the Problem?**
4 × 4

5 × 5 (other solutions are possible)

6 × 6          8 × 8

## Page 2

**Around the World**
Results of the investigation will vary.

**The Puzzler**
There are 12 unique solutions. However, if allowing different orientations of the same unique solution, i.e. rotation and reflection, there are a total of 92 solutions. This is one solution.

**Let's Investigate**
S = maximum number of segments
C = number of chords

$$S = \frac{C(C + 1)}{2} + 1$$

## Page 3

**Famous Mathematicians**
Can the networks be travelled?

| | |
|---|---|
| No | Yes | No | No |
| Yes | No | Yes | Yes |

Euler's rules:
- A network can be travelled if it has two odd vertices. However, the travelling must begin at one of the odd vertices and finish at the other.
- A network with more than two odd points cannot be travelled without retracing a line twice.
- A network with no odd vertices (only even vertices) can be travelled along each line once, and only once.
- The journey can start at any point and will always finish at the same point as it started.

Children's own networks will vary.

## Page 4

**The Arts Roundup**
Designs will vary.

**Technology Today**
Designs will vary.

**Construct**
Designs will vary.

**Inquisitive ant**

surveying
To make a detailed map of an area of land, including its boundaries, area and elevation. It involves the use of, among other elements, geometry (including angles) and finding distances.

### Prerequisites for learning

- Solve problems by collecting, selecting, processing, presenting and interpreting data, using ICT where appropriate
- Construct and interpret frequency tables, bar charts, line graphs and pie charts
- Recognise approximate proportions of a whole and use percentages to describe and compare them

### Resources

pencil and paper

Resource sheet 2: My notes (optional)

Resource sheet 3: Pupil self assessment booklet (optional)

Resource sheet 5: 1 cm squared paper

ruler

newspapers

pair of compasses

protractor

calculator (optional)

data handling software

computer with Internet access

## Teaching support

### Page 1

#### The Arts Roundup

- This activity highlights the different interpretations that different people can have of the same set of data. What is important however is that children are able to recognise and logically explain the trends that the line graph displays. Therefore, once the children have completed the first part of this activity, conduct a group discussion providing an opportunity for each child to describe their interpretation of Oliver's graph.
- The second part of this activity provides the children with an opportunity to create their own partly labelled graph, and to answer questions and interpret similar graphs constructed by other children.

#### Focus on Science

- Children will need to have access to the Internet to complete this activity.
- If appropriate, ask the children to construct their bar chart or graph using ICT.

### Page 2

#### Focus on Science

- Children will need to have access to the Internet to complete this activity.
- If appropriate, ask the children to construct their bar chart or graph using ICT.

#### Let's Investigate

- Depending on the sport and aspect of the investigation, children may need to have access to the Internet to complete this activity. However, if the children are finding out the results from a newspaper, they may need to have access to newspapers over a period of time.
- If appropriate, ask the children to construct their bar chart or graph using ICT.

#### The Language of Maths

- Similar to 🐝 The Arts Roundup activity on page 1, this activity involves children recognising and explaining the trends that each of the graphs display. Once the children have completed the activity, conduct a group discussion providing an opportunity for children to read and compare statements.

### Page 3

#### The Puzzler

- Most children should find this puzzle relatively easy to solve. The important aspect of this activity is the children writing about how they worked it out.

### In the Past

- This activity is concerned with interpreting data displayed in a line graph, drawing reasonable conclusions, and making and justifying likely predictions based on the trends displayed in the graph.

## Page 4

### Looking for Patterns

- For some children, this may be the first time that they have come across a scatter graph. If this is the case, you may need to spend some time with the children briefly highlighting the connections, relationships and trends displayed in the graph.

### The Language of Maths

- Some children may need assistance in converting the data in the graph or table into percentages before presenting the information in the pie chart.
- Children can either draw the pie chart or use ICT.

## AfL

- What can you tell me about the information displayed in the graph / chart / table?
- What relationships / connections / trends do you notice?
- What conclusions can you draw from this data?
- Explain to me the results of your investigation.
- Why did you decide to present your data in this way? How else could you have displayed the data?
- What predictions can you make in light of the trends that this graph shows?

# Answers

## Page 1

**The Arts Roundup**
Descriptions, graphs, questions and statements will vary.

**Focus on Science**
Results of the investigation will vary.

## Page 2

**Focus on Science**
Results of the investigation will vary.

**Let's Investigate**
Results of the investigation will vary.

**The Language of Maths**
Statements will vary.

## Page 3

**The Puzzler**
More children live in Rickety Towers than there are flats.

**In the Past**
Reports, reasoning, conclusions and predictions will vary.

## Page 4

**Looking for Patterns**
Reports will vary.

**The Language of Maths**
Pie charts will vary depending on the data used.

**Inquisitive ant**

spreadsheet
A computer program that displays numerical data in cells in rows and columns, in which computer formulas can perform calculations on the data.

# Issue 35

## Statistics

### Prerequisites for learning

- Describe and interpret results and solutions to problems using the mode, range, median and mean
- Solve problems by collecting, selecting, processing, presenting and interpreting data, using ICT where appropriate
- Construct and interpret frequency tables, bar charts, line graphs and pie charts
- Write a short report of a statistical enquiry, justifying choices and conclusions
- Understand the concept of and symbol for square root, and use the square root key on a calculator

### Resources

pencil and paper

Resource sheet 2: My notes (optional)

Resource sheet 3: Pupil self assessment booklet (optional)

Resource sheet 5: 1 cm squared paper

ruler

selection of food packages showing recommended number of servings, e.g. cereal boxes, orange juice container, ground coffee (optional)

selection of different types of newspaper, i.e. broadsheets and tabloids

calculator

data handling software

computer with Internet access

## Teaching support

### Page 1

**Let's Investigate**

- This activity is best undertaken as a group task as it involves children collecting traffic data at an intersection near the school.
- Children can present their statistical evidence using ICT.

**Sports Update**

- The total of the scores is 90, i.e. 3 × 30 (number of darts × mean).

  Therefore the two other darts must total 80 (90 – 10).
- Draw children's attention to the dartboard and how scores greater than 20 are achieved using the double and triple rings, and the two centre rings.

### Page 2

**Around the World**

- "If the world was a village of just 100 people" is a concept that children may have come across before. If not, it is worth spending time before children work independently on this activity discussing it with them.
- Encourage the children to use the information in the table to display the information that is most relevant to them. They should also compare the village of 100 people with populations that mean something to them.
- Investigate "If the UK was a village of just 100 people".

**Let's Investigate**

- If crisps are sold in school, you may want to discuss with the children how they could involve other children in the class / school to help them with the investigation.

### Page 3

**Sports Update**

- Ensure children understand the meaning of mode, median and mean.
- The total of the scores is 90, i.e. 15 × 6 (number of games × mean).
- Children write a similar problem of their own.

### The Puzzler

• Children give more than one answer.

### Sports Update

• Tell the children that there are two possible sets of scores and ask them to find both sets.

### At Home

• You may wish for the children to undertake this activity in school rather than at home. If so, have available a selection of food packages showing recommended number of servings, e.g. cereal boxes, orange juice container, ground coffee …

• If the children do undertake this activity at home, once they have completed the task, ensure that there is an opportunity in class for pairs or groups of children to discuss their results.

## Page 4

### Let's Investigate

• Children should investigate different types of newspapers, e.g. broadsheets and tabloids, as well as different newspapers, e.g. *The Daily Telegraph*, *The Times* and *The Guardian*.

### Focus on Science

• Ensure children understand and can use the formula to determine a person's reaction time.

• Children present their results using ICT.

### AfL

• What are the results of your investigation? How did you go about collecting the necessary data? What do your results tell you?

• Are your results reliable? How can you be sure?

• What is the answer to this problem / puzzle? How did you work it out?

# Answers

### Page 1

**Let's Investigate**
Results of the investigation will vary.

**Sports Update**
Keith's other two scores were 26 (double 13) and 54 (triple 18).

### Page 2

**Around the World**
Results of the investigation will vary.

**Let's Investigate**
Results of the investigation will vary.

### Page 3

**Sports Update**
Answers will vary for the scores of the 15 games. One possible combination is: 1, 2, 2, 3, 3, 4, 4, 5, 7, 7, 7, 10, 11, 12, 12.

**The Puzzler**
Answers will vary for the different ages of the family members. One possible answer is 32, 35, 10, 7, 5, 1.

**Sports Update**
Scores for each match could be either: 2, 3, 6, 6, 8 or 1, 5, 6, 6, 7.
The team need to score 11 goals in the next match to raise their mean score to 6.

**At Home**
Results of the investigation will vary.

### Page 4

**Let's Investigate**
Results of the investigation will vary.

**Focus on Science**
Results of the investigation will vary.

**Inquisitive ant**

primary and secondary sources
A primary source is data collected first-hand through observations, tests, experiments or other similar methods. A secondary source is data collected from reference books, newspapers, websites, CD-ROMs and so on.

# Issue 36

## Statistics

### Prerequisites for learning

- Find percentages of whole-number quantities
- Understand compound units for speed, such as metres per second, metres per minute, miles per hour and kilometres per hour
- Solve problems by collecting, selecting, processing, presenting and interpreting data, using ICT where appropriate
- Construct and interpret frequency tables, bar charts, line graphs, conversion graphs and pie charts
- Write a short report of a statistical enquiry, justifying choices and conclusions

### Resources

pencil and paper
Resource sheet 2: My notes (optional)
Resource sheet 3: Pupil self assessment booklet (optional)
Resource sheet 5: 1 cm squared paper
ruler
selection of newspapers
pair of compasses
protractor
calculator
electricity bill (optional)
stopwatch
tape measure
data handling software
computer with Internet access

## Teaching support

### Page 1

#### Around the World

- Total rainfalls are:
  Summer: 78 + 102 + 118 = 298 mm
  Autumn: 130 + 126 + 121 = 377 mm
  Winter: 131 + 98 + 82 = 311 mm
  Spring: 69 + 77 + 84 = 230 mm
  Yearly: 1216 mm

  Therefore, angles are:
  Summer: $\frac{298}{1216} \times 360 = 88 \cdot 223 \ldots (88°)$
  Autumn: $\frac{377}{1216} \times 360 = 111 \cdot 611 \ldots (112°)$
  Winter: $\frac{311}{1216} \times 360 = 92 \cdot 072 \ldots (92°)$
  Spring: $\frac{230}{1216} \times 360 = 68 \cdot 092 \ldots (68°)$

- Children can either draw the pie chart or use ICT.

### Page 2

#### Construct

- In working out which arrangements of the 21 dots are better than an ordinary 1–6 dice, it is the ratio of wins to loses that is important, not the proportion of wins to the total number of rolls.

- One method of working out alternatives is to use a 6 × 6 grid similar to those below to show all the possible outcomes of a particular pair of dice.

2 ordinary 1–6 dice:

| | | | | | |
|---|---|---|---|---|---|
| $\frac{1}{1}$ | $\frac{1}{2}$ | $\frac{1}{3}$ | $\frac{1}{4}$ | $\frac{1}{5}$ | $\frac{1}{6}$ |
| $\frac{2}{1}$ | $\frac{2}{2}$ | $\frac{2}{3}$ | $\frac{2}{4}$ | $\frac{2}{5}$ | $\frac{2}{6}$ |
| $\frac{3}{1}$ | $\frac{3}{2}$ | $\frac{3}{3}$ | $\frac{3}{4}$ | $\frac{3}{5}$ | $\frac{3}{6}$ |
| $\frac{4}{1}$ | $\frac{4}{2}$ | $\frac{4}{3}$ | $\frac{4}{4}$ | $\frac{4}{5}$ | $\frac{4}{6}$ |
| $\frac{5}{1}$ | $\frac{5}{2}$ | $\frac{5}{3}$ | $\frac{5}{4}$ | $\frac{5}{5}$ | $\frac{5}{6}$ |
| $\frac{6}{1}$ | $\frac{6}{2}$ | $\frac{6}{3}$ | $\frac{6}{4}$ | $\frac{6}{5}$ | $\frac{6}{6}$ |

Wins: 15 Lossses : 15

1 ordinary dice / winning dice with 21 dots arranged as 0, 0, 5, 5, 5, 6

| | | | | | |
|---|---|---|---|---|---|
| $\frac{1}{0}$ | $\frac{2}{0}$ | $\frac{3}{0}$ | $\frac{4}{0}$ | $\frac{5}{0}$ | $\frac{6}{0}$ |
| $\frac{1}{0}$ | $\frac{2}{0}$ | $\frac{3}{0}$ | $\frac{4}{0}$ | $\frac{5}{0}$ | $\frac{6}{0}$ |
| $\frac{1}{5}$ | $\frac{2}{5}$ | $\frac{3}{5}$ | $\frac{4}{5}$ | $\frac{5}{5}$ | $\frac{6}{5}$ |
| $\frac{1}{5}$ | $\frac{2}{5}$ | $\frac{3}{5}$ | $\frac{4}{5}$ | $\frac{5}{5}$ | $\frac{6}{5}$ |
| $\frac{1}{5}$ | $\frac{2}{5}$ | $\frac{3}{5}$ | $\frac{4}{5}$ | $\frac{5}{5}$ | $\frac{6}{5}$ |
| $\frac{1}{6}$ | $\frac{2}{6}$ | $\frac{3}{6}$ | $\frac{4}{6}$ | $\frac{5}{6}$ | $\frac{6}{6}$ |

Wins: 17 Lossses : 15

Key: win | draw | lose

### Focus on Science

- The first part of this activity is concerned with interpreting and comparing data presented in two pie charts. The second part involves the children using the information presented in the pie charts to make and justify predictions, and drawing an appropriate pie chart.
- Children can either draw the pie chart or use ICT.

### The Language of Maths

- Children may need to look through several newspapers before they find information displayed as a graph, chart or table. Encourage the children to find information that has meaning and relevance to them.

## Page 3

### Focus on Science

- For the second part of this activity children need to bring an electricity bill into school. Alternatively, children can complete this part of the activity at home, or you could bring in an electricity bill of your own.

### Sports Update

- Some sensitivity may need to be taken into consideration with this activity. However, results can still be presented ensuring anonymity, and conclusions made.
- Suggest the children present their results in a graph chart or table, using ICT if appropriate.

## Page 4

### Around the World

- Children will need to have access to the Internet to complete this activity.

### Sports Update

- Ensure children are familiar with line conversion graphs, e.g. converting from metric to imperial units or from degrees Fahrenheit to degrees Celsius, and exchange rate conversion graphs.
- Children construct their line conversion graphs using ICT.

### Sports Update

- Discuss with the children how they are going to find out their average walking speed in m/sec, m/min, m/hr, km/h. Are they going to work out one or two and use these to calculate the others?
- Children can investigate for themselves the Olympic and World record holders. Limited data is available in Issue 22.

## AfL

- Talk me through how you drew your pie chart. How did you work out the angles?
- Tell me the results of your investigation.
- Why did you present the information in this way? Why did you think it was the best way?
- What do these graphs / charts show? What conclusions can you draw from them? What predictions can you make? How can you justify your predictions?
- Why is this data best presented in this way? What benefits does it have over other types of graphs / charts?

# Answers

## Page 1

### Around the World

## Page 2

### Construct
The two best arrangements are:
0, 0, 5, 5, 5, 6
0, 0, 4, 5, 6, 6.
One better arrangement than an ordinary 1–6 dice is 0, 1, 4, 5, 5, 6.
Other answers are possible.

### Focus on Science
Report and pie chart will vary. However continuing the trend from 1980 to 2000, the 2020 pie chart should show a greater percentage of 'Bioenergy and waste'.

### The Language of Maths
Conclusions will vary depending on the data used.

## Page 3

### Focus on Science

| | |
|---|---|
| Cold appliances | 697 kWh |
| Cooking | 574 kWh |
| Lighting | 656 kWh |
| Audio visual | 533 kWh |
| ICT | 246 kWh |
| Washing/Drying | 574 kWh |
| Water heating | 328 kWh |
| Other | 492 kWh |

Results of the investigation at home will vary.

### Sports Update
Results of the investigation will vary.

## Page 4

### Around the World
Results of the investigation will vary.

### Sports Update
Conversion graphs will vary.

### Sports Update
Results of the investigation will vary.

**Inquisitive ant**

grouped frequency distribution
When there is a large set of data it can often be difficult to show every data value as there will be too many to display in a table or on a graph. So the data can be grouped into class intervals (or groups) to help us organise, interpret and analyse the data.

# *Stretch and Challenge 6* Record of completion

**Class/Teacher:** _____

| Domain(s) | Topic | Stretch and Challenge Issue | Names | | | | | | | | | | |
|---|---|---|---|---|---|---|---|---|---|---|---|---|---|
| Number: – Number and place value | Number | 1 | | | | | | | | | | | |
| | Negative numbers | 2 | | | | | | | | | | | |
| Number: – Addition, subtraction, multiplication and division | Addition | 3 | | | | | | | | | | | |
| | Subtraction | 4 | | | | | | | | | | | |
| | Multiplication | 5 | | | | | | | | | | | |
| | Division | 6 | | | | | | | | | | | |
| | Mixed operations | 7 | | | | | | | | | | | |
| | Mixed operations and algebra | 8 | | | | | | | | | | | |
| Number: – Fractions (including decimals and percentages) | Fractions | 9 | | | | | | | | | | | |
| | Fractions | 10 | | | | | | | | | | | |
| | Decimals | 11 | | | | | | | | | | | |
| | Percentages | 12 | | | | | | | | | | | |
| | Percentages | 13 | | | | | | | | | | | |
| Ratio and proportion | Ratio and proportion | 14 | | | | | | | | | | | |
| | Ratio and proportion | 15 | | | | | | | | | | | |
| | Ratio and proportion | 16 | | | | | | | | | | | |
| Algebra | Algebra | 17 | | | | | | | | | | | |
| | Algebra – The Financial Issue | 18 | | | | | | | | | | | |

| Domain(s) | Topic | Stretch and Challenge Issue | Names | | | | | | | | | |
|---|---|---|---|---|---|---|---|---|---|---|---|---|
| Measurement | Length | 19 | | | | | | | | | | |
| | Mass | 20 | | | | | | | | | | |
| | Volume and capacity | 21 | | | | | | | | | | |
| | Time | 22 | | | | | | | | | | |
| | Area | 23 | | | | | | | | | | |
| | Perimeter | 24 | | | | | | | | | | |
| | Measurement | 25 | | | | | | | | | | |
| Geometry: – Properties of shapes | 2-D shapes | 26 | | | | | | | | | | |
| | 3-D shapes | 27 | | | | | | | | | | |
| | Movement and angle | 28 | | | | | | | | | | |
| Geometry: – Position and direction | Reflections | 29 | | | | | | | | | | |
| | Translations | 30 | | | | | | | | | | |
| Geometry: – Properties of shapes – Position and direction | Geometry | 31 | | | | | | | | | | |
| | Geometry | 32 | | | | | | | | | | |
| | Geometry | 33 | | | | | | | | | | |
| Statistics | Statistics | 34 | | | | | | | | | | |
| | Statistics | 35 | | | | | | | | | | |
| | Statistics | 36 | | | | | | | | | | |

**s&C** Volume 6

# The Maths Herald

Name:

Date:

Date of starting issue:

Date of finishing issue:

My notes

My notes

Inquisitive ant

2

My notes

3

2

My notes

3

# The Maths Herald

**S&C** Volume 6

Name:

Date:

Date of starting issue: _____  Date of finishing issue: _____

## What have you learned?

## What did you use to help you?

## Any other comments?

## Your teacher's comments

What did you enjoy the most?

What did you enjoy the least?

Did you find the work:

too easy?

just about right?

too hard?

What would you like to learn next about this topic and why?

# Scale drawing

Example

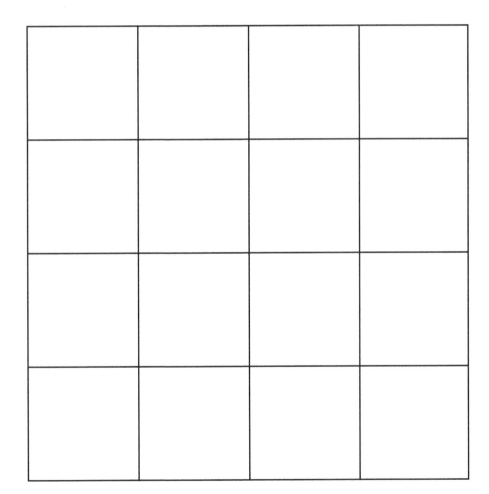

# 1 cm squared paper

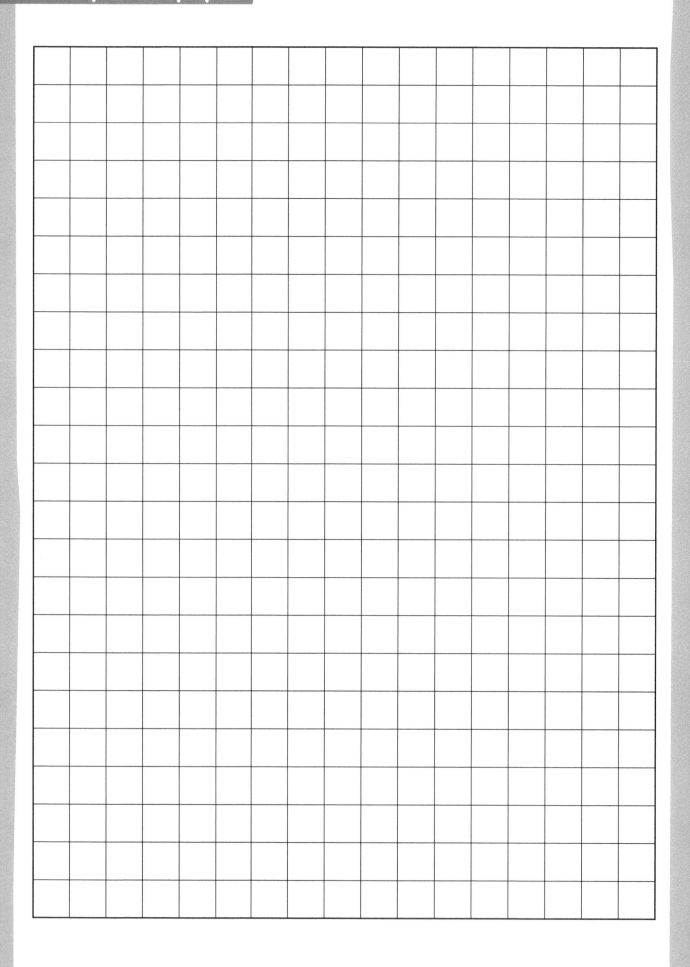

# 0·5 cm squared paper

# Squared dot paper

# Triangular dot paper

# Isometric paper

# Diamond paper

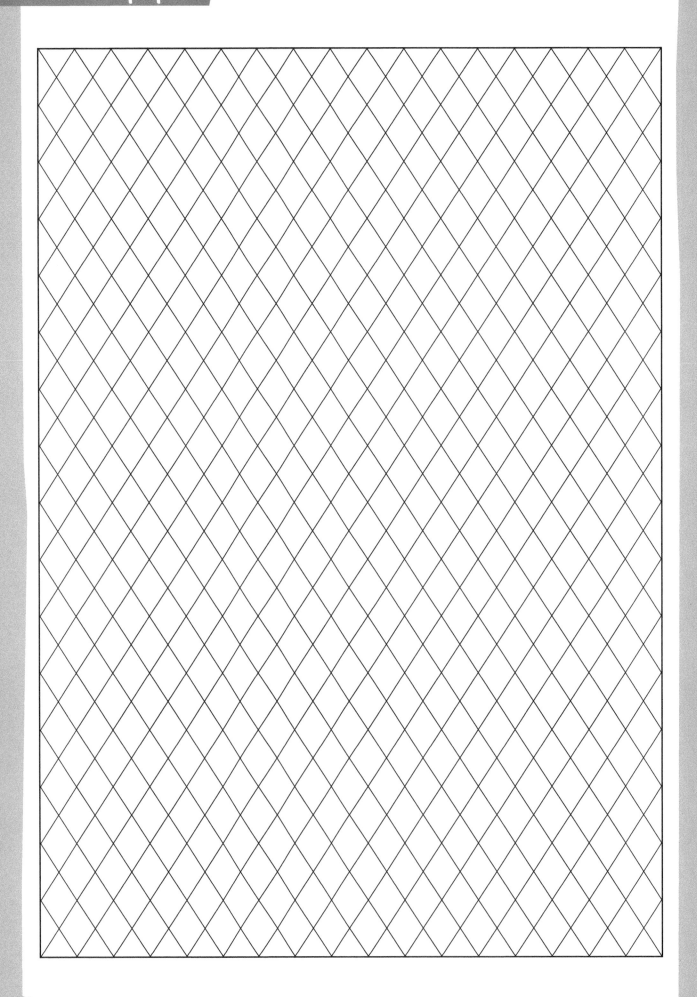